Psychologisation in Times of Globalisation

Today more than ever, our understanding of ourselves, others and the world around us is described in psychological terms. Psychologists deeply influence our society, and psychological discourse has invaded companies, advertising, culture, politics, and even our social and family life. Moreover, psychologisation has become a global process, applied to situations such as torture, reality TV and famine. This book analyses this 'overflow of psychology' in the three main areas of science, culture and politics.

The concept of psychologisation has become crucial to current debates in critical psychology. De Vos combines these debates with insights from the fields of critical theory, philosophy and ideology critique, to present the first book-length argument that seriously considers the concept of psychologisation in these times of globalisation.

The book contains numerous real-world examples making it an accessible and engaging analysis that should be of interest to researchers, postgraduates and undergraduate students of psychology and philosophy.

Jan De Vos is a researcher at the faculty of Philosophy and Moral Sciences at Ghent University, Belgium.

Psychologisation in Times of Globalisation

Jan De Vos

Routledge
Taylor & Francis Group

LONDON AND NEW YORK

First published 2012
by Routledge
27 Church Road, Hove, East Sussex BN3 2FA

Simultaneously published in the USA and Canada
by Routledge
711 Third Avenue, New York NY 10017

Routledge is an imprint of the Taylor & Francis Group, an informa business

© 2012 Psychology Press

British Library Cataloguing in Publication Data
A catalogue record for this book is available from the British Library

Library of Congress Cataloging-in-Publication Data
Vos, Jan de, 1967–
    Psychologisation in times of globalisation / Jan De Vos.
        p. cm.
    Includes bibliographical references and index.
    1. Psychology. 2. Human behavior. I. Title.
    BF121.V59 2012
    150–dc23   2011048690

ISBN13: 978–0–415–68201–5 (hbk)
ISBN13: 978–0–415–68202–2 (pbk)
ISBN13: 978–0–203–11545–9 (ebk)

Typeset in Times by
Swales & Willis Ltd, Exeter, Devon

Paperback cover design by Andrew Ward

Printed and bound in Great Britain by the MPG Books Group

For my family, Vera, Max and Celine (†)

Contents

Preface

This book sets out, in a lucid but complex argument, three lines of research and the interrelationship between them. Jan De Vos makes us reflect on how the birth of psychology might be understood as a necessary aspect of modern sciences and so modernity itself. He shows us how psychologisation of other disciplinary and cultural domains might be understood, and brings us face to face with how this psychologisation is grounded in politics, specifically under conditions of globalisation. De Vos poses these lines of research as questions, but we come to learn as we travel through the book that they cannot be answered separately, and each of the chapters addresses one side of this triangle of questions while forcing the reader around the triangle in order that they may grasp how one depends on the others.

Our author reviews in detail, and with many compelling examples, the psychologising trap that awaits the reader as they attempt to make sense of their own journey through psychology. This is the trap of imagining that the view they have obtained of the triangle of questions is from an external vantage point, or from within a flexible multi-perspectival superior position that the modern subject who is positioned as an 'expert' in our globalised world is invited to aim for when they start to learn about psychology. We see, for example, how psychoanalytic ideas that are usually shut out of mainstream psychology can be used tactically to free ourselves from psychology, including from the psychological discourse of psychoanalysis itself. The book weaves its way through the highways and byways of psychology, and it disrupts a conventional academic understanding of what the end-point of this kind of work should be. The labyrinthine journey repetitively turns around the place from which this inquiry is conducted, inhabiting and questioning the academic gaze upon the outside world (here, psychology in the world outside the university) and its puzzled reflections upon itself (here, what psychologists are doing inside the university).

Psychology is inside us now as well as being around us wherever we look, and here we have some resources to question how the relation between 'inside' and 'outside' is constructed. In this book, *Psychologisation in Times of Globalisation*, Jan De Vos provides a wealth of critical conceptual resources for us to be able to move into a realm 'outwith' psychologisation. These are crucial resources for mapping our place inside the discipline of psychology and in the everyday psychology that suffuses discourse and practice in the outside world.

Ian Parker
Discourse Unit
Manchester Metropolitan University

Acknowledgements

This book is written in a dialogue with many other people: psychologists, ex-psychologists, non-psychologists, anti-psychologists. My special thanks for suggestions, remarks and support goes out to Erica Burman, Tom Claes, Ronald Commers, Marc De Kesel, Boris Demarest, Pauline Mottram, Calum Neill, Eli Noë, André Ockerman, Ian Parker, Nimisha Patel, Isabel Rodriguez and Gertrudis Van de Vijver.

Some parts of this book are based on previous published journal articles. Chapter 2 is partly based on De Vos, J. (2009a) 'Now That You Know, How Do You Feel? The Milgram Experiment and Psychologization', *Annual Review of Critical Psychology*, vol. 7; De Vos, J. (2010b) 'From Milgram to Zimbardo: the double birth of postwar psychology/psychologization', *History of the Human Sciences*, vol. 23, no. 5. The final, definitive version of this paper has been published in *History of the Human Sciences*, vol. 23, no. 5, December 2010 SAGE Publications Ltd. All rights reserved. © Jan De Vos 2010; and De Vos, J. (2011a) 'Depsychologizing Torture', *Critical Inquiry*, 37(2), 286–314 © 2011 The University of Chicago Press. Chapter 3 is partly based on De Vos, J. (2009b) 'On Cerebral Celebrity and Reality TV. Subjectivity in Times of Brain-Scans and Psychotainment', *Configurations*, vol. 17, no. 3. And chapter 4 is partly based on De Vos, J. (2011c) 'The psychologization of humanitarian aid: skimming the battlefield and the disaster zone', *History of the Human Sciences*, vol. 24, no. 3. The final, definitive version of this paper has been published in *History of the Human Sciences*, vol. 24, no. 3, July 2011 SAGE Publications Ltd. All rights reserved. © Jan De Vos 2011.

Introduction

Deadlocks in the critique of psychologisation

A scene from the past: a pupil is daydreaming behind his desk. The teacher shouts his name; first name and surname. How many times has he already had to do this today? Now he shouts only the surname. He throws a piece of chalk at the pupil. Startled the pupil looks up and hears the teacher say: write me the school rules five times over and report immediately to the prefect's office. The same scene today: the daydreaming pupil is now seated in the circle. It is circle time, the teacher talks about the shooting of yesterday in a school in the capital. Carefully he follows the procedure devised by experts. He opens the educational box and asks: could you tell the group how you feel about it? The daydreaming pupil is not aware that the teacher holds out four masks to him: happy, sad, frightened or angry. The teacher repeats the question, pronouncing the first name of the pupil each time a little louder. After lunch break the school psychologist enters the class: would you mind joining me in my office? If the old-time discipline did not leave you much space to breathe, now the therapeutic zeal is claiming even the refuge of your inner thoughts.

Such forms of *psychologisation* are not restricted to the sphere of the school but have spread over almost every societal field. Psychologisation can here preliminarily be defined as psychological vocabulary and psychological explanatory schemes entering fields which are supposed not to belong to the traditional theoretical and practical terrains of psychology. Is it then not to be observed that, psychologists have penetrated deeply in our society, and apart from them, the psy-discourse has invaded in an unprecedented way companies, advertising, culture, politics, up to our social and family life? To put it bluntly: even the bedroom is no longer psychology-free: one just has to take a look at the glossies on the bedside tables, aimed at both men and women. This psychologisation moreover has become a global process. Be it a Chilean mine collapse or an earthquake in Christchurch, New Zealand, in both countries psychologists and officials presented in the media the same discourse on the symptomatology and the prognosis of the Post Traumatic Syndrome. 'Little do they know we are bringing the plague.' Thus runs the comment attributed to Freud when, together with Jung, he sailed to the USA for the first time. Today it seems that it is psychology rather than psychoanalysis which has achieved global contagion. In this book we shall follow this ever expanding action-radius of the psy's (the psychologists, the psychiatrists and every other psycho-social professional) as we will join them in the torture chambers of Guantánamo and Abu Ghraib, in the production rooms of reality TV, and in the military C-130 on their way to the famines in Africa and traumatised populations in the war zones.

But let us first take a step back. It is clear, the critique of psychologisation appeals to the imagination. It promises to open the door to something we have lost; a more genuine and authentic presence with ourselves and the world. If only we could get rid of all this psychologising! Without doubt, psychologisation can be objectified, as one could quantify the invasion of the psy-disciplines and measure the proliferation of psy-speak. One could, for example, count the psy-signifiers in the media. One could map the intake of first-year students in psychology departments. Or one could assess the economic weight of the psy-industry and its related sectors. All this to prove that we are subjected to the psy-disciplines from before our birth (the pre-maternity classes) until our death, where the psy is seeing to it that our last breath is drawn properly. Today, more than ever, our understanding of ourselves, others and the world comes in psychological terms. We receive a psychological analysis on top of everything: e.g. the man behind the politician, a psy-profile of the school-shooter, and the psychological characteristics of the trauma-experience (be it an earthquake or even a financial crisis). So let us leave all this psychologising behind and return to the things themselves!

However, a note of caution is necessary here. For what would keep the outcry *there is too much psychology and there are too many psychologists* out of the dynamics of psychologisation itself? Let us scrutinise how even the very conceptualisation of psychologisation might in this way turn out to be problematic. The concept of psychologisation traditionally encompasses a critique of a specific discourse originating in the *psy-sciences* and their related praxes (all those sciences and praxes which, in one way or another, are concerned with the psychic and the subjective). Broadly speaking this critique concerns the fact that the psy-discourses are becoming increasingly hegemonic as they furnish the human being with particular signifiers and particular discursive schemes (assigning particular positions) with which to look upon itself and its world. However, despite the fact that this definition directly captures certain contemporary phenomena, various problems arise as soon as we ask from which position the critique emanates. For it seems that, invariably, it issues from a meta-psychological perspective which might, in the end, simply bounce back into psychologisation: *this is why people tend to psychologise* is nothing but the *nec plus ultra* of psychologisation. The question thus becomes one of whether any critique of psychologisation does not, in the end, promise the same thing as mainstream psychology; i.e. a grasp of the world, the others and yourself delivered through revealing what they are really, *really* about? This, however, should not be the end of the discussion. The wager of this book is that the very discernment of the specific and inevitable impasses inherent in the critique of psychologisation can allow us to approach the phenomenon of psychologisation, and thus the phenomenon of psychology itself, anew. Moreover, I will claim that the era in which we live offers us a specific window. That is to say, the time of globalisation with its undoubtedly heightened and intensified forms of psychologisation offers a chance of understanding the very interchangeability of psychologisation, the critique of psychologisation and psychology. The question *who are we that we need so much psychology* is eventually structurally missed by psychology itself. Or, in other terms, in the time of globalisation psychologisation eventually reveals itself as the very paradigm of psychology, if not, as we will see, its hidden, obscene truth. However, as said, the critique of psychologisation only becomes viable if it can bring its own deadlocks into the equation.

Psychologisation: three possible critiques, their deadlocks and how to transcend them

Let us start with determining three possible critiques of psychologisation, each of them addressing a particular field which is supposed to be affected by the overspill of the psy-discourse. The first concerns the critique of psychology where, as a discipline, it would occupy terrains which are, viewed from another perspective, not psychological. This is the critique emanating from other sciences (medical sciences, sociology, anthropology . . .) on psychology's misappropriating of certain presumably extra-psychological realities.[2] A second approach criticises psychologisation not only as an illegitimate claim to jurisdiction but, foremost, as the impertinent overflow of psychology to the broader fields of society. Consider the overspill of psychology via education and the media to culture and society in general. This spread of psychological discourses could be regarded as littering the human life-world, allegedly obstructing straightforward and genuine ways of living. The third critique not only regards improper uses of psychology, as in the first two critiques but, moreover, a *misuse* of psychology.[3] This critique addresses the, structural or otherwise, entanglement of psychology with power mechanisms, be it purely political (psychology effecting individualisation and preventing engagement in politics proper) or broader politico-economical (e.g. big pharmaceutical companies requiring psychologised subjects).

These three, often combined, critiques – the scientific critique, the cultural critique and the political critique – are, however, ridden with deadlocks. Let us first scrutinise the two possible outcomes they envision. On the one hand, one could argue that, despite the misguided overflow of psychology to science, culture or politics, psychology is still a positive and legitimate science. Or, in contrast, one could argue that psychology, as such, is an obsolete theory and praxis. Both options are problematic. Let us start with the first one, the one which still grants psychology a place and, thus, amounts to a plea for hygiene. Returning to the three possible critiques of psychologisation this hygiene exercise would mean, first of all, in the case of the scientific critique, urging psychology and psychologists to avoid overspill and engage in a parsimonious theory and praxis respecting the other sciences. Secondly, concerning the cultural critique, a psychology capable of constraining itself would also be capable of avoiding and contesting popularisations which both distort the theory of psychology and obstruct more 'natural' human and social interactions. Lastly, regarding the political critique, a psychology conscious of the pitfalls of psychologisation would also be fit to oppose the misuse of psychology and its entanglement in power mechanisms. Let us take a closer look at those three different versions of a plea for hygiene.

On the level of a scientific critique, the paradox of this plea for hygiene is that it amounts to a denial of the premises of psychology itself. For, if psychology concerns the subjective side of being in the world, then this inevitably means that every sublunary aspect of the world falls under its jurisdiction. The biological, sociological, anthropological and any other dimension of human existence necessarily pass over the subject and thus fall *de facto* under the expertise of psychology. A psychology denying this cannot but engage in a manifold of paradoxes. Is psychology then not condemned to constantly shift over a slave/dominatrix scheme, submitting itself to other scientific paradigms and, in this submission, come to dominate them? As such, it is clear that psychology cannot but claim the throne in the castle hall of the sciences. Any modesty is misplaced here. If this might be the ambition of other sciences too (economy, sociology, or even mathematics), psychology at the least has proven to be the most successful in occupying the throne. As such, the fact that psychologisation outruns the other -isations is an issue we have to address in this book.

Regarding the cultural critique, the plea for a hygienic psychology is in danger of amounting to a rather strange, wistful looking back to a supposed pre-psychologised time. Just consider how therapists themselves sometimes reminiscence of such eras in which they supposedly received clients or patients naïve in respect to psychological theories, presenting, as it were, pre-theoretical symptoms. This, however, opens up a problematic and paradoxical nostalgia for the pre-modern subject. It positions the expert in an ethnographic stance vis-à-vis the client whose pre-modern authenticity should, on the one hand, be kept free from academic interferences but, on the other, paradoxically requires the expert to verify and guarantee it. Against this I argue that psychologisation is not only about the spilling over of a discourse, polluting everyday life with psy-signifiers. Rather, psychologisation is above all testifying how in modernity the discursive positions themselves have radically altered. This book aims to show that to plea for keeping psychology within the confines of psychology departments and their laboratories disregards the fact that the human zoo out there precisely concerns the modern *de facto* academicised and psychologised subject. The modern subject is not merely immersed in a full life-world but, rather, its engagement in everyday life is always already mediated, no longer by a religious discourse, but instead by a scientific one. Hence, the advice *don't psychologise, be yourself* cannot but be taken up starting from the same position. *Yes, I have to be more authentic* only repeats and confirms the stance of psychologisation. For, being one's own expert, as the injunction runs, only re-establishes the academic gaze, precisely by turning it inwards.

Concerning the political terrain, then, a plea for a hygienic operation entails the rather problematic dichotomy of *bad psychology* being lured into power plays (or simply openly collaborating), versus *good psychology*, either viewed as psychology staying neutral (being beyond ideology and merely sticking to its scientific vocation) or as psychology directed towards the ethical, the good and the emancipation of humankind. However, both *good psychology* options foster the unquestioned assumption that psychology is a relevant body of knowledge and postulate the importance of psychology qua *knowledge*. In both views psychology is believed to harbour a dangerous potential which should be supervised by ethical committees so as to prevent its inappropriate use. The first thing to deconstruct here is not the content of psychological knowledge as such, but the position of the Olympian vantage point of psychology and the psychologist claiming to be able to extract valuable knowledge from human beings which then would have to be safeguarded from foul and inappropriate uses. Should we thus label some parts of psychology as secret and classified? But it seems more likely that it is precisely these kinds of omnipotent fantasies which recently have propelled one of the most infamous entanglements of psychology with power, namely the involvement of psychologists in torture at sites such as Guantánamo and Abu Ghraib (I will address this at length in Chapter two).

This brings us to the more radical position of denouncing psychology in itself as obsolete both in its theory and in its praxis. Let us again explore this in three movements. With respect to the alleged colonisation of other sciences, the argument could be that today psychology is rendered irrelevant by the hard scientific data which shows the human being as a function of neurology, genes and evolutionary mechanisms. Nikolas Rose for example observes how the birth of the 'neurochemical self' entails 'the waning of psychology' (Rose, 2008, p. 460). Thus, is there no need for psychology anymore? However, this is again a problematic stance. For, if one denounces, for example, the free will as an illusion, almost immediately a subjective dimension pops up in another place. As Slavoj Žižek contends, if a neurobiologist shows you a genomic formula stating that 'this is you', this encounter with your objective self might be the experience of the gap of subjectivity at its purest (Žižek and Daly, 2004, p. 57). In other words, the formula *that is what you are* opens up the (albeit problematic) perspective of a subject looking puzzled at itself as an objectified thing. This paradox further entails that the rejected psychology invariably re-enters the scene. Just consider how precisely as the human being is denied psychological qualities, the biological substratum of the genes get anthropomorphised and psychologised, as preferences and desires are attributed to neurons and genes. Furthermore, despite the anti-Freudianism rampant in these approaches, it does not take long for a kind of unconsciousness to re-emerge. When, for example, love is explained as being deceived by chemistry, or solidarity feelings are reduced to the trick of the altruism gene (e.g. Bachner-Melman et al., 2005), this cannot but entail that we are again lured by something; if not by the Freudian unconscious, then by neurotransmitters or the genome. Still presupposing another scene, the indebtedness to Freud's 'andere Schauplatz' (the other scene) is far greater than generally admitted.

Regarding the critique of psychologisation as the overflow to everyday life, an anti-psychological stance also does not offer a perspective as this too almost invariably leads to the neurological outlook. Not only do the neurosciences psychologise the material substratum, they also engage in a neurologisation, or better, a neuropsychologisation of culture and everyday life. That this amounts merely to old wine in new bottles is nowhere more apparent than in the case of ADHD. Since the 1980s, when it was 'voted into existence' as a category of the DSM (Diagnostic and Statistical Manual of Mental Disorders) (Timimi and Radcliffe, 2005, p. 64), massive information and education campaigns to inform the public have been successfully implemented by governmental and other agencies. Like the psy-discourse, the neuro-discourse spreads its signifiers and assigns the discursive positions. Here the anti-psychological discourse trades the psycho-educational discourse for a neuro-educational one. If one takes a look at the many official and unofficial websites on ADHD[1] it seems that the first and most important lesson for a sufferer, parent or other involved party is that ADHD is a disorder with no psychic determination whatsoever. Are we not facing here a kind of allergy to any psychological dimension as such? Is the psychic the annoying symptom, the scandal to be expelled? This is perhaps what the mainstream neurological discourses share with the mainstream psy-sciences: they do not want the psyche, even though they cannot really get rid of it. Could it be that the psychic and subjective dimension has to be contained by the mainstream discourses because of the dangerous, political dimensions they harbour? This brings us to the third critique, concerning psychology's entanglement with power mechanisms and economic processes. Here it can once again be observed that an anti-psychological discourse seems virtually incapable to supersede the psychological discourse. Critiques of, for example, the psychologisation of humanitarian aid inevitably take recourse to psychologising arguments to make their case. Consider, for example, Pupuvac who, in her critique of the trauma-approach, cannot avoid calling the discourse on trauma *traumatic* for the persons involved (Pupavac, 2002). I shall discuss this amply in the fourth chapter. But here it seems already clear that psychology is a tenacious discourse. Perhaps, the simple plea to de-psychologise politics misses the true bond between psychology/psychologisation and contemporary politics. Just consider how the manifold so-called politicisation and democratisation movements in various fields themselves rapidly tilt over to psychologisation with its clear un-emancipatory and even alienating effects. One can, for example, claim that the idea of bringing more democracy into parenting led to more psychology in education. Similarly, more democracy in schools brought psychology to the schools. Likewise, more democracy in business environments introduced psychology into their enterprises and factories. And finally, more democracy in the South has led to a psychologisation of the South (e.g. the already hinted at psychotherapeutic turn in humanitarianism).[2]

Are we thus lost in psychologisation? Is there no outside of psychology and is this the end of the critique of psychologisation? This book's answer is no, as it claims a methodology starting from the very deadlocks of the critiques. Let us hereto consider three assumptions, following again our threefold distinction. First, where the hard, non-psychological sciences claim the authority and the expertise to fence psychology in by defining and narrowing its jurisdiction, one can say that they are struggling foremost against their own inner demons. Is not the function of psychology precisely to contain and to master the problematic subjectivity which structurally haunted scientific objectivity since it emerged in Modernity? It is there, I claim, that psychologisation, as a kind of secondary symptom, enters the scene to fix the failing of the solution. Historicising and reconstructing instances of psychology's structural bond with psychologisation in relation to the advent of the modern sciences thus opens a new perspective on the critique of psychologisation. I shall tackle this historical side in the first chapter. The second chapter is then a further elaboration of this starting from a contemporary issue.

This leads us to the second assumption. Underneath the psychologisation of culture and society there is no Everyday Life as an authentic domain to be rescued. Everyday life is suffused, if not saturated, with science and technology: the imagery of a real, de-psychologised and authentic everyday life is furthermore itself part of psychology. *Be the real you*, as the authenticity discourse says, is the central tenet of today's psychologisation of culture. Is it then not significant that Philip Zimbardo, former president of the American Psychological Association and known for his Stanford Prison Experiment, considers reality TV as a *via regia* to disperse 'real psychology' to the population (cited in Mason, 2001)? The similar dispersing of psychology via the widespread praxis of psycho-education indicates that psychologisation might be the very core activity of psychology. The third chapter will deal extensively with these issues.

The third assumption is that psychology is not only mixed up in power mechanisms and economic processes, but that psychology is the very paradigm and the discourse of modern biopolitics. Michel Foucault's understanding of biopolitics as that power takes life itself and exploits it (Foucault, 1978, pp. 142–143), certainly makes psychology a key science in the disciplines of life. What I will argue for in this book goes still one step further, that is, psychology is not merely put into use of politics and economics in their managing of life; in modernity politics and economics are themselves always already psychological. As power instead of merely exercising its right to death, seized life itself as its object, modernity became psychological and psychologised. Especially in these times of globalisation it is to be observed that politics are psychology. By this I do not mean that you should know psychology to do politics. Rather what I mean is that today politics, as it has become de-politicised, technocratic and allegedly beyond ideology, has become psycho-politics. Leaving the decisions which matter to the market or rather, to the supra-national organisations, politics restricts itself to psy-matters, passing legislation on bullying, diversity, dress-codes and so on. But – and this is of course the most interesting thing – economics has also become psychological: just consider how the daydreaming pupil mentioned before was called to order via the voice of authority in the same way as in the factory the worker in conflict with his colleagues was urged to return to the assembly line. Now both are probed and have to account for their emotional status within a psychologised discourse. This is believed not only to enhance, respectively, education and the production process; this psychological dimension is, foremost, considered the ultimate goal, product and thus commodity of both education and economy. This psycho-economy is the subject of chapter four.

As these three assumptions will guide us in the rest of this book it is important to spell out the hypotheses and the epistemological premises and engagements on which they are based.

Hypotheses and further epistemological premises and engagements

To summarise: to consider psychology as a discipline always at risk of an inappropriate overspill has not proved to be a viable critique concerning the phenomena of psychologisation. For, the fact that one can only define what would be the proper boundaries of the psy-theories and the psy-praxes in psychological terms means that one cannot but repeat the psychologising stance. The circularity which arises here urges us to seek other grounds for a more structural critique. The premise that psychology not only spreads its signifiers, but also alters the discursive positions of subjects can be a first guiding principle, as precisely this is not thoroughly addressed by the traditional critiques. Here the central hypothesis is that psychology and psychologisation are two sides of the same coin: as psychology enters the scene, it inevitably and decisively alters the coordinates of subjectivity. Hence, and this is the second hypothesis, modern subjectivity as such might be understood as a doublet: it is both psychological and psychologised. Following from that, the third hypothesis is that the double figure of psychology and psychologisation not only permeates but actually defines and structures the fields of modern science, modern culture and modern politics.

Hence, I will argue not only that psychology/psychologisation is contingent on the advent of modernity, but also, as already mentioned, that the heightened phenomena of psychologisation in post-modernity and globalisation offer us a chance to disentangle the phenomenon. If, as Ian Parker contends, Cartesian modernity leads to the opposition individual/social becoming primordial and hence to the psy-complex to individualise all sorts of problems (Ian Parker, 1995, p. 61), it is clear that in these times of globalisation that opposition is taken to new grounds. Just consider that it is only today that psychologisation seems to have reached its height. Today psychologists are everywhere: in schools, at work, in the courts, etc.; the psy-discourse has become central in understanding everything from school failure, suburban riots and bomb attackers, to the effects of short-selling on the global financial market. Here, with regard to this psychologisation in times of globalisation, my central epistemological premise is not that psychologisation would constitute a cognitive mapping for a world having lost its former referential frameworks, such as religion or ideology. This line of thinking would only lead to the pitfalls already described. For, although the psychologising discourses attempt to give meaning and structure to our post-modern world, it is important to understand psychologisation not as a symbolic-imaginary operation tackling the *real* world (supposedly laid bare by a globalisation which erodes local cultural and religious frameworks). Rather, psychologisation tries to reconcile us with the *virtuality* of globalisation itself. We need so much psychology because our life-world is de facto *virtualised*. Hence I do not call for a de-psychologisation: behind the heavy veils of psychologisation there is no promised land of authenticity: not in terms of the scientific, the cultural, or the political. Recall Žižek's summary of Marx: it is not that we have the wrong idea about how things really are, we have the wrong idea of how in reality things are mystified (Žižek, 2005). With respect to psychologisation, one should not focus on the supposed real life behind it, but instead try to show how in reality life gets psychologised; what we take for reality is always already psychological. Marx's aim was not to prove that behind religious formations, for example, there lurks a real, material and social reality. He primarily asserted that behind the commodity, which appears to us as a real thing, something is operating at the level of the fetish, at the level of the imaginary. According to Žižek, this means that the fetishist illusion resides in our real social life, not in our perception of it. For example, one knows that money is not a magical thing, that it is just an object standing for a set of social relations, but one nevertheless acts in real life as if money were something magical (Žižek, 2005). In the same way, we know psychology is not the real thing, that it is just a representation of life as it is. But this is precisely the fetish; the belief that there is a life beyond psychology obscures how modern life as such is psychologised. Just consider reality TV and *psychotainment*; the real, authentic life that the media cater for is exactly the core of psychologisation. Does this not reveal the hidden paradigm of psychology itself? Is psychologisation not showing us that psychology instead of a more or less accurate map of real life is essentially a fetishisation of real life? If you want to know the human, don't study psychology, study psychologisation.

But, am I not forgoing the fact that psychology can hardly be seen as a monolithic science with a unified praxis? The field of psychology is not a heterogeneous field, but is ridden with many different approaches, schools and factions. So which psychology am I targeting? Should I not differentiate between all these dispersed currents and praxes? Yet, my response is surprisingly simple; the diversity of the psy-field notwithstanding, there is a common denominator which does hegemonise the field, and that is psychologisation: psychologisation unites all these different strands within the psy-sciences. Here my critique not only connects to the conceptualisation of the *psy-complex*, defined by David Ingleby in a broad way as an ensemble of agencies traversing the family, school, work place and thus the social itself (Ingleby, 1984, p. 43),[3] it also argues that what precisely unites this ensemble is the paradigm of psychologisation. This is what this book will attempt to show: psychology not only invariably leads to psychologisation; it is its very *modus operandi*. In short: psychology *is* psychologisation. Therefore I consider it not really interesting to seek to differentiate between good and bad psychology, and every position in-between, according to the extent a certain approach is more or less connected to psychologisation. I want to ask the reader, from the one who is critically interested in psychology, over the true psy-aficionado up to the professional psychologist to consider how psychologisation is inextricably bound to the discipline of psychology. For, the principal question is not whether the assertions of the psy-sciences are right or wrong because another question displaces and distorts every possible answer. This question is: *what does it mean for modern man to live his own life as a psychologist, anthropologist, or whatever?* The issue is not whether the psy-sciences, for example, correctly assess the importance of parents playing with their children and reading them stories. The real question is what it means that parents themselves consider this a *quality time* activity which enhances the development of their offspring's *personal and social skills.*

In this book I will try to show that it is in modernity that the vantage point to look upon oneself became an academic one and that precisely here psychology and psychologisation come in. The modern subject is hailed to adopt an academic gaze and this actually pulls it out of everyday life and thus out of psychology itself. Looking upon itself as a psychological thing, the subject, as the bearer of that gaze, itself testifies to a *zero-level of psychology.* This might be the central point I will try to make in this book, one I will have to approach from different angles and which will lead us to sometimes winding paths, but which in the end will turn out to be the only possible end point of our quest to understand the relation between psychology and psychologisation. For the time being let me found the idea of a zero-level of psychology in the following argument: the stance *this is the psychological-neurological-biological being you are,* as such constitutes a different subject looking at itself. This new subject scrutinising itself as an object of psychology cannot but situate itself beyond psychology, that is, it assumes a zero level of psychology, neurology and biology.

However – and here I have to make yet another shift in order to spell out my methodology – the only way to keep the abyss of the zero-level of psychology empty and not fill it in with meta-academic constructions which today come mainly in variants of neuro-xyz (neuropsychology, neuroethics, neuroeconomics . . .) is to jump over the empty gap in order to avoid getting stuck in its unfathomable muteness. My epistemological engagement and commitment here is the following: if one wants to say something about psychologisation without succumbing to the temptation to re-psychologise, one has to use . . . psychoanalysis. For while psychoanalysis is commonly seen as the *mother of psychologisation*, this is not an impediment, but rather, the right point of entry in order to understand psychologisation.[4] Psychoanalysis will prove a fruitful tool thanks to its peculiar position: not wanting to be a psychology it nevertheless claims to be a theory on the psyche. This is why in the course of its history psychoanalysis not only tilted over to the psychological discourse, one can also argue, as Robert Castel and Jacques

Donzelot did, that it gave a decisive turn to the phenomenon of psychologisation.[5] The way this book will understand this is by showing that there are good arguments to consider psychoanalysis as the first important theoretical praxis of modern subjectivity, making it thus an essential means of opening up the radical research terrain of the modern *homo psychologicus*.

The radical research terrain of the homo psychologicus: an outline

As modernity and the Enlightenment spawned the modern subject, I aim to demonstrate how this necessarily entailed the birth of the discipline of psychology together with its *skandalon* – that is, what psychology wants to deny but is for ever haunted by – a zero-level of psychology. Or, put differently, I want to explore how psychology via psychologisation processes produces subjectivity as excluded from itself. Here we can take recourse to Giorgio Agamben's conceptualisation of the paradigm. Agamben, working from Plato, contends that a paradigm concerns one singular example which makes the object or class intelligible. For Agamben, this leads to the essentially paradoxical status of the example:

> What an example shows is its belonging to a class, but for this very reason, it steps out of this class at the very moment in which it exhibits and defines it. Showing its belonging to a class, it steps out from it and is excluded.
>
> (Agamben, 2002b)

One can use this formulation to understand that in modernity being a human passes over the sciences – as science becomes the ultimate signifying horizon of everything under the sun – and that this entails the subject itself becoming the paradigm of the sciences, hence falling out of the human order and only in this way exhibiting its belonging to humanity.[6] The way how, in these times of globalisation, a study of psychologisation processes can reveal this zero-level of subjectivity, can be illustrated by (what else?) an example. Consider, for instance, the structural similarity of the Islamic fundamentalist with the Western *homo psychologicus*. The fundamentalist is not a traditionalist as such. As Marc De Kesel claims, it is not the tradition which defines his being a Muslim, if he professes traditional Islam, this is done as a sovereign choice for that tradition. Today's fundamentalist thus starts from a point beyond tradition, and that point, De Kesel claims, is the modern position (De Kesel, 2007). This is completely analogous to the Western human being, for whom, as I would claim; *being human* itself is a choice. Not starting from tradition or intuition, the Western human being inserts him- or herself into everyday life, into being as such, via academic knowledge, via the life-sciences, via psychology, via the academic gaze. This is the modern position which the *homo psychologicus* shares with the Muslim fundamentalist.

Again, engaging in this research terrain of the *homo psychologicus* it is crucial to fully address the emptiness of the modern position. At the zero-level of subjectivity and of psychology we do not find a subject which could be fleshed out again psychologically, sociologically nor neurologically and perhaps not even culturally or politically. This is the crux of my critique against mainstream psychology, as I argue that it is as such not up to this task of acknowledging a zero-level of psychology. This zero-level of subjectivity, as it drives psychologisation processes, is psychology's blind spot, or as already said, its *skandalon*, its unacknowledged principle which must remain hidden.[7] Only by radically emptying out this zero-level of psychology a critique of psychologisation becomes again possible.[8]

That will be the guiding principle in the following chapters. Let me give a brief outline. In chapter one we will trace the origins of the *homo psychologicus*. For if in late-modernity the *homo psychologicus* has become full grown, this allows us to question its birth in modernity and the Enlightenment. This journey to the past will reveal that already in the very beginnings of psychology one can discern a non-acknowledged paradox, the fact that psychology is directly connected to the de-psychologising processes of psychologisation. The three following chapters will trace the vicissitudes of the *homo psychologicus* in the respective fields of science, culture and politics (remember the three possible critiques). In each of these chapters psychologisation is analysed via the exploration of a concrete phenomenon that will bring us directly into the heart of the matter. In Chapter two I will take up the question whether psychology is a science. The phenomenon, from which I start, is the involvement of psychologists in torture practices in Guantánamo and Abu Ghraib. A close reading of the experiments of Stanley Milgram and Phillip Zimbardo will allow both a new critique on the participation of psychologists in torture and an answer to the question: what are the sciences for psychology and what is psychology for the sciences? Chapter three deals with the overflow of psychology into culture. It juxtaposes the phenomenon of '*psychotainment*' (reality TV, celebrity culture and other instances of psychologised entertainment), with the mainstream contemporary theories of consciousness such as those of Daniel Dennett. An understanding of the central place of image culture in psychology will make it possible to question the so-called neurological turn. The fourth chapter deals with the psychologisation of politics: it starts from an analysis of the psychological turn in humanitarian aid and then proceeds to a critique of psychologisation as the central paradigm of contemporary biopolitics. In the final concluding chapter the key themes of this book will be rehearsed in order to answer how psychologisation is related to globalisation. Hereto I will bring in Sigmund Freud's *das Ewig Weibliche* (the eternal feminine) in order to provide, not a full closure of the book, but, rather, a seal meant to block off any possible simple return to psychology.

Notes

1 For one example see http://www.nimh.nih.gov/health/topics/attention-defecit-hyperactivity-disorder-adhd/index.shtml.

2 Of course, this cannot but bring to mind Alain Badiou's radical thesis that the name for the ultimate enemy is not capitalism but democracy, or Mario Tronti's idea that democracy is the death of politics *tout court* (for a discussion of these points of view see Mandarini, 2009). As such, it is clear that the so-called democratic illusion, the idea that everything should be questioned and can be democratically decided upon, often comes in psycho-social robes. Just consider the fact that, in its death throes after the fall of the Berlin Wall, democratic socialism often embraced a de-politicised psycho-social Socialism-lite.

3 Ingleby describes the psy-complex as an ensemble of agencies 'whose discourses are not confined to particular sites of professional intervention' (Ingleby, 1984, p. 43). Rose understands this in a Foucaultian way: it is not the state which exercises power over the population and subjectivity, rather, 'state' power becomes diffused through the population and has to be seen as a complex network of strategies (Rose, 1985).

4 Maybe today the only possible way left of doing psychoanalysis, is to do a critique of psychology and psychologisation (see also De Vos, 2005)

5 According to, for example, the Foucault-inspired French sociologists Robert Castel and Jacques Donzelot (Donzelot, 1977), the turn to the psychological was brought about by psychoanalysis. As Castel et al. argued 'psychoanalysis was the main instrument for the reduction of social issues in general to questions of psychology' (cited in Ingleby, 1984)

6 As Agamben writes: 'If we define the exception as an inclusive exclusion, in which something is included by means of its exclusion, the example functions as an exclusive inclusion. Something is excluded by means of its very inclusion.' (Agamben, 2002b)

7 Here I lean on Agamben writing on the paradigm: 'The fallacy which remains unseen in the common usage of hypothesis is that what appears as a given is in reality only a presupposition of the hypothesis which would explain it. Thus the origin, the unpresupposed principle, remains hidden.' (Agamben, 2002b)

8 Compare, for example, Žižek's presupposition of a zero-level of ideology as the very condition to do ideology critique: 'Ideology is not all; it is possible to assume a place that enables us to maintain a distance from it, but this place from which one can denounce ideology must remain empty, it cannot be occupied by any positively determined reality – the moment we yield to this temptation, we are back in ideology' (Žižek, 1994, p. 70).

1 The birth of the homo psychologicus
The chronicle of a death foretold

We must start the search for the origins of the *homo psychologicus*, somewhat paradoxically, with its apparent death. For, we can observe that the psychological, or put more correctly, the psychic or the subjective, today has little or no space anymore in mainstream *Academia*[1] nor in the mainstream psy-practices. Let me illustrate the widespread phobia for the psychic with a little anecdote. Once at a broad philosophical conference I gave a paper on emotions in politics with the title carrying explicit references to psychoanalytic authors. Apparently this had drawn the attention of a notorious Freud and Lacan-basher who I saw taking the first row at my session. 'Emotions,' thus he started after my paper, 'are nothing more, nothing less than brain activity. The rest are stories!' I answered politely that stories constitute a legitimate field of studies in their own right – which made little impression to be honest. It was only afterwards – it is always afterwards that the good arguments come – that I thought that I should have referred to the movie *The Matrix*. In that science-fiction movie machines and technology have become autonomous and for their survival they tap electricity and energy from the human beings. The humans are held prisoners in embryonic water-filled cradles and serve as batteries. However, as the first such 'human resources' died en masse, the human beings were connected to a supercomputer which generated a virtual reality. This virtual life keeps 'the crops' alive. How to understand this? It is clear that the psychic life as such is needed to make the system work. Hence, is it not the radical conclusion to make that, instead of body warmth and electricity, the machines foremost feed on the psychical and subjective life – in other words, the stories – produced by the humans? The humans live the (albeit virtual) life the machines themselves lack. Perhaps we can find here a basic scheme: if in *The Matrix* the machines live by proxy of the humans, this shows how the human being itself experiences life. Life is always somewhere else, with someone else, in another space, in another time. We do not have an immediate, unmediated access to life. Maybe this is precisely why we need psychology: it allows us to think the life to which we ourselves have no access. We need these stories, be it the elaborate novelist stories in the vein of psychoanalysis, or be it the stories on genes and neurotransmitters, reassuring in their supposedly firm and certain ground. Today however, we are no longer so keen on the novelist stories. Could it be that the uneasiness or even the anger they provoke should be read as the signs of our times? Today the mainstream psy-experts *talking* about brain scans, neuro-transmitters, and senso-motor skills can hardly be said to be the advocates of the psychical dimension. *It is not about the stories; it is about body warmth and electricity, nothing more!* This emotionality involved in discarding the subjective dimension might indicate that we are not merely assisting the death of the *homo psychologicus*; maybe its death should be classified as a suspicious death. Those who proclaim the end of the human of the stories at least do not give this species much breathing space. The subjective and the psychic dimension is like a strange disease, an obscene secret that has to be discarded and denied. Of course, the inquiries in this book will in the end reveal that the *skandalon*[2] will always return: the death of the *homo psychologicus* can only be a staged death: the new neuro-biological man has not freed itself from psychologisation, on the contrary: as we will see, it is still ridden by unavowed stories. But for now, this first chapter will try to disentangle the different story lines and assess the possible motives of the fall of the *homo psychologicus* by turning the gaze backwards to its origins. And there we will see that if the birth of the *homo psychologicus* has not already brought us a stillborn child, then at least its story reads as a chronicle of a death foretold.

The homo psychologicus: the birth

As such the *homo psychologicus* can be said to be rather young. It is the product of the Enlightenment and the advent of the modern sciences. In modernity the human being came to look upon himself not any longer from a religious or ideological vantage point, but from an academic perspective. The sciences and especially the psy-sciences produce a new reflexive gaze: *brain research has taught us that . . . according to questionnaires 60 per cent of the population suffers from . . . in psychology we call this repression . . .* Psychologisation, or the inducing of the psychological gaze, thus seems the inevitable effect of psychology. Unwittingly or not, psychology structurally exhorts the human being to adopt a psychologising gaze and to look upon itself in terms of brain areas, percentages or repression mechanisms.

Looking for a genealogical explanation one easily winds up with putting the blame on Sigmund Freud. For his *Psychopathology of Everyday Life* (Freud, [1914]1957) seems to be a decisive framework for late-modern man turning the gaze inwards in a psychologising way. In this key work Freud wrote about forgetting proper names, mistakes in speech and other everyday faulty acts, to which, as the common reading goes, he attributed some deeper psychological meaning. If one is to speak of a gradual colonisation of everyday life, it is clear that Freud as such made an inaugural step. For *Psychopathology of Everyday Life* had a vast cultural impact: the *oops, a Freudian slip of the tongue* is still quite widespread. Although quite paradoxically that exclamation almost invariably means that the speaker is *not* going to engage in understanding his lapse: Freud is exactly invoked to whisk it away. One can even say that today in broad Academia, Freudian theory itself is whisked away: Freud's study on the trivial waste products of psychic life is now itself considered wasted time. The alleged deeper meaning is replaced by neurological short-circuits, cognitive processes or just chance events. There is no message or meaning to be looked for: the contemporary cigar is always but a cigar.

But it might be a misunderstanding to think that Freud was looking for a *deeper meaning* in the pathology of everyday life, in dreams or in the suffering of his patients as such. One can argue that Freud was more interested in the subject, that is, in what it meant to be *subjected* to meaning. Although the Freudian subject is connected to hermeneutics, coming from both without and within, the subject itself always resurfaces as having nothing to do with all this meaning. The subject is the result, or better, the remainder of all that: the subject is that almost mythical empty point which is left behind when all the stories are told. In this way the subject is the proverbial dog watching a sick cow. This beautiful Flemish saying originally meant to watch eagerly something one wants, but eventually it became to mean to watch something with bewilderment, being incapable to grasp it or to connect with it. Thus the subject is the asymptotic zero level of meaning; watching for example his own brain activity and believing the rest to be mere stories. Maybe it is precisely this disturbing meaninglessness which today is rejected and which is replaced with mainstream academics' more manageable stories, meant to provide a total, closed account of the human being. Claiming that all is brain activity is not telling too little, it is telling too much, it is not robbing the subject of meaning; it is overstuffing the subject with stories.

Is it hence not the meaninglessness as such which consequently comes to haunt us? Consider so-called random violence such as freeway shootings, hate crimes and wilding, which worry policy makers, educators and community workers (see for example Best, 1999). We could downplay this as mere media hype playing on the fears of the public and reinterpreting phenomena which always existed but which we did not yet grasp or account for. But this of course would be the easy way out. Maybe meaningless violence is not to be linked to our lack of understanding, but rather to be understood as the effect of *too much* understanding and meaning. Today everyday life is overstuffed with meaning leaving almost no breathing space: *what you experience, that is called in psychology* . . . So perhaps the escape from this straitjacket can only come in the dimension of the meaningless. Recall the example of Slavoj Žižek: the typical skinhead who repeats the well-known psycho-sociological platitudes on his own situation in front of the camera. This youngster is the prototype of the post-modern academic subject: after the interview – bringing up 'diminished social mobility, rising insecurity, the disintegration of paternal authority, the lack of maternal love in his early childhood' – he returns to the mob not in the least hindered by his academically correct self-assertions (Žižek, 2008b, p. 241).

This example shows that it is important to discern the educational and schoolified aspects of psychologisation. Through psychologised discourses we are addressed as students in human behaviour – as if we were all aliens who have to be taught how to move within a human environment. Post-modern man has to be informed; we need to know the figures: *20% of our children* . . . as we read in the headlines of our popular newspapers. The information of the psy-sciences gives us meaning; it structures and outlines our post-modern world. The theorisation of life is in fact post-modern life itself, life at the level of the virtual. It is thus no surprise that psychologisation is a main tenet in today's schools. The psy-factor is considered primordial in education and this requires the psy-theories to be taught *verbatim* to the pupils. Recently I saw on TV children explaining to the interviewer '*we have to respect one another and um, this also means that we have to be assertive in a, um, positive way, and there was something about emotions but I've forgot.*' These kids were using precisely the tone and manner of speaking that children traditionally used to adopt when reciting some kind of classical standardised knowledge. Thus the *homo psychologicus* has a twin, namely the *homo academicus*. In order to assess this twin, we have to move backwards in time once again.

The homo academicus: the twin

To understand psychologisation in the sense of the dissemination of 'psy-terminology', one should recall that the basic paradigm of the school as such is the theorisation of life. In opposition to this, and especially since the Enlightenment, many philosophers and pedagogues (such as Rousseau, Pestalozzi, and Froebel) promoted *real life learning*. Education was considered too artificial; teachers were therefore supposed to bring their pupils in contact with real life and take them, as Pestalozzi and Froebel would have it, as much as possible to the garden, the fields and the forests. But this could only have paradoxical effects: *real life* cannot be experienced without mediation; this is the classical (Hegelian) difference between man and animal:

we experience reality via a medium, whether it is language, culture, society or history. In addition, this loss of man's immediate and unmediated presence in the world – and how to re-mediate or simply deny it – can easily be called one of the basic themes of religion, literature, philosophy, and science. Every call for a return to *real life* is hence accompanied by a new and frequently unperceived theorisation. Thus *real life learning* was mediated first and foremost by philosophers' and pedagogues' theories of what *real life* was. What stands between Rousseau's *noble savage* and nature is Rousseau himself and his romantic theories about the noble savage.

Rousseau's ideas furthermore have laid the base for the modern notion of childhood. His model starts from the innocence of the child (in contrast to the religious view of the original sin) and its proximity to nature (Burman, 2008, p. 73). Not only can this be said to be the departure point of child psychology, but it also directly paved the way for an educational method which addresses this child of nature precisely by feeding it theory! For, as we still see today, *real life learning* begins from the *theories* of the nature of life. Moreover, what today especially becomes clear is that it is above all the human sciences and especially psychology which provide the lessons of natural life. *We're um, also meant to be assertive in a, um, positive way, and there was something about emotions but I've forgotten it.*

This kind of psycho-education has meanwhile spread far beyond the schoolyard: through the mass-media and governmental campaigns, psychologisation has found its way into the broad spectrum of society. The basic idea is that knowledge helps and empowers: *what you are going through is what psychology calls* ... The administration of theory is supposed to have preventive and even curative effects. *Knowledge* must therefore be spread, while in the meantime it is has to be obscured that our relation to reality is mediated. One of the chief characteristics of today's psychologisation lies precisely in the way we all have become psychology students, through school, work (e.g. the discourse of human resources), television and magazines. Yet again psychology claims to bring us back to the unmediated real thing: to the real you and to the things that really matter in your life. Do you want to become a parent? Take a parenting course. Problems with drugs? Enrol in a rehabilitation course. Sex problems? Consider a master-class. Are we here facing, as Johannes Beck puts it, the threatening prospect of life reconstituted as a series of learning modules (Beck, 1999)? We seem to be condemned to never grow up and remain forever under tutelage.

Sometimes the infantilising stance is breathtakingly blatant. Flanders educational specialist, the psychiatrist Professor Dr Adriaenssens[3] for example, uses a very simple scheme in his advice for parents of adolescents. He argues that it is normal for adolescents to engage in black-and-white thinking, considering 'how the brains of a teenager function'. A music-choice, becoming a vegetarian fanatic, racist talk . . . all this is connected with the fact that 'teenager brains [are] not yet fully developed' (Adriaenssens, 2007). It is simple: no fuzz, no stories, it is about brain activity. Equally clear and simple are his words of advice: 'Do not say: "Just wait and see, you still have to learn a lot!", but say: "'You've got me perplexed here, I honestly do not know what to think"' (Adriaenssens, 2006). In this way, parents of adolescents will achieve much more according to the expert. Of course, here already the stories come in; stories meant to pre-script your life, providing you with your role and your lines. But can you imagine yourself pronouncing those artificial and mannered prefab sentences? Of course the expert anticipated any hesitance on that ground, as Dr Adriaenssens contends: 'although today's generation of parents has not learned to communicate, it can be trained' (Adriaenssens, 2006). It is clear; this psycho-social part of Lifelong Learning as it has been fully deployed in the last decades by governmental agencies, the educational system, resource centres, the media, etc., is gradually transforming our postmodern habitat, our public sphere and our everyday life in a general and psychologised Academia. But, again, how did we come here? Let us take a further step into the past.

Ecce Homo: the labour pains

The Belgian historian Jacques Claes argues that psychology emerged because there was a need to reconnect man with, as Claes coins it, a 'receding world' (Claes, 1982, p. 31). Before the Enlightenment, man lived in a world where God was present in everything, whether living or not. This *emanation*, God as the common denominator, mediated the human being's presence and its being in the world. When, in the Renaissance, the word psychology was coined – traditionally attributed to Rudolf Goclenius (1547–1628) – something must have changed. As Claes puts it; through a gradual process of secularisation the human being became more and more disentangled from the world, and it is there that psychology emerged as the mediator, the means to position the subject once again in a meaningful relation with the world.

As such it is clear that in modernity *ecce homo* (behold the man) got a reflexive twist. In a secularised world the human being was solicited to contemplate himself, and there he only found a doubting and thus reflexive being. Remember how René Descartes (1596–1650) grounded modern subjectivity in the very act of doubting: *I doubt, therefore I think, and therefore I am.* However, this gaze turned inwards is quite problematical: if I am the one who doubts and thinks, who is then the *I* speaking? The answer is: I am the I who says he is the one who doubts and thinks. But then who is that I? In other terms: who is that storyteller always shifting a place? Descartes still relied on God to get a grip on this infinite shifting of the reflective perspective. The Cartesian radical split between *res cogitans*, the thinking agent, and *res extensa*, the outside world, is guaranteed by God: God is acting as the go-between (think of the occasionalism of Nicolas Malebranche assuming God as the only causal agent: even in the case of lifting one's arm a divine intervention must be presupposed.).

Later Julien Offray de La Mettrie took up Descartes' problem in such a decisive way that his book *L'homme machine* (*Man Machine*) (La Mettrie, 1996 [1747]) provided science with a basic paradigm which is respected to this day. La Mettrie solved Cartesian dualism by denying the *res cogitans* any substance as such: for La Mettrie, all the aspects of the soul have to be considered as aspects of the *res extensa*. 'Man' is a machine; thinking, willing, feeling are but bodily reactions and functions; soul is something material, observable in the nerves and in the brain. Or, also stories are brain activity! La Mettrie grounded his argument on future research; once our knowledge and techniques will be refined enough to prove that the soul is but the function of the body. A very modern academic stance indeed: just think about the history of ADHD: first denominated Minimal Brain Damage, it became Minimal Brain Dysfunction – because no lesions were found – till finally it became ADHD: solid in its abbreviation of merely behavioural symptoms, it carries in its core the ever postponed promise to find the organic base of this disturbance in some undefined future.

La Mettrie's materialism was criticised from the beginning as it undermines any religious or moral dimension; when man is a machine only the law of nature prevails. But this debate on moral nihilism often misses the central paradox of equating 'man' to animal as well as to machine. Since in the equation, the question of what the human being is cannot but persist: even when we would have charted the whole brain and would understand fully the mechanics and chemistry, the image would be equally puzzling: the human being as that strange creature asking the question *who is man* while holding his brains in his hand and contemplating it from all sides. Considering 'man' as a machine-animal cannot but reveal the human as that mysterious being who came to look upon himself as a machine-animal. As Marc De Kesel contends, La Mettrie's solution of reducing the *res cogitans* to the *res extensa* left that problematic mythical point – situated beyond *res extensa* – intact: the point from which the human being looks upon himself (De Kesel, 2008). La Mettrie made of 'man' a sick cow, but the puzzled (and puzzling) gaze of the dog remained. La Mettrie only made it clearer that the modern, Cartesian subject relates to himself and the world via the academic gaze. Furthermore, as De Kesel argues, this zero level of subjectivity is also the neutral and objective point that science presupposes when engaging in scientific research (De Kesel, 2008). The modern subject is an academic subject, the unbridgeable gap between himself and the object in the world outside, eventually also bears on himself and on his self-experience. The subject always falls between two chairs. Maybe it is in this way that we can understand that La Mettrie eventually adopts a seemingly amoral hedonistic stance. In his writing *L'Art de Jouir* he says that if you kill a man or rape a woman, it should not bother you, you could not have helped it; so do not let remorse upset you (La Mettrie, 1987). Having reduced the subject to a zero level, and the question of subjectivity however still persisting, La Mettrie thus comes up with a very *Sadean* answer to disavow this gap: *have no remorse, just follow the law of nature.* But, it should be clear, considering man as a machine-animal does not open the path to an uncomplicated natural way of being. For the human to be one with nature cannot but come in a perverted way: the human can only play or mimic the animal driven by nature. La Mettrie, covering up the zero level of subjectivity with a natural subject, thus ends up with the sadomasochistic subject. Incidentally, the filiation between La Mettrie and Sade was proclaimed by Sade himself. Perversion is a way to deny the abyss of the human subjectivity, for which as Sade shows us, a whole corpus of knowledge, *la philosophie du boudoir*, is needed to enable this enactment (De Sade, 1990). Sade thus reveals how knowledge and academia itself are potentially structured as a perversion: the dogma of there is nothing but brain activity is not an innocent story (De Vos, 2011b).

Modern culture's way of handling the question of what is the human being is fundamentally marked by La Mettrie and De Sade. Consider for example that in our globalised day and age we are flooded with the Sadean pre-scriptions *Enjoy! It is your Duty!* These commands are clearly grounded within science. For example, although today in advertising, the serious, non-ironic use of the man in the white coat has almost disappeared (notwith-standing the obvious exceptions of toothpaste or washing powder ads); the frame of science is omnipresent. The consumer is invariably addressed as a proto-scientist, having adopted the scientific gaze to look upon him or herself. For example, Flora spread has on its official website[4] next to the home button, three other buttons *know your heart, heart healthy living, cholesterol advice*: food consumption is for the everyday consumer a scientifically informed business. We are far removed here from a natural subject; we are fully in the midst of mediation, if not to say, in the midst of stories, scientific stories. It could, moreover, be argued that advertisement increasingly appeals to consumers' familiarity with the *psychological* storyboard. As Daunton and Hilton write 'it is now something of a duty to explore personal identity through consumption' (Daunton and Hilton, 2001, p. 31). L'Oréal's 'Because You're Worth It', for example directly refers to the self-esteem and self-worth discourse in psychology. Nike's 'Be Real, Be You, Be True' – and, design your own custom shoe – on its turn appeals to the authenticity injunction, the (paradoxical) psy-command par excellence. It is crucial to understand that we are not dealing with clever advertisers who use psychology to address our subconscious emotions or hidden drives, no, they directly appeal to the consumers' familiarity with the widespread imagery of psychology, to its own proto-scientific position.

It is in this way that we are addressed, not only by consumerism, but also by the medical specialist, the omnipresent psychologist, the social worker, or the teacher (who has to combine all these professions), all bombarding us with stories and instant academic answers serving our insatiable quest for authentic being. The fact that we are that much flooded with answers is maybe what inspired José Saramago in the epigraph of one of his last novels: 'we will know less and less what is a human being' (Saramago, 2008). Saramago testifies of today's discontents if not of a crisis in our academicised and psychologised culture. However, before we return to the present times, we still have to clear some things up. For, if it is now clear that modernity brought us the modern psychological/psychologised subject, the question has still to be made explicit: how to understand the relation between subjectivity and the sciences, and what is the place of psychology as a discipline in all this? Let us therefore turn to Edmund Husserl, who writing in the interwar period, also saw a crisis, or better, a redoubled crisis: a crisis in the sciences and a crisis in psychology. His understanding of the origin of these crises can bring us to the moment of procreation of the *homo psychologicus*; a procreation predestining its birth as a de-subjectivised subject.

The de-subjectivised subject: the procreation

In his Vienna lecture of 1935 entitled *Philosophy and the Crisis of European Man*, Husserl tries to account for what was then considered as the 'European Crisis'. In the twentieth century it became clear that, after the debacle of the First World War, a new global catastrophe was in the making. Husserl, making the diagnosis that the European nations are sick and that Europe itself is in a critical condition, asks why the sciences fail to provide remedies or solutions. His answer is that the sciences themselves are in a crisis and that this is directly responsible for the broader *crisis of the European man*.

In his work *The Crisis of the European Sciences and Transcendental Phenomenology* Husserl traces the origin of the crisis of the sciences in their inability to deal with the fact that consciousness, rather than merely being an object in the world, is also a subject for the world (Husserl, 1970, p. 178). This failure is for Husserl particularly visible in psychology, which had explicitly sought to become 'the universal science of the subjective' (Husserl, 1970, p. 112). Psychology, because of its naturalism, misses the radical and genuine problem of the subject, or as Husserl calls it, 'the life of the spirit' (Husserl, 1970, p. 299). This is Husserl's harsh but concise diagnosis: as science deals with objectivity, it cannot take subjectivity into account. This is where psychology must come in. However, for wanting to be a science as the others, psychology fails as per definition.

From this we can infer that subjectivity is not that what precedes the sciences, it is not something which is there in the world and unfortunately does not fall within the range of science. For in the latter position the conclusion would be that we should just promote an extra-academic and extra-scientific psychology. This would open the way for New Age or other kinds of religious or spiritual psychologies. In contrast, drawing upon Husserl the only possible conclusion is that the procreation of modern subjectivity is inextricably linked to the advent of modern sciences. Modern subjectivity is precisely the result of the objectivations of the natural sciences. To explain this let us start from Husserl's insight that the crisis of science lies in the loss of its meaning for life (Husserl, 1970, p. 5); that is, science 'abstracts from everything subjective' (Husserl, 1970, p. 6). Husserl dramatically presents this alienation of modern man – in an 'all that is solid melts into air'-way – as follows: '. . . all the shapes of the spiritual world, all the conditions of life, ideals, norms upon which man relies, form and dissolve themselves like fleeting waves, [. . .] reason must turn into nonsense, and well-being into misery' (Husserl, 1970, p. 7). Science envisions the mastery of the totality of being 'without anything left over' (Husserl, 1970, p. 22). Hence, the charting of the world does not add meaning, it deprives it of meaning. Does the dimension of the subjective not crumble away here? In contemporary terms: if you are but a function of brainwaves and evolutionary mechanisms, then in the end there is not much *you* or subjectivity left. Science is the disenchantment of all human and social realities as they are reduced to objectified and measurable mechanisms. On the other hand, it is maybe exactly in this zero-level of subjectivity that the modern subject as such sees light. For, can we not say that the sick cow of the sciences creates the gaze of the startled and baffled dog? In other words: science's *this is what you are* engenders an extra point *beyond* the explanation, a point from where the answer can come: *oh really, is that me?* In short: the de-subjectivating effects of the objectivations of science result in a surplus: the modern subject as the carrier of the scientific gaze. If science creates a *human zoo* this also means the procreation of a new subject; the de-subjectivised spectator: *look at me, it must be my genes/that really fits my cognitive map /I probably have repressed that.*

In Husserl's writing it is furthermore clear that the double movement of de-subjectivation and subjectivation actually constitutes the very condition of science as such. For, the expulsion of the subject is the primary condition for objectifying mathematical science as such. The man or woman in the white coat must him or herself be de-subjectified, as he or she must do away with all the 'cultural properties which are attached to things in human praxis' (Husserl, 1970, p. 51). Thus while on the one hand the emptied subject is spawned by science and its advancing objectivations, on the other hand, this zero-level subject is the very condition for science: it is the point from where the objectivations can be done.

It is here that we find psychology, and consequently, according to Husserl, its 'tragic failure'. For, as the enigma of subjectivity spawned by modern science needs a psychology, psychology according to Husserl wrongly adopts the methodology of the mathematical or natural sciences. Psychology thus tries to solve the problem of subjectivity with the very tools that engendered it. Psychology is the paradoxical business of trying to objectify subjectivity, the latter itself the result of objectification. Just consider how today subjectivity is always the object of newer and more enhanced brain-scanning techniques. Contemporary psychologists thus seem caught in a catch 22: as they claim the independent status of psychology by taking over the neurological paradigms.

So if we return to Jacques Claes' idea that psychology had to connect man with a receding world, then now we can complete the picture. Offering the subject a vantage point to look upon itself and the world, psychology connects the modern subject not to itself but to its double, the *psychological homunculus* it is said to be. The latter can thus be said to only be a presupposition and a construction of psychology itself. Psychology in this way is as such the praxis of psychologisation: it creates the psychological gaze as well as the psychological imagery to look at. It is this that may only become fully clear in the late-modern phenomena of psychologisation. Consider for example psychotainment shows on television: *please join me and watch closely what has happened*, thus says the *Supernanny* as she invites the parents to look at the recorded footage. The parents are thus supposed to adopt the academic expert-gaze of the Supernanny and watch together with her the *psychologoids* on the screen. It should be clear, this is not just about televised infotainment, this video-method is already being advised for parents to use at home: tape your kid's behaviour and talk to him or her about it in front of the TV set. The psychologised human being assumes a de-psychologised, zero-level position beyond the alleged psychological reality.

Psychologisation in late modernity: the afterbirth

This short genealogy of the *homo psychologicus* can allow us to better situate today's phenomena of psychologisation in their relations to science, culture and politics. For, it is only now, in the turn to late modernity, that the *homo psychologicus* becomes full blown, exactly where he loses any psychological or psychic quality. Psychologisation culminates in these times of globalisation in its opposite, it depicts us the human being at the end of all stories. In this foretold death of the psyche, the modern psychological human being itself might thus have played the role of the vanishing mediator. The disappearance of Man, in the words of Foucault, 'erased, like a face drawn in sand at the edge of the sea' (Foucault, 2002, p. 442), hence seems to pass over psychology and psychologisation. Here psychoanalysis, as the paradigmatic psychological theory of modernity, can be said to have played a central, mediating role, but one which makes it very apt to use for a critique of psychologisation. For, Freudian psychoanalysis, equally proclaimed death, is at its best a theory and a praxis which does not close the gap between psychologisation and de-psychologisation, between subjectivation and de-subjectivation. Freud's endeavour was precisely to assess the human being from within this gap, this *Spaltung*, as the place of the faulty acts, the dreams, the symptoms, in short, the place of the modern subject as such. However, in the building of a corpus of knowledge, psychoanalysis also became, as said, the mother of all psychologisation, fuelling various attempts to fill the abyss of subjectivity. Moreover, even if it can be said that before the becoming popular of psychoanalysis psychology already had found its way into multiple places of human life, one can argue that only with psychoanalysis the psy-discourse finally reached everyday life. For, by drawing issues such as faulty acts and dreams into the explanatory framework, the psy-discourse realised a quasi-omnipotent and all-encompassing grip on human reality. In this way psychoanalysis gave an important impetus for a revival of the psy-sciences and academic psychology in the beginning of the twentieth century.[5] In the wake of the success of psychoanalysis, the psy-sciences claimed a psychological explanation for things until then not analysed within a psychological framework – or not analysed at all.[6]

This colonisation hence led to a pan-psychologisation: nothing could escape the field of fire of psychology. And where everything is psychological, the concept threatens to lose its sharpness and every point of significance. This is where pan-psychologisation shifted to an opposite position, as it led to understanding all humans under the sun in a narrow biological and neurological framework (see De Vos, 2008). As already said, the mainstream psychologist today does not believe in the psyche, but in the genome, the neurotransmitters and the heritage of our past as hunters-collectors: the rest are believed to be stories. Novelist psychoanalysis definitely has had its time: its complex theorems like narcissism, polymorph-perverse sexuality, or the death-drive are dismissed. For the contemporary psy, the human being and the world are fairly simple things: ADHD for example is a disturbance in the stimuli management in the brain, the remedy is medication, psycho-education and empowering of the network. Depression? A problem with neurotransmitters, the remedy: medication, psycho-education and empowering of the network. In short: life itself is a biological disturbance which asks for medication, psycho-education, and empowering of the network. The rest are stories. One should be careful not to wave all this aside as a caricature: of course biological and neurological research is far more complicated and a lot of the psychological academic theories are more nuanced, but it suffices to look at the majority of practices in everyday psycho-social praxis and education to know which models are the hegemonic ones and influence and shape the actual policies. Those models are invariably so transparent and so perspicuous that they tend to obfuscate human reality and thus seem to realise Saramago's already mentioned dictum that we will know less and less what is a human being.

The fact that the waning of the novelist and hermeneutic approaches is taking place on the threshold of the twenty-first century should also be understood in relation to the alleged end of history and of the grand narratives in politics and ideology. Today's dismissal in psychology of the psyche is thus closely connected with the dismissal of another central point in the heritage of the Enlightenment: the political dimension. Since the fall of the Berlin Wall, the substantiation of the fundamental Other in politics ceased to exist. The European-American model of democracy became not only the sole player but rapidly wanted to get rid of its ideological garb. Fused with market capitalism, the Western political model came to understand itself as something near to the normal, natural state of affairs. In this way politics evacuated the element of ideological choices and became reduced to the art of expert administration, or, as Žižek contends, it became politics without politics (Žižek, 2004a). The political space opened up by modernity thus threatens to be closed down. Descartes' idea of the *res extensa* entailed the paradigmatic disclosing of a space where God was no longer involved, God's role was reduced and limited to furnish the keystone to Cartesian dualism. This desecrating of the world made science as well as modern politics possible. *Res extensa* thus came to harbour two things: the birth of the autonomous State, and the autonomous Individual (yet in the Cartesian perspective both against the background of respectively God's Empire and the Soul). The conceptions of both State and Individual were closely connected: no State without the autonomous Individual (the principle of democracy) and no Individual without the autonomous State (the rule of Law). Modernity thus created a *psycho-political subject*. In today's politics however any beyond seems lost, Descartes' idea to ground the reality *sub sole* transcendentally with God's Empire and the Soul, is left behind. Academia is our sole space and covers our whole reality. While in pre-modernity the reflexive gaze was incorporated and bound within a religious discourse (God knew all your thoughts), in modernity this position shifted to science and to knowledge. And where

Academia renounced every transcendentalism, the State and the Individual were thus reduced to units (identical to themselves) to be managed by academic and expert ways of handling things. This is what only culminates in late-Modernity. Furthermore, with the end of the Cold War and the falling away of a concrete other side of Western democracy, the circle has been made round. However, we should not be trapped in the illusion that this is a smooth process. For is what we now witness not the return of the beyond: do the transcendent God and Soul of Descartes not return in meaningless violence, in terrorist threats and fundamentalist intolerance stemming from both Christian and Islamic sides? However, it is important not to regard these instances as a mere return to pre-modern, religious forms of subjectivity or to some naturalistic essence of the human being. Rather, these are all instances of the modern condition. They are all testifying that where a naturalised approach on the human and on society becomes hegemonic the zero-level of subjectivity (understood on both the individual and social level) returns in a violent way. Or in others words: it is precisely when the death of the *homo psychologicus* is declared that its afterbirth is coming to haunt us.

So maybe we have to reinvent *res extensa*, starting from reopening the impossible Cartesian gap. Thinking beyond Academia we have to reinvent politics and the psycho-political subject, we have to reinvent psychology, we have to reinvent psychoanalysis: we have to think again the zero level of subjectivity. If not, the obverse of our Academic truth and conceit will again and again resurface and haunt us. If for Illouz, referring to Weber's theory on *theodicy* (why do the innocent suffer and the wicked prosper?) psychology is the first cultural system that deals with the theodicy problem (Illouz, 2008), one could argue against this that the supposed solving of the problem of theodicy only gave the problem a peculiar (modern) twist. Namely the theodicy problem became: why does Academia as the successor of the religious discourse itself engender suffering and wickedness despite its best intentions? Psychology in its vocation to be the keystone of the paradoxical modern subjectivity clearly has its structural dark shadows. This is what we will explore in the next three chapters, as these will deal with psychologisation in the respective fields of science, culture, and politics.

Notes

1   In this book I conceive of Academia not simply as the academic world or the universities. Academia, rather, stands for a specific modern discourse in which scientific knowledge is the point of departure for what is said and what is done (in Lacanian terms this is the *discourse of the university*). For, although expertise and knowledge historically has a role in a variety of praxes and power relations (e.g. shamanism), it can be argued that only in modernity does objective knowledge become a totally separate realm which in its own right claims

sovereignty. This claim can be assumed by various agents within a whole array of societal spheres. The psy-discourse and hence the psy-complex are in this way a part of Academia – albeit, as we will see, a central part.

2   For the use of the word 'skandalon' I am inspired by René Girard who connected the Greek word *skandalon* (an obstacle that one cannot avoid) to Freud's conceptualisation of desire: linked to a particular obstacle, desire always returns to what it collides with (Girard, 2002).

3   A similar academic expert on education, widely known with the public is, for example, Robert Winston in the UK.

4   At the time of writing.

5   For a more elaborate account of psychoanalysis' entanglements with psychology and psychologisation see my article 'Psychologization or the Discontents of Psychoanalysis' (De Vos, 2011d)

6   The history of psychology is characterized by subsequent rebirths. As said, the term psychology itself saw light in the renaissance with Rudolf Goclenius (1547–1628). But it is only with the psychophysics of Fechner in the nineteenth century that psychology claimed an independent position within the hard sciences (Claes, 1982). The next big rebirth can be situated after the impact of the Freudian movement, which necessitated a repositioning of the psy-sciences.

2 Psychologisation and the sciences

Is psychology a science? This question heated many debates and, one could argue, at its own assured psychology's place within Academia, albeit only in the argument that up till now, there are some unscientific aspects in psychology, but in the not too far away future psychology will be taken up in the 'rise of the sciences'. One could also claim that when psychology will reach its rightful place in the premiere league of Academia, this will also entail the end of psychologisation, here understood as the end of the unhappy overflow or colonisation of the other sciences. To surpass this rather unfruitful hypothetical debate, another, double, question can be asked: what are the sciences for psychology and what is psychology for the sciences? Here the issue is not the future fully assured scientific tenure of the discipline – or, as the opposite alternative, its complete disappearance and incorporation in the neurosciences – but, rather, the historical vicissitudes of the place of psychology in Academia. How did psychological theory and praxis evolve with the unfolding of the history of the project of the modern sciences, and more broadly, the project of modernity? As argued in the first chapter, modern subjectivity is a function of the objectifications of modern science: psychology is the attempt to both give form, to contain and to master the modern subject, the subject of the sciences. Hence it is important to look back at the moments where this project ran into crisis and to scrutinise how this affected and was affected by the discipline of psychology.

This is also the wager of Edmund Husserl, who we discussed in the first chapter. Husserl understood the crisis of Europe in the interwar period as a crisis of the modern sciences and pointed to the crucial place of psychology. His verdict was simple: psychology from the very beginning chose the wrong path by trying to objectify the problem of subjectivity. It is worthwhile to take a look at attempts made in the broader social sciences to grasp the important and vast changes at the turn of the nineteenth century which dramatically changed the coordinates of the human and its life-world. Especially before and just after the debacle of the First World War we can witness the rise of so-called social psychology. This new branch of psychology wanted to account for the immense societal changes and their impact on the individual which neither classic individual psychophysical and functional psychology, nor the emerging disciplines of behaviourism and psychoanalysis seemed able to assess. Gabriel Tarde's inter-individual psychology (Tarde, 1989 [1901]) or Gustave Le Bon's psychology of the masses (Le Bon, 2002 [1895]) can for example be said to have greatly influenced Sigmund Freud's attempt to get a hold on the social level and its meaning in psychoanalysis in for example *Culture and its Discontents* (Freud, 1955 [1930a]).

The impact of the Second World War on the social and psy-sciences might easily be said to have been even greater. The more than 60 million casualties, of which more than 6 million perished in the Holocaust, the unimaginable horror of the use of the atomic bomb on civilian populations . . . all this defied any account from within the established frameworks. Science fell short of any explanation, let alone that it could provide solutions or offer any prophylactic approach to prevent the repetition of the atrocities. Some even asked a more radical question: what if the project of Modernity itself harbours the very potential leading up to these catastrophes of humanity? If this was the stance Adorno and Horkheimer were drawn to (Adorno and Horkheimer, 1989 [1944]), the more traditional academic disciplines rather attempted to restore the belief in the project of the sciences: the atrocities of the Second World War solicited a renewed effort to get a hold on human nature. As in the case of the First World War, psychology was again summoned to deliver both a psychological explanation and the means to prevent repetition. Once again, psychology was to deliver the cornerstone of the endangered scientific-technological edifice of modernity.

In this chapter I will first turn to the social psychologist Stanley Milgram's attempt to get a grip on what the Second World War showed modern humanity capable of. In general one can say that the originality of Milgram was that he was able to span two opposed sets of explanation. On the one hand the psy-sciences turned to the personality of the 'perpetrator'. Adorno for example, even with his radical conclusion of the Second World War as the inherent outcome of the Enlightenment, still sought in *The Authoritarian Personality* (Adorno et al., 1993 [1950]) for an individual, psychoanalytical explanation of the perpetrator. On the other hand, other scholars attempted to understand the barbarities people proved to be capable of in terms of situational facts. Milgram provided the link between these two explanations with his experiments on obedience. This *tour de force* meant that his experiments incited much interest far beyond the university walls. It can easily be said to be the most popularised experiment of the post-war period and thus as such a central example to scrutinise the phenomenon of psychologisation. In this chapter I will engage in a close reading of the experiment together with that other famous experiment, Philippe Zimbardo's Stanford Prison experiment, which as I will argue, should be seen as the twin experiment, the necessary sequel to the Milgram experiment. My thesis is that juxtaposing the two experiments will allow us to assess how the discipline of psychology reinvented itself after the Second World War.

Thus rather than a full historical study, I opt here for a paradigmatic approach. My arguments to elevate the experiments of Milgram and Zimbardo into seminal examples for psychology are threefold. First, I am not the only one to do so: one of the American Psychological Association's most prominent presidents, George Miller, considered the two experiments crucial for psychology. In his presidential address in 1969, Miller pleaded to 'give psychology away', claiming this is the royal road towards 'psychology as a means of promoting human welfare'. For Miller both the Milgram and the Zimbardo experiment were the ideal means for psychology to disseminate its knowledge to a broad audience (cited in Blass, 2000, p. 208). From this it already follows that the two experiments show in a condensed way how post-war psychology reasserted itself as a science after the deadlock of the two world wars, precisely by 'giving itself away' which is, of course, a concise definition of psychologisation. The fact that indeed a vast audience has knowledge of the experiments is therefore significant. A second reason to consider the experiments as paradigmatic is that a close reading of the twin experiments of Milgram and Zimbardo furnishes us with a scheme which enables us to lay bare the structure of the main currents of the discipline of psychology up till today, that is, they lean on the paradigm of psychol-ogisation. The third argument is handed to us via the recent history of psychology in which both experiments were constantly evoked and referred to, testifying to their importance and, at least in my reading, to their seminality for the whole discipline of psychology. For, as 2007 APA president Ronald F. Levant echoed Miller and pleaded to make 'psychology a household word' (Levant, 2007), psychology was indeed spread worldwide during his presidency. That is, Northern American psychology was exported with the help of US intelligence to the US detention sites all over the world, with Guantánamo and Abu Ghraib as the most-known examples. It is precisely there that we re-encounter Milgram and Zimbardo: as they were repeatedly invoked to explain the collaboration of psychologists in the so-called enhanced interrogation techniques via the psychological explanatory scheme itself.

This infamous history of psychologists working in the US detention sites I shall address in the second part of this chapter, where I shall claim that with the recurrent psychologisation of its involvement in torture, the discipline of psychology once again missed its encounter with history. In the third part of this chapter I will further explore this post-cold war (non?)-crisis in psychology in order to return to the question *what are the sciences for psychology and what is psychology for the sciences?* If our answer will be that psychology/psychologisation is the structural blind spot of the project of the modern sciences, then it will be clear that the stakes of the debate are high.

From Milgram to Zimbardo: the double birth of post-war psychology

Milgram's shocking answers

In Stanley Milgram's experiment on obedience a naive subject finds himself in a room together with another person who is actually a confederate of Milgram's. An experimenter in a grey lab coat tells them that they take part in a learning experiment to study the effects of punishment on learning. A rigged draw assigns the naive subject the role of teacher and the confederate the role of learner. The latter is strapped into a chair with one arm connected to the so-called shock generator. The teacher, in the baseline condition of the experiment, is seated in an adjacent room behind a switchboard. He is instructed to conduct a word-pair test via the intercom and to punish each wrong answer with an electric shock, increasing the shock by one level after each failure. The experimenter, in his lab coat, takes place behind the naive subject and, whenever the test subject protests or refuses to go on, he intervenes with pre-scripted phrases such as *the experiment requires that you continue.*

In an attempt to understand the horrors of the Nazi epoch, Milgram devised the experiment to study people's willingness to obey an authority figure who gives instructions which conflict with their personal conscience (Milgram, 1974, pp. 114–115). While Gordon Allport called it the *Eichmann Experiment*, Milgram himself indicated that Hannah Arendt's conception of the banality of evil came close to his own experimental findings (Milgram, 1974, p. 6). The first thing we need to look more closely at, then, is how Milgram understands or, better, *stages* authority. Yannis Stavrakakis contends that Milgram understood that it is not the substance of the command but the source of authority that is decisive. This source is supported by a scenario, or, as Stavrakakis puts it in Lacanian terms, by a *fantasy scenario*. For Stavrakakis it is clear that the phantasmic frame in the experiment is science itself. The command is taken seriously by the naive subject insofar as it comes from Scientific Research (Stavrakakis, 2007, p. 175). We should understand this as meaning that the subjects are not actually naive in the sense that they would be pre-Enlightenment creatures unschooled in the ways of science. They are already addressed as subjects familiar with and marked by science.

Moreover, if Milgram obtains obedience with academic currency, he does not think this through. He chooses science as a mere contingent example of authority, as he suggests that he also could have used military or religious authority (Milgram, 1974, p. 142). This choice becomes particularly problematic when he additionally chooses *psychological science* – the subjects are told they are participating in an experiment on the psychology of learning – as the focus of the experimental set-up. In this way the experiment is pervaded by all kinds of unquestioned loops.

Quite surprisingly, these short-circuits are missed in mainstream critiques and, in this way, the real problematic core of Milgram's experiments remains out of sight. For, while the experiments have been criticised as a mere triumph of social engineering (e.g. Edward E. Jones, cited in I. Parker, 2000, p. 112)[1] or as a mere dramatisation of people's capacity for violence (Brannigan, 2004), the question of what exactly it is that is being enacted in the experiment seems to be overlooked. An enactment or a dramatisation presupposes a script, and as Stavrakakis pointed out, this is related to the (fantasy) scenario of science. To this, I add that it is psychology in particular which is providing the script for the Milgram experiment. So let us first discern how the scenario runs and, secondly, which roles or discursive positions are played out.

Concerning the baseline of the scenario, the key is to understand the didactic candid-camera moment when Milgram himself enters the room to lift the veils of deception, disclosing the *learner* as a confederate. The paradox is that, while Milgram wanted to show that obedience to authority is situational, in the moment of revelation the core of the experiment is revealed to be, surprisingly, *individual psychology*. In the post-experimental debriefing the use of standard questions such as *Do you feel upset?*, *What did you feel?*, or *Now that you know, how do you feel?* shows how Milgram ends up psychologising the issue of obedience. That is, the candid-camera moment not only reveals the gaze of the big Other of Academia, it also invites the participants to subject themselves to the discourse and signifiers of the psy-sciences. *Now that you know, how do you feel?* In this light we can understand Milgram's triumphant proclamation that the participants on the whole viewed the experiment as an opportunity to learn something about themselves and the conditions of human action (Milgram, 1974, p. 196). Milgram's experiment thus shows that looping effects in psychological research are not secondary but primary: in the debriefing the script of psychology (underlying the whole experiment) reasserts itself in full vigour. Or, with Milgram, psychologisation is the dramatic, enacted means by which psychology asserts itself as a science.

Let us now turn to the roles and the subject positions at play in the enactment. To start with, the naive test-subject is, surprisingly, put in the role of an experimental learning psychologist carrying out a word-pair test. While it is rather illogical to be asked to conduct an experiment, strangely enough not one of the participants questions this. Perhaps we have 100 per cent obedience here because the assignment of this role simply repeats general psychologisation processes in which everyone is turned into a proto-psychologist and encouraged to adopt a scientific gaze. Moreover, it is exactly in the role of psychologist that the participant is cast as the obedient bureaucrat inflicting torture and pain! However, if it is 100 per cent obedience that we are looking for, there might be a much easier place to find it. Namely, Milgram got his 100 per cent from the *experimenter* who instructed the test-subject with his monotone prompts such as *You have no other choice, you must go on.* Milgram's film footage shows an experimenter mechanically and emotion-lessly repeating his scripted phrases while the obviously agitated and stressed subjects express their desire to stop (Milgram, 1965a). So, while Milgram dismisses the Freudian explanation of aggressive and destructive tendencies (Milgram, 1974, p. 165), do these not re-emerge unexpectedly on the side of the experimenter? One must conclude that the obedient bureaucrat-torturer was already written twice into the experiment. As Dannie Abse suggests, Milgram, looking for little Eichmanns, constructed a scene with an experi-menter in the role of Himmler (cited in Brannigan, 2004). The role of the obedient bureaucrat-torturer is situated both with the naïve subject, as the proto-psychologist, and with the experimenter, in the role of senior psychol-ogist. This leaves us with Milgram's own role. Is he not the figure of the ultimate malevolent scientist collecting from his participants the *surplus-value* of his scripted experiment? His post-experimental *Now that you know, how do you feel?* is meant to harvest the psychologising answers to make his case on obedience. In the debriefing he invariably explains his theory on obedience for which the test subjects have provided the scientific data. Hence, are Milgram's subjects not de-subjectivised as they are reduced to the obedient objects of the power of psychological knowledge? Milgram reports proudly that a large number of subjects spontaneously requested to be *used* (sic) in further experiments (Milgram, 1965b, p. 58). Consumed in the candid-camera moment, the test-subjects become the mere objects of the psy-sciences. Milgram's promised emancipation from blind obedience is actually the mere imposition of the powerful and un-emancipatory discourse of psychology. However, as an enactment, Milgram's *shocking answers* (Zimbardo's quip) to the incomprehensible horrors of the Holocaust still needed an amendment; in order to ground them in something more than a mere dramatisation and a looped and pre-scripted analysis. This is where Zimbardo comes in.

Zimbardo's psychological *study of prison life*

Historically, Zimbardo's prison experiment cannot be seen apart from Milgram's experiment on obedience.[2] Zimbardo himself recognises his indebtedness to Milgram and acknowledges various parallels between the Stanford Prison Experiment and Milgram's research on obedience (see especially Zimbardo, 2006a). Nevertheless, Zimbardo's experiment contests Milgram's thesis that authority is central in phenomena of obedience and instead puts forward that people blindly enact what is expected of them in their role as group members. In this section I will explore the parallels and the differences between the two pieces of research and try to assess in which ways Zimbardo is departing from the Milgram paradigm only, as we will see, to return to it in the end. My focus is thus not so much the historical link, but rather, the paradigmatic link, which, as I will claim, can be understood as Zimbardo's experiment being the necessary logical sequel to Milgram.

To begin with, perhaps the most striking parallel between Milgram and Zimbardo is how the discourse of psychology occupies a central, albeit unquestioned, place in both experiments. That said, considering their respective advertisements to recruit participants, something has clearly changed in the time between the two studies. While Milgram needed people 'for a study of memory', Zimbardo recruited explicitly for 'a *psychological* study of prison life' (Haney, Banks, and Zimbardo, 1973, p. 73, my emphasis). With Milgram it may have been clear to the participants that the experiment was situated within science, but it is only at a particular moment that psychology itself entered the scene, with the question *Now that you know, how do you feel?* It is only here that the subject is explicitly drawn into psychological discourse. As such, the Milgram experiment illustrates the shift in late-modernity from the *master discourse* (with a master figure as the agent) to the *university discourse* (where knowledge itself is the agent).[3] Milgram's psychologising question *Now that you know, how do you feel?* leaves behind the old *master*, exemplified in the authoritative figure in the lab coat, and opens the way for the *university discourse*, in which the knowledge of the psy-sciences takes the prominent role. Milgram, in this way, does indeed conduct an experiment on obedience. He shows or, better, enacts how, in the psychologisation processes of late modernity, humankind is called upon to *subject* itself to the psy-sciences. Zimbardo takes this logic one step further. With Zimbardo, psychology is no longer called upon to structure the scene in a second moment. From the very beginning the scene is set within a psychological discourse: 'male college students needed for psychological study of prison life.'

So where Milgram has his psychologising de-briefing moment, Zimbardo has his psychologising *pre*-briefing. The selected students were divided randomly (this time for real) into guards and prisoners, and the first group had to attend a so-called *guard orientation* meeting the day before the actual experiment. There Zimbardo addressed the guards:

> You can create in the prisoners feelings of boredom, a sense of fear to some degree, you can create a notion of arbitrariness that their life is totally controlled by us, by the system, you, me – and they'll have no privacy . . . We're going to take away their individuality in various ways . . . We have total power in the situation. They have none.
>
> (Zimbardo, 1989, my transcription)

This is surely quite directive. However, Zimbardo's co-researcher Craig Haney strongly downplays this, arguing that the guards were only told that they were not allowed to use physical punishment or aggression (Haney, Banks, and Zimbardo, 1981). Also Zimbardo invariably minimises this step. In his latest book, *The Lucifer Effect*, he maintains that the guards' orientation did not encourage them to follow a prescribed path (Zimbardo, 2007a, p. 54). But while this passage is criticised by many authors (e.g. Banyard, 2007; Brannigan, 2009; Haslam and Reicher, 2008), surprisingly none of the critics appear to see that the participants are effectively asked to take on the role of experimenter. Zimbardo literally tells the guards that it is up to them to produce the 'required *psychological* state in the prisoners' (Zimbardo, 2007a, p. 55, emphasis added). There is no doubt that the experiment is scripted, but we should not miss the fact that the script is psychological. The student-guards are asked to play the role of social scientists conducting an experiment. Banyard is right in stressing the awkward use of the pronoun *we* in *we have total power* (Banyard, 2007), but this should not be understood as *we the guards* but, rather, as *we the psychologists*.[4] While with Milgram we have a similar scenario of the test-subject being put in the place of the scientist, Zimbardo brings this scheme to a logical completion. The Milgram experiment does not really involve role play. The naive subject agrees to perform an assignment in which he effectively remains himself (in the naive sense). It is only at the end that it is disclosed that he has been playing a role. With Zimbardo it is all out in the open. Not only is it clear who is playing which part, but it is also clear to everybody that it is all a role play. The essential trick of role play is the staged lucidity within a redoubled role: Zimbardo's students are not so much instructed to play guards, rather, they are instructed to play psychologists pretending to be guards.

Another point of comparison between the experiments concerns the role of the victim. Zimbardo's shift here is to introduce the role of the prisoner, where he effectively fleshes out the victim-role which in Milgram was still played by a confederate. But there is something particular to be discerned in this shift. For, do we not find here another instance of something that while remaining concealed with Milgram was laid bare with Zimbardo; namely the aspect of humiliation? With Milgram the humiliation is implicit and only emerges in the de-briefing, where the test-subject is confronted with his reprehensible behaviour and is reduced to a mere object of social psychology. In this way, the ingenious and powerful science of psychology manages to extract from the test-subject valuable knowledge. In Zimbardo's experiment the humiliation is made explicit and primary as it shifts to the category of the prisoners. This is how Haney and Zimbardo describe the 'induction':

> A degradation procedure was designed in part to humiliate prisoners and in part to be sure they weren't bringing in any germs to contaminate our jail. The prisoners were deloused and decontaminated, they were made to wear baggy uniforms without underwear, they had to wear stocking caps to conceal their hair . . .
>
> (Haney et al., 1981)

This de-humanisation and de-subjectivation of the prisoners had started already with the staged arrests, as the students were unexpectedly picked up at their homes by local police officers while surprised and curious neighbours looked on and then, blindfolded, they were driven 'in a state of mild shock' to the 'Stanford County Jail'. Let us follow the experiment from here to see where Zimbardo's restructuring of the aspect of humiliation leads. Initially nothing much happens, things only start to unravel on the second day. The prisoners remove their stocking caps, rip off their numbers and barricade themselves inside the cells. Zimbardo writes that he was stunned. He had not expected a rebellion and it was not clear to him what they were rebelling against. But, one is tempted to see Zimbardo's surprise as feigned: for were not these kinds of events what he had hoped for? Zimbardo, however, is convinced that he sees the 'real thing' and does not appear to understand the dynamics of his own script and its loops. With Milgram the script entailed the juxtaposition of authority and conscience, which was then transcended by the psychologising disclosure of the de-briefing. Zimbardo, on the other hand, sets out with the assumed power of psychological discourse itself and what results from this is the creation of an opposition between those within this discourse and those outside it. In other words, while the guards' orientation constitutes a class of those informed by psychology, in the same movement, it constitutes the prisoners as the humiliated and debased objects of the psychological discourse.

This is precisely what Reicher and Haslam miss in their BBC Prison Study (Reicher, 2006). Their study challenges Zimbardo's theory that behaviour is determined by assigned roles and criticises the underlying message that resistance is futile. Consequently, the BBC Prison Study focuses on the 'manipulations of theoretically relevant variables' rather than assigned roles (Reicher, 2006, p. 7). Summarising their findings, Reicher and Haslam state that it is powerlessness and a failure of the group that makes tyranny psychologically acceptable. That these results seem to prove what had to be proved is not the issue here. More important is that Reicher and Haslam psychologise the situation even more than Zimbardo. Every day, the participants were subjected to psychometric testing and swabs of saliva were taken in order to ascertain cortisol levels. They knew they were being video- and audio-recorded at all times (the experiment was broadcast as a reality TV show) and that two clinical psychologists were monitoring the study throughout. Is this not the paradox of psychology as the ultimate tyrannical Big Brother? The remark of one of Zimbardo's participants that the Stanford Prison was 'a prison run by psychologists' (Zimbardo, 2007a, p. 160), gets fully realised with Reicher and Haslam. In controlling every theoretically relevant variable, they assess and control even the psycho-social determinants of the emancipatory potential. In this way, the double bind position of Zimbardo's prisoners is effectively generalised with Reicher and Haslam: every participant is the excluded–included subject of the hegemonic psycho-logical discourse. But staging absolute control makes Reicher's and Haslam's experiment rather dull since it cannot really provide anything like Zimbardo's high-pitched dramatics.

In Zimbardo's experiment it gradually becomes clear that the psychol-ogising of the guard–prisoner opposition is the very motor of the drama. While Milgram himself did the psychologising, with Zimbardo this task is assigned to his participants. This is how we can understand that, after crushing the initial rebellion, the guards announced that they were going to resort to 'psychological tactics instead of physical ones' (Zimbardo, 1999). This is, of course, nothing more than the signifier *psychology* taking yet another tour on the merry-go-round of the experiment, preparing us for yet another turn, as the brutal guard nicknamed *John Wayne* comes to the foreground, the one who was going to set the stage for the final showdown of the experiment.

For Zimbardo *John Wayne* exemplifies 'the point in time when an ordinary, normal person first crosses the boundary between good and evil' (Zimbardo, 2006b), illustrating that it is not authority but role assignment which explains obedience and consequent reprehensible and shocking behaviour. Many commentators focus on *John Wayne* to launch critiques of the experiment as a pre-scripted role play. Zimbardo eventually concedes that acting was the first step in the student Dave Eshleman's becoming *John Wayne*, but he argues that, by living the part for eight hours a day, Eshleman began 'internalis-ing his character' (cited in Zarembo, 2004). Acknowledging the first part of Zimbardo's argument, however, the question becomes again what is the baseline of the scenario and who plays which part? Eshleman's own explanation was that he drew his inspiration from the fraternity hazing he had just gone through:

> And a lot of these things I'm sure just sort of popped into our heads to see, you know, we were kind of testing the limits. You know they did anything we told them. Where's the point where they would stop and object?
>
> (Cooper, 2004)

If we take this seriously, then this puts a big question mark over Zimbardo's claim that the behaviour *John Wayne* displayed can be understood as authentic and independent of the experiment itself. For, hazing always takes place in relation to the absent authority. It is this authority that those conducting the hazing assume and of which they, as Eshleman himself contends, act to test the limits. Slavoj Žižek points out that in hazing the mimicking of the absent authority clearly reveals the obscene underside, the obscene surplus already present in the regular authority (Žižek, 2004b). In order, then, to discern what kind of authority is really being mobilised in the Stanford Prison Experiment, Eshleman's remarks are very helpful. In an interview he explains that he was acting to help Zimbardo get results. He tells us that the first night he was struck by the fact that everybody was treating the study like summer camp: 'I decided that nothing was really happening in this experiment and that in order for this experiment to get any results that somebody had to start to push the action and I took it upon myself to do so' (Cooper, 2004). Strangely enough, almost the same words return with Zimbardo: 'On the first day, I said, this is not gonna work. I mean, the guards felt awkward, giving orders. And they'd say, okay, line up, and repeat your numbers. And the prisoners would [start] giggling' (Sundance Channel, 2006).

This is not the only discursive short-circuit. Zimbardo states that he borrowed the idea of the guards wearing sunglasses from the movie *Cool Hand Luke* (Haney et al., 1981) and then Eshleman mentions the same movie as the inspiration behind his prison guard character (Cooper, 2004). Is this a case of trading places? *John Wayne* seems to be the uncanny double of Zimbardo, revealing a problematic core of the psy-sciences. Eshleman, for example, argues that he was running a little experiment on his own. Concluding that the experiment was put together to prove a point about prisons being cruel and inhumane, Eshleman decided 'to help those results come about' (Zarembo, 2004).[5] In this sense, the brutal *John Wayne* appears not as the figure of the derailed guard, but, rather, as the gestalt of the mad scientist.[6] So if the experiment reveals something about evil, as Zimbardo claims, is this not about evil emerging in the relation between the social and human sciences and the discourses of power? Evil is, then, the inevitable dark side, the underlying truth of a discourse which claims to be human and to do good. In Milgram's experiments evil was acted out in different places. It first appears with the test-subject who, in his role of experimental psychologist, is lured into bureaucratically performed cruelty. It is then located with the experimenter who, as a mad scientist, presses the poor, naive test-subject to continue. Finally, it is located with Milgram himself, as he enters the room to disclose the experimenter as the embodiment of malevolent science and to exchange the *master discourse* with the *university discourse*. Here Milgram proves to be the ultimate demiurge; having extracted valuable knowledge from his subjects, materialising it into psy-knowledge, he leaves the test subject behind, humiliated and subjected to the pseudo-emancipatory psy-discourse. With Zimbardo this power over the *homo psychologicus* is entrusted to the guards, their cruelty is ultimately the cruelty of the psy-sciences.

Zimbardo's experiment takes up the issue where Milgram leaves off, showing what happens when the scenario operates entirely under the *university discourse*. It is in this context that we can understand Zimbardo's excuse for having inflicted real pain on his participants. He admits that he got carried away in his role and was beginning to think like a prison superintendent rather than a research psychologist (Zimbardo, 1999). Is not this contention, however, based on the role-theory he precisely wants to prove with his experiment, the ultimate excuse for not having to deal with his problematic role as experimental psychologist? Maybe we should simply hold Zimbardo responsible for being carried away as a *psychologist*.

It is this we should keep in mind when we come to the *grand finale* of the experiment: where Zimbardo claims that the full immersion of each of the participants in their role leads to the encounter with the very core of the human being. This scene takes place when Zimbardo's girlfriend visits the experimental prison. Christina Maslach, who had just earned her doctorate in psychology under Zimbardo, is confronted from the open door of Zimbardo's superintendent's office with the 'toilet run chain gang', the line of hooded prisoners being led to the lavatory. Zimbardo urges her to look and relates her answer:

'I already saw it'. And she looked away again.

I was shocked by her seeming indifference.

'What do you mean? Don't you understand that this is a crucible of human behavior, we are seeing things no one has witnessed before in such a situation.'

(Zimbardo, 2007a, p. 169)

Zimbardo seems convinced he is looking at *bare life* itself, showing his girlfriend as it were the laboratory version of the Big Bang, the genesis of vibrating and pulsating life. Zimbardo appears as the sovereign, mad scientist with the life of his monster or the unmediated Real in his hands. Christina Maslach looks away in disgust and understands that to pull Zimbardo back to reality she has to introduce love into the equation by making Zimbardo choose between the fascinating Siren-like *crucible of human behaviour* and her love in the actual world. Maslach describes how she told Zimbardo that he had become a stranger to her, that she did not recognise 'the caring and compassionate person' she once knew: 'I'm not sure I want to, you know, have anything to do with you if this is the real you' (Sundance Channel, 2006).

For Zimbardo this was a slap in the face, 'the wake-up call from the nightmare that [he] had been living day and night for the past week,' and he decides to call the experiment off (Zimbardo, 2007a, p. 170). Maslach reports that a great weight was lifted from both of them and from their personal relationship (Zimbardo, 2007a, p. 171). So the story ends and they married and lived happily ever after? At least the dramatic end scene provided the perfect *deus ex machina* to close the experiment. Remember Zimbardo's hunch at the beginning of the experiment that it was 'not gonna work' (and Eshleman adding that somebody had to push the action). Should the sub-sequent escalation not then be seen as a dramatisation of 'pushing the envelope,' as Eshleman called it, to reveal the true face of humankind in a violent Armageddon? The dramatic denouement of closing down the experiment might thus, above all, have served to bring the experiment (which involved substantial expenses) to a nice conclusion, complete with Zimbardo's *mea culpa*, a moving romance and the scientific achievement of having laid bare the core of the human being.

Conclusion: how Zimbardo complements Milgram

Milgram attempted to deal with the horrors of the Nazi era, as it was there that the Western world was confronted with the deadlock of the project of Enlightenment and the impotence, or even the implication, of the scientific discourse. Milgram's experiments are the *mise-en-scène* of the departure from the master discourse and the attempt to reground science within the university discourse, in which the subject, called upon to adopt a scientific gaze, becomes a psychologised subject. Milgram testifies that the turn to the university discourse in late modernity structurally glides over the discourse of psychology and, thus, over the problematic status of subjectivity. Psychology aspires to be the meta-theory of science, resolving the breach of subjectivity in the constructions of science. Husserl already pointed to the problematic position of psychology appropriating the same objectifying paradigms that engendered the problem of subjectivity (Husserl, 1970). It can be claimed that Milgram is caught in the same paradox. In his experiment, the paradoxes of modern subjectivity not only do not return, but his experiment, moreover, shows how these paradoxes result in post-Second World War psychology being caught in a fundamental and structural psychologisation. In other words, Milgram's paradigmatic experiment lays bare how psychology cannot but ground itself in an auto-enactment and the looping of a pre-scripted situation. George Miller's call to spread psychology in this way reflects mainstream psychology's choice to re-establish itself as a science via psychologisation. In the experiments of both Milgram and Zimbardo, psychology is indeed given away; it is the very motor of the experiments.

This analysis enables us to grasp that the underlying paradigm of a whole array of theoretical and practical approaches in contemporary psychology relies on feeding psychology into the field of research or the field of action. One telling example here is the psychologisation processes of children and youth: via all sorts of media and institutions psychology is given away to parents, teachers, educators, and, last but not least, to the children themselves. Consider for example what the novelist Doris Lessing wrote commenting on Milgram:

> Imagine us saying to children: 'In the last fifty or so years, the human race has become aware of a great deal of information about its mechanisms; how it behaves, how it must behave under certain circumstances. If this is to be useful, you must learn to contemplate these roles calmly, dispassionately, disinterestedly, without emotion. It is information that will set people free from blind loyalties, obedience to slogans, rhetoric, leaders, group emotions.'

> (Lessing, 1986, p. 60)

Well there it is, in all its bluntness: let us turn the children into calm, emotionless, objective (and thus obedient) psychologists.

While Milgram can be seen as setting up the scene, Zimbardo starts from the already scripted scene. There Zimbardo is pushed to find a way to ground and fix the looping of the script of psychology in a mythical heroic journey into the underground of the Real of Man. In this way Zimbardo's enacted *passage à l'acte* affirms Milgram's paradigm of psychologisation. Zimbardo's assigning psychology the power to reveal the human as he really is moreover allows us to understand the centrality of the imagery of the real of man in processes of psychologisation. Just consider the authenticity trope in psychologisation processes: children, women, lovers, employees, consumers, politicians . . . all are summoned to get in touch with their real and true being (e.g. McGowan, 2008). We also see it in reality TV and *psychotainment shows* that supposedly lay bare the real, authentic psychological human condition. But of course the more sophisticated place of the real human today is the 'neuro-chemical self' (Rose, 2008). Coming in brain-charts and genome-patterns this new homunculus can be said to have taken the lead role in today's psychologisation processes, seemingly bypassing the paradoxical fact that the (post)modern subject is the enigmatic leftover of the process of objectification. The real you in the end is always there where you are not.

The fact that the rebirth of psychology after the war had to come in two steps – Milgram and then Zimbardo – might appear as a repetition of the original double birth of psychology as postulated by the aforementioned Jacques Claes. For Claes, psychology first emerged in the Renaissance where this new discipline had to reconnect the human with a receding, increasingly secularised world. Psychology's second birth comes with Gustav Theodor Fechner's psychophysics (Claes, 1982). Fechner regrounded psychology within the hard sciences and conceived of the human being as a psycho-physical being in order to reconnect man to a world from which he grew estranged, this time due to the fast and thoroughgoing changes brought about by technology in the nineteenth century. The second birth is a repetition, but one that consolidates the first birth within the emerging dominant framework in society. Post-war psychology, in the same way, is characterised by a double birth. Milgram, in the passage from the master discourse to the university discourse, re-grounded psychology as a science that psychologises its subject. Zimbardo warranted this process of psychologisation claiming access to the *real* of the human and hence prepared psychology's subordination to the dominance of the neurological paradigm.

Given all this, we should seriously question the recent reappearance of Milgram's and Zimbardo's experiments in the debate concerning the enhanced interrogation techniques devised in the War on Terror launched by the Bush Jr. administration in the aftermath of the 9/11 catastrophe. At least it seems doubtful whether mainstream psychology could ever, as Dan Aalbers puts it, be part of the 'clean-up crew' (Aalbers, 2008) striving to stop the abuses in contexts such as Abu Ghraib and Guantánamo where it has actually informed them.

Guantánamo and Abu Ghraib: the case of scientifically based torture

Psychology as the last holdout

In May 2006 the American Psychiatric Association banned all direct participation by psychiatrists in intelligence interrogations: 'No psychiatrist should participate directly in the interrogation of person[s] held in custody by military or civilian investigative or law enforcement authorities, whether in the United States or elsewhere' (quoted in Soldz, 2008b, p. 601).

In June 2006 the American Medical Association (AMA) stated: '(P)hysicians must neither conduct nor directly participate in an interrogation, because a role as physician-interrogator undermines the physician's role as healer and thereby erodes trust in the individual physician-interrogator and in the medical profession' (quoted in Soldz, 2008b, p. 601).

In the meantime, however, the American Psychological Association (APA) allowed their members to participate and even saw an important role for psychologists in such interrogations. It was only after the steadfast opposition of APA activists and an enforced referendum that the APA was made to change its policy. Stephen Soldz, founder of the Coalition for an Ethical Psychology, posted a press release on his website on 17 September 2008:

> Today, the membership of the American Psychological Association [. . .] passed a referendum banning participation of APA member psychologists in US detention facilities such as Guantánamo or the CIA's secret 'black sites' operating outside of or in violation of international law or the Constitution.
>
> (Soldz, 2008a)

The question we need to ask is why did psychology remain the last holdout? Many have pointed to the entrenched political interests and the dependency of the APA on military research funding (Summers, 2007). But beyond this explanation, critics and commentators invariably and inconspicuously resort to the explanatory framework of psychology itself to account for the latter's involvement in torture (for examples, see below). I want to argue that the fact that critics tend to psychologise the close link between psychology and the military is not without its problems, especially as this loop remains largely unquestioned. My thesis is that the psychological perspective, when not dealing with its own inevitable ouroborosian moment, might thus become part of the problem rather than simply one point in the conjunction of the military and psychology. That is, it is precisely the logic of psychologisation which might be seen as providing the very framework for today's practices of torture. As the (in)famous CIA Kubark manual puts it, contemporary interrogation methods cannot be meaningfully comprehended without psychology (CIA, 1963).

Our way in here is to scrutinise how the experiments of Stanley Milgram and Philip Zimbardo are repeatedly referred to, albeit often briefly, to explain the involvement of psychologists in torture. The experiments have been invoked in order to explain, for example, why psychologists obey orders that run counter to their personal and professional ethics – drawing upon Milgram

– or how psychologists find themselves on the slippery slope where 'good people turn evil' – drawing upon Zimbardo (Zimbardo, 2007a). However, there are authors who critique such psychologising explanations. Nimisha Patel, for example, points to the fact that psychological research can also be invoked by perpetrators of torture as a defence, wherein they argue that in particular social contexts and circumstances anyone can become aggressive and engage in torture practices (Patel, 2007). But perhaps there is more to be said about the recurring use of Milgram and Zimbardo regarding the involvement of psychologists in the War on Terror. The simple fact that these experiments would no longer be sanctioned by any research ethics committee and would thus be forbidden – if not illegal – points to the problematic and puzzling link between psychology and torture. It is through an analysis of the failure of psychology's current self-assessment – starting from the questionable idea that psychological knowledge is dangerous in the wrong hands – that we can begin to grasp why psychology has come to be 'the most militarized among the social or biological sciences,' as Alfred McCoy puts it (McCoy, 2006, p. 32). In this way it will become clear that the relation between psychology and the discourses of power is much more troubling than the indictment of a psychological association securing its interests in a lucrative bargain.

Milgram's blueprint for psychological torture

Jerome Bruner's foreword to the latest edition of Milgram's book *Obedience to Authority* points to the treatment of Iraqi prisoners at Abu Ghraib as proof of the relevance of Milgram's experiment (Bruner, 2005, pp. xi, xiii). Various authors consider this link as self-evident: '(A)s every graduate of introductory psychology should know from the Milgram studies, ordinary people can engage in incredibly destructive behaviour if so ordered by legitimate authority' (Fiske et al., 2004, p. 1483).

In the same vein Barbara Ehrenreich evokes Milgram to explain that 'we know that good people can do terrible things under the right circumstances' (Ehrenreich, 2004). But where there is so much supposed knowledge, it is important to go beyond a passing reference to Milgram, as most papers connecting Milgram with Abu Ghraib or Guantánamo do.

Take for example the idea that the central constellation of the Milgram experiment – the triad of learner, teacher, and experimenter – is being repeated in Abu Ghraib in the form of the detainee, psychologist, and military command (Olson et al., 2008). But maybe here the obedience of the Guantánamo or Abu Ghraib psychologist is too quickly explained by equating him to Milgram's test subject in the role of the 'teacher'. For, as said, in the experiment the most central instance of 100% obedience is to be found with the experimenter in his lab coat, mechanically repeating his prompts in order to make the 'teacher' continue. Does this role not come closer to the psychologists in Guantánamo and other military sites, who advise and instruct those doing the actual torture? But we still have to go one step further, that is, to amend the triad with a fourth term. Remember how Milgram obtains obedience with academic currency, and more particularly, borrowing it from the discipline of psychology. There the experiment is caught within an unrecognised short-circuit: the set-up of the experiment and the explanatory framework are one and the same, that is, psychology. The unquestioned fourth term backing up the triad is hence embodied by Milgram himself, as the representative of science and of psychology. This suggests that the Abu Ghraib triad of detainee, psychologist, and military command has to be amended with the fourth term of the discipline and the discourse of psychology, represented in the debate by the APA. It is a thorough reflection on the fourth term that, I claim, is missing in both the Milgram experiment and in the critical movement of psychologists against torture. So let us recapitulate Milgram's role in his experiment. The key moment is when Milgram enters the room to lift the veils of the deception. Here the gaze of psychology is revealed, as the set-up of the experiment becomes the final framework of the analysis. Milgram's question, *Now that you know, how do you feel?* harvests the induced psychologising answers in order to back up his theory on obedience which hence ultimately rests upon the prior psychologisation of the whole experimental setting. Coming back to Guantánamo and Abu Ghraib, is it not exactly the same circularity that returns in the critique of psychologists involved in torture? Again, it is assumed that psychology can facilitate both an understanding and a remedy. But the problem, as in Milgram's experiment, is that psychology is already in place; today's torture is already informed by psychology. Put differently, the problem with a psychologised understanding of today's torture practices is that it leans on the same psychological canons that inform the torture. Of course, the Milgram experiment explains a lot; it is a core element of the operative script in military settings.[7] Guantánamo and Abu Ghraib precisely revealed the use of so-called psychological torture and the actual involvement of psychologists in the practice of torture itself, and this makes a naive psychological understanding of torture highly problematic.

To push this argument to its limits, is psychology's involvement in torture not the actual realisation of Milgram's experiment? For in Milgram's experiment obedience to authority actually boils down to obedience to psychology, an obedience that results in the inflicting of harm on another human being. That is, the test subjects were asked to 'torture' for the sake of psychological research! Milgram's experiment thus seems to be the prelude to the alliance of psychology and torture; he prepared the setting for

Guantánamo. It is thus no mere happenstance that Milgram's research is central to the canonical literature that informs the enhanced interrogation of the military. The experiment itself is structured as torture, for in the moment of disclosure and debriefing, Milgram tries to extract the truth from test subjects in order to produce scientific data. It is here that we have to situate the ultimate dehumanisation and desubjectivisation, where the subject is reduced to the unemancipatory position of the object of the psy-sciences, frozen in a *Candid Camera* moment.

This sheds particular light on Olson and others' recourse to Milgram when they argue that although experiments like Milgram's are now rightly blocked for ethical reasons, they still have something significant to say about the events in Guantánamo and Abu Ghraib (see Olson et al., 2008). Are these remarks not structurally similar to the arguments used by proponents of coercive interrogation? The common idea is that the use of unethical and transgressive methods can extract the truth from subjects. In this way we cannot fail to be suspicious of the plea to remove the military psychologists and bring in the trauma psychologists. Soldz, for example, contends that psychologists should take 'the lead in forming a truth and reconciliation process facing up to the roles our profession has played in these dark times' (Soldz, 2008b, p. 597). Dan Aalbers wants psychologists to be part of the 'cleanup crew' to stop the abuses in, for example, Guantánamo. He wants to get 'the psychologists that are working for the detainers' out and bring the 'psychologists who are working for the detainees in' (Aalbers, 2008). There is a clear echo of the military discourse here from the APA's 'task force' that will look into the involvement of psychologists, and Aalbers 'cleanup crew,' to Olson's phrasing that 'fighting powerlessness and trauma should be a highest priority' (Olson et al., 2008, p. 12). Are we not here close to declaring a war on trauma? More importantly, these pleas to bring in 'good psychologists' are structurally analogous to the moment of debriefing in Milgram's experiment, which should lead us to expect little from them in the way of emancipation. In terms of our analysis, the idea of bringing in the psychologists leads us moreover to Zimbardo's Stanford Prison experiment, as it is Zimbardo's experiment that initiated a further introduction of psychology and psychologists to the American penitentiary system.

Zimbardo's prison run by psychologists: the general rehearsal

Also Zimbardo's experiment has been invoked repeatedly to explain how psychologists could be drawn into reprehensible practices in Guantánamo and Abu Ghraib. Frank Summers, for example, contends that the Stanford Prison experiment shows 'the ease with which people will inflict pain on each other' (Summers, 2007, p. 85). But this explanatory relevance has also been questioned. Banyard, for example, explicitly criticises Zimbardo's own contributions to the debate, arguing that there is a direct road from Zimbardo's experiment to Abu Ghraib; behind the scenes in these military prisons psychologists were feeding the guards ideas on how to deal with the prisoners (Banyard, 2007, p. 495). Zimbardo's interventions in the debate are indeed problematic for a few reasons. Zimbardo appeals to the standard concepts of social psychology, pointing to the 'slippery slope of initial commitments,' 'camaraderie, "group think," and the 'diffusion of responsibility' (Zimbardo, 2007b, p. 69). Psychologists in intelligence settings, he argues, are locked into social psychological mechanisms and are therefore not able to make distinctions between permissible and impermissible interrogation (cited in Rubenstein, 2007). Does Zimbardo not locate psychology in a peculiar position here, as *the* science above all other sciences, including itself? Zimbardo seems able to assess how psychologists in military service are in the grip of systemic influences and how these mechanisms also impede the APA in realising a fully informed and balanced ethical stance. But what should stop us from concluding that Zimbardo and other critics are also in the grip of systemic influences precisely insofar as they claim an Olympian perspective? Soldz points to the dangers of this assumed meta-perspective, commenting on the previous APA policy (which advocated that psychologists could keep interrogations '*safe, legal, ethical and effective,*') (Moorehead-Slaughter, 2006) he questions the assumption that psychologists have some unique moral quality that makes them able to resist situational pressures (Soldz, 2008b). But of course, in a further twist, the same critique can be made of Soldz. Are there not always situational factors to be discerned that might invalidate his claim to be able to see through things and see clearly where 'bad psychology' goes astray? In other words, what makes us critics safe from psychology?

The only way out of this loop is to decentre the naiveté and to situate it with everyone who, from a meta-perspective, thinks to look upon naive human behaviour. Take, for example, a typical assessment that draws upon Milgram and Zimbardo and urges us to rid ourselves of the naive notion that torture is perpetrated by individual monsters: '(T)these horrific acts are often perpetrated by seemingly ordinary individuals, acting within systems that allow and encourage it' (Keller, 2006, p. 567). Is it not equally or even more naive to speak in these late modern times of 'ordinary individuals' in the grip of mechanisms that psychology could lay bare? To put it bluntly, the naiveté is on the side of the psychologist who – resembling a naive anthropologist – looks down from a meta-position onto supposedly naive and ordinary persons. Zimbardo's Stanford Prison experiment, however, shows that such an ivory-tower psychology is necessarily based on a totalitarian psychologisation of the terrain surrounding the tower. After which, the psychologised terrain is considered as the true and naive reality. The Zimbardo experiment in this way is more than just feeding the guards ideas on how to deal with the prisoners; the experiment positions the guards in the position of psychological researchers. Their brutality is in the first place the reflection of the brutality linked to the processes of psychologisation. The Stanford Prison was, thus, fully staffed with guard-psychologists, with Zimbardo himself joining the crew in the role of superintendent. We thus move from Milgram's script to a general rehearsal.

Moreover, the whole ambiguity of Zimbardo, more or less denouncing his experimental setup but still claiming to have laid bare the truth of the human species, is, as it was with Milgram, strictly homologous to the structure of torture: if you want to know something, you have to transgress some boundaries. Here still another aspect becomes clear, for when in Zimbardo's experiment the scenario derails and the players start to run amok, a perverse stance enters the experiment. However, and here we have to perform yet another decentring, this perverse element does not primarily occur with the guards, but with Zimbardo himself. For is not the scene where he exclaims to behold the abyss of humanity as it really is, marked by a certain pleasure or even *jouissance*? In getting carried away, Zimbardo transgresses all boundaries and believes he has glimpsed what no mortal should: bare life. The gist of the Lacanian concept of *jouissance* is that it is to be distinguished from mere pleasure; *jouissance* is what is envisioned in a transgressive movement beyond the pleasure principle. For our purposes, Zimbardo's exalted cry of having seen 'the crucible of human behavior' should be understood within the framework of perversion and its economy of the *jouissance*. As the orgasm as the ultimate instance of *jouissance* shows, in *jouissance* the subject disappears. The trick of perversion, therefore, is to assume the place of the object of the *jouissance* of the Big Other (Lacan, 1978, p. 185). That is where we find Zimbardo, as he seems able to withstand the painful gaze of Medusa and still return to mortal life and considers his ordeal something that he has to go through for the sake of science: 'we are seeing things no one has witnessed before in such a situation' (Zimbardo, 2007a, p. 169). This idea of being the mere servant or instrument of a higher cause – be it for the sake of science or to obtain information that can save the country – links the Zimbardo experiment to torture practices via the paradigm of perversion. In the case of Zimbardo, reducing oneself to an instrument of science is strictly homologous to the position of the pervert. As Lacan states, the pervert occupies the place of the object for the benefit of another 'for whose *jouissance* he exercises his action as sadistic pervert' (Lacan, 1978, p. 185).

Thus the experiment is not about brutality as enacted by ordinary people or circumstantial sadism – an all-too-readily invoked argument in the case of Abu Ghraib – but, rather, it is about perversion and *jouissance* as operative in psychology as a scientific practice itself.[8] Perhaps this is also at stake in the shift between Guantánamo and Abu Ghraib. In Abu Ghraib the per-petrators were not part of the official interrogation team. They were military police who were asked informally by military intelligence to prepare and 'to soften up' prisoners for interrogation (Hersh, 2004, p. 29). Just like Zimbardo's students, they quickly understood what was expected from them, and they re-enacted and mimicked the official enhanced interrogation techniques. The untrained MPs were thus neither involved in *sadism on the nightshift* nor improvising or drawing upon their own allegedly *natural* sadistic impulses; rather they were acting out the military manual and its forms of torture which are the result of semi-clandestine research on the part of the American intelligence agencies in cooperation with the psy-sciences after the Second World War (McCoy, 2006). What Abu Ghraib reveals, as Žižek has remarked, is the dimension of *jouissance* involved in these practices (Žižek, 2004b). If Guantánamo stands for the ordered use of torture (informed by psychology), Abu Ghraib reveals the *jouissance* – the obscene underside and the perverse core – of the methods informed by psychology.[9]

The shift from Guantánamo to Abu Ghraib is in this way an echo of the shift from Milgram to Zimbardo. In Milgram's paradigm the autogenesis of psychology is laid bare for anyone to see, as it is founded on a mere loop. Zimbardo attempts to consolidate and to legitimate this via a mythical heroic journey into the underground of the Real of humankind. It is precisely there that the potentially perverse core of psychology fully reveals itself. Psychology is not so much a dangerous knowledge as it is a dangerous fantasy. Scrutinising these two propositions should enable us in the next section to deal with de-psychologising torture.

Conclusion: de-psychologising torture

Psychology is not a dangerous knowledge, it is a dangerous fantasy

Is it not clear that, even when one would succeed in keeping psychologists – the bad and the good – out of intelligence settings, psychology as a theoretical framework would still be used and would thus still inform the interrogation techniques and technologies? Are we thus led to the absurd conclusion that, in addition to the interdiction against psychologists working for the military, there should be an embargo on (a certain part of) the knowledge of psychology itself? But, of course, the real issue at stake is the question of whether or not psychology really constitutes a critical and thus a dangerous knowledge.

Working from Milgram and Zimbardo, this conclusion is to be doubted. For if one is to maintain that they delivered sound scientific research and reliable knowledge, one should ask whether they could have gathered this data in any way other than through their transgressive experiments. The answer is clearly negative. Their findings cannot be detached from the transgressive structure that produced them. Milgram's experiment would be impossible without the deception and the inherent humiliation that are close to the structure of torture itself. Zimbardo's experiment in turn needs the enacted transgression (Eshleman becoming the brutal and sadistic *John Wayne*) to lead to the unveiling of the so-called 'crucible of human behavior'. Milgram and Zimbardo's experiments are not about a dangerous knowledge that might potentially be misused; rather, they are performances of a technology of conduct posing as science. They do not deliver the theoretical framework or modern techniques for torture but, rather, its rationale – its practical framework – precisely in their claim to have discovered a knowledge that should be prohibited from being used for foul ends. It is this construction of an illusion that is the most dangerous aspect of both Milgram and Zimbardo's experiments.

One should thus pose a simple question: has psychology 'improved' torture? Has it brought new and more effective forms of torture? Even Peter Suedfeld, a psychologist who has acted as a consultant to, among other agencies, the Canadian Department of National Defence and NASA, has his doubts: 'Psychology as a discipline appears to have played no verifiable role in the development of torture techniques . . . There does not seem to be much that psychologists could add, or have added, to the tools already at hand' (Suedfeld, 1990, p. 105). Maybe Suedfeld has a point here. Considering the outcome of scientifically informed torture resulting from the CIA-sponsored 'Manhattan project of the mind,' as McCoy calls it, one is inclined to say that the harvest has been quite poor (McCoy, 2006, p. 7). At most, torture has become a bit less bloody as the focus has been to leave no marks, and perhaps this is the most concise way to describe psychological torture. But what can be attributed to the input of psychologists is that they to a great extent have helped to systematise torture, a point supported by the Red Cross report on Guantánamo that stresses the formalisation and the systematisation of interrogation techniques (Lewis, 2004). And, furthermore, the psychologisation of torture served as the legalistic *coup de theatre* of the Bush administration. Torture was redefined as any practice leading to organ failure or death, and this opened the way for the 'enhanced interrogation techniques' (McCoy, 2006, p. 123). Psychology here was an ideal partner in this newspeak operation, as became clear in the already mentioned APA policy, psychologists were supposed to keep interrogations '*safe, legal, ethical and effective*' (Moorehead-Slaughter, 2006).

The first step in a critique, therefore, is to expose and deconstruct the very concept of psychological torture and state that psychology only provided the systematisation and refinement of torture techniques. For if one concedes that psychologists have valuable knowledge that can be misused, then psychologists are de facto not guilty. This is the stance of Suedfeld: 'If torturers use dental drills on healthy teeth, this does not imply that researchers and practitioners who develop, improve, and use such drills in the course of ethical dental practice should feel guilty' (Suedfeld, 1990, p. 106). How dubious such comparisons are can be showed with Jack Vernon who in the 1960s conducted similar research on sensory deprivation as Donald Hebb. Vernon contends that 'while our goal is pure knowledge for its own sake, we have no objection to someone's use of that knowledge' (Vernon, 1966). Does this celebration of neutral knowledge not sound rather hollow and hypocritical? As noted above, it is precisely the claim to be merely serving science that drives psychology into the perverse structure. In this light, locking someone up and depriving them of any human interaction is at least a peculiar way of searching for neutral knowledge. Even if one doubts the direct military involvement of academic psychologists engaged in research on sensory deprivation, their ruthless objectifying and technologising of human subjects still stand out. Is furthermore this desubjectivising stance not in fact a structural characteristic of mainstream psychology? Reading, for example, the post-9/11 APA document 'Combating Terrorism Responses from the Behavioral Sciences,' (APA, 2004) one is struck by the cold techno-rationality, the ambitious psychosocial engineering and the eagerness of psychologists to be involved in the War on Terror.

The thesis that psychology is not a dangerous knowledge but a dangerous fantasy can also help us to understand a strange twist in the recent history of torture. US intelligence, during the urgent period following 9/11, devised their enhanced interrogation methods by reverse engineering their own programmes that aimed to train their own personnel to resist coercive interrogation and torture. The SERE (Survival, Evasion, Resistance, and Escape) programme that included forced nudity, stress positions, isolation, sleep deprivation, sexual humiliation, and exhaustion (M. Benjamin, 2007), thus became the main inspiration in devising enhanced interrogation techniques. The CIA put the two developers of the original SERE program, psychologists James Elmer Mitchell and Bruce Jessen, in charge of adapting the tactics to use on detainees in the global War on Terror. Mitchell and Jessen were directly involved in training interrogators in brutal techniques, including waterboarding (Eban, 2007). As such, we are here led to see the switch of the good use of psychology based on a defensive patriotism to the deviant use of psychology based on an offensive patriotism. But this obscures the more fundamental question of why the US intelligence services needed the detour of the reverse engineering. Would this not be similar to devising biological weapons starting from an antiserum? Why not just use the real stuff?

Let us take a closer look at the SERE program. During SERE, trainees are subjected to harsh and abusive treatment modelled upon the cold-war era so-called *psychological torture* techniques used by China, North Korea, and the former Soviet Union (Olson et al., 2008). However, with these forms of torture allegedly invented by the Communists, we enter the misty realm of cold-war fantasy. McCoy points to the fact that the CIA interpreted the success of the public show trials in the USSR as demonstrating that the Soviets had discovered more subtle techniques than traditional physical torture, 'including psychosurgery, electroshock and psychoanalytic methods' (McCoy, 2006, p. 23). This engendered the myth of so-called brainwashing and resulted in the CIA beginning to fund experimental psychological research in order to give the US an advantage in 'brain warfare' (Welch, 2007, p. 481). The psychologist Irving L. Janis, advised the CIA in 1949 to engage in a systematic investigation of drugs, electric convulsive treatments, and other techniques for weakening the resistance of detainees to 'duplicate the public confessions obtained in Soviet-dominated trials' (McCoy, 2006, pp. 22–23). Dick Anthony contends further that the pseudoscientific theory of brainwashing was also used as a propaganda device to combat communism. Brainwashing was said to explain why some US prisoners of war appeared to convert to communism while imprisoned in Korea (Anthony, 1999, pp. 421–456). Public announcements of the CIA's 'battle against Communist brain warfare' and several popular articles stoking public fears about mind control (McCoy, 2006, p. 24) thus ensured a place for the evil Communist *Dr Psy* in the public imagination.

So one should carefully untangle the knot of the enhanced torture techniques being devised by reverse engineering the SERE programme. US intelligence did not go back to enemy (Communist) forms of psychological torture, as has been claimed in the media (Shane, 2008), nor did the US resort to alternatives developed in-house. The US variant of psychological torture, rather than based on any actual evidence from the mysterious forms of tortures supposedly used by the enemy, has its foundations in what the US *fantasised* the enemy was capable of. And here psychology is the vehicle, the discourse in which the terms of the fantasy of Communist mind control were constructed. Besides being useful as propaganda, the imagery of psychological torture served as the basis for training soldiers to resist torture, which can be understood foremost, as Brad Olson contends, as a programme to foster aggression and de-individuation in US soldiers, a sort of hazing that would make them more likely to kill in battle (Olson, email to author, 25 November 2008). In a final turn of the screw, psychologists reverse engineered the fantasy to give psychological torture a scientific rationale and a thorough systematisation. Thus psychology does not potentially fuel dangerous fantasies as much as it carries in its very core the dangerous fantasy itself.

Evidence of this historical lineage can be found in the recent disclosure of a chart that systematises the application of coercive techniques (including sleep deprivation, prolonged constraint, and exposure) used by military trainers at Guantánamo in 2002. The chart is actually an excerpt from an article written in 1957 by the social scientist Albert D. Biderman on forced false confessions by Communists (Biderman, 1957, pp. 616–625). While Biderman's chart is nothing more than the schematising of interviews of US prisoners of war who have been tortured, it has come to be known as Biderman's principles, a schematic protocol for the implementation of psychological torture. So one cannot even call this applied psychology: elevating a mere scheme to *Biderman's principles* means that the signifiers of psychology are above all used to give torture a scientific *cachet*. In this way Lawrence Hinkle, Jr. and Harold Wolff, contemporaries of Biderman, are correct when they state that, regarding torture in communist countries:

> (I)n no case is there reliable evidence that neurologists, psychiatrists, psychologists or other scientifically trained personnel have designed or participated in these police procedures. There is no evidence that drugs, hypnosis or other devices play any significant role in them. The effects produced are understandable in terms of the methods used.
>
> (Wolff and Hinkle, 1957, p. 609)

The neurologists, psychiatrists, and psychologists, indeed, were only brought in by the US, with Hinkle, Wolff, and Biderman as the first. Drugs and hypnosis would follow later with, for example, the infamous psychological research of Ewan Cameron in Canada (McCoy, 2006, p. 42). What Biderman, Hinkle, and Wolff initiated was a mode of thought, that is, psychology as a way of making understandable what they thought, inferred, and fantasised about the Communist maltreatment of prisoners.

One should not underestimate the role of fantasy in the legitimisation of torture. Consider, for example, Antonin Scalia's (an Associate Justice of the Supreme Court of the United States) defence of heavy-handed interrogation tactics by referring to the popular TV series *24*, where the protagonist Jack Bauer repeatedly engages in torture in ticking-time-bomb scenarios. 'Jack Bauer saved Los Angeles,' Scalia said, 'Are you going to convict Jack Bauer?' (quoted in Eban, 2007). This ticking-time-bomb scenario, of which Alan Dershowitz (2003) is the most well-known advocate, is refuted by many authors for its high implausibility and the slippery slope risk it carries with it of legitimising torture in less clear-cut circumstances (see Brecher, 2007; Costanzo et al., 2007; Rejali, 2007). What is so remarkable in for example Suedfeld's attempt to defend the ticking-bomb scenario is how determined he is to rescue the scenario as such. Suedfeld accuses the opponents of the ticking-time-bomb logic of a politicised bias and of making absolutist and simplistic arguments, countering them with basically one argument: reality is more complex than you think. Suedfeld desperately tries to rescue the scenario qua scenario, that is, the fantasy of a transgressive hero that does the abhorrent dirty work for the better of humankind. 'Having accepted that torture is a last resort, the pain of the tortured suspect may be less abhorrent than not doing everything possible to save all those innocent lives' (Suedfeld, 2007, p. 60).

Are we not led to the conclusion that wherever there is psychology there is a scenario, a script, and thus a fantasy to be saved? To be clear, the suggestion is not that there could somehow be a reality free of fantasy. This is exactly the reproach that can be made of mainstream psychology; it claims to be able to assess the human being as it really is (in terms of neurotransmitters, evolutionary patterns, emotions, skills, brain areas, childhood traumas, cognitions, rapid eye movements, and so on). Here, as I already did in my introduction, I endorse Žižek's claim that it is not that we have the wrong idea of how things really are but, rather, that we have the wrong idea of how things are mystified (Žižek, 2005). Mainstream social science analyses may well be the material from which today's mystifying veils are made. The centrality of the script and the fantasy of having access to the real thing – and how this is disavowed – is exactly what we have learned from Milgram and Zimbardo. It is this fantasy of being able to touch upon real life, which makes mainstream psychology very suitable to deliver the rationale for psychological torture, or more in general, for today's forms of biopolitics.

If one fails to take this into account, one cannot understand the paradox of torture being so widely employed despite its ineffectiveness in obtaining reliable information. This is where a lot of critics unluckily take recourse to psychology and once again fail to provide the much needed political analysis. McCoy, for example, ends his historical analysis quite disappointingly by attributing the persistence of state-sponsored torture to 'its deep psychological appeal, to the powerful and the powerless alike, in times of crisis' (McCoy, 2006, p. 207). Hinkle and Wolff also already had resorted to psychologising explanations that link the turn to torture to feelings of insecurity and the pressure to produce speedy confessions (Wolff and Hinkle, 1957). Similar psychologising arguments have mentioned frustration and desperation on the part of the interrogator (see Costanzo et al., 2007). Other authors point to torture as a tool of *psychological* intimidation both on an individual level, in terms of the prisoners, and on a social level, instilling a constant threat within the population (see for example: Klein, 2007; Rejali, 2007). Jerry Piven resorts to a psychoanalytically inspired psychologisation, asserting that neither Arendt (the banality of evil), Milgram (the obedience to authority), nor Zimbardo (the adoption of assigned roles) can account for the 'fervor and excess of murder, genocide, or sadistic cruelty' in torture. To explain why the US persists in torture despite it being obviously ineffective, Piven engages in post-Freudian interpretations, by understanding perpetration as a strategy of punishing and destroying loathsome aspects of the self projected onto the other. Piven concludes: 'this is why torture must be understood psychologically' (Piven, 2007, pp. 4, 10). The fundamental error of authors who psychologically interpret the question *why torture?* is that in so doing they merely repeat the stance of the CIA. Both opponents and proponents share the same fantasy, namely, that psychology allows direct access to human reality. The scientific rationale of both parties obscures how this paradigm is the base of today's biopolitics. Can we escape this endless psychologising and come to a truly political assessment?

Psychology and homo sacer: the matrix of (de)psychologisation and (de)politicisation

If psychology has a tendency to depoliticise and to swap the socioeconomic level for the individual level and consequently to obliterate the material conditions of existence and power imbalances, must we then, in response, leave the subjective dimension behind? Against this, considering distress as something personal might not necessarily, as Ian Parker puts it, be a bad thing. Parker argues that we need to develop 'a response to social problems which works at the interface of the personal and the political instead of pretending that society is something separate from us' (Ian Parker, 1999, p. 104). Can it not be observed that it is precisely this link between subjectivity and politics which is obscured or even neutralised by the individualising tendencies of mainstream psychology and psychologisation as its shadow? As such it is clear, re-politicising this issue does not mean rejecting the question of subjectivity. Quite the opposite. It means reinvigorating it.

This is why critique of psychology and psychologisation necessarily has to start from a theory of the psyche. My choice for psychoanalysis has its roots here: for, as stated earlier, psychoanalysis can be called the mother of all psychologisation – consider how Freudian terminology rapidly found its way into everyday life. This accords it the position of privileged partner, the one that can take psychologisation seriously, in contrast to mainstream psychology, which structurally has to obscure the fact that its central paradigm is that of psychologisation. In this way, a Lacanian approach to the late modern subject as the psychological-psychologised doublet can make it possible to resuscitate the entanglement of subjectivity with politics.

To make a first step into that field – I will attend to the issue of politics in Chapter 4 – let us consider Giorgio Agamben's analysis of Guantánamo.

Agamben's notion of *homo sacer* attempts to critically amend Michel Foucault's notion of biopolitics. Foucault argued that at a certain point in history the era of discipline came to an end and the era of biopolitics began. Biological life as such began to be drawn into the sphere of politics, becoming the subject of knowledge on which power could be exerted. In biopolitics, power takes life itself and exploits it (Foucault, 1978, pp. 142–143). For Foucault this was the end of sovereignty, as power was no longer strictly localisable; power is now everywhere and comes from everywhere (see Foucault, 1978, p. 93). Agamben's point, however, is that sovereignty and the sovereign use of power is still apparent in biopolitics. He moreover argues that the exceptionality of sovereign power – the fact that the law by definition has to ground itself in a point beyond the law – rests upon a similar exceptional state at the other end of the power spectrum (Agamben, 1998). The included/excluded sovereign is structurally in need of an equally included/excluded counterpart. Agamben situates *homo sacer* and what he calls *bare life* as this counterpart. In Roman law a person who was declared *homo sacer* was a person banished in terms of law and religion; anyone could kill him or her with impunity and he or she could neither be sacrificed nor buried according to religious rituals. Thus *homo sacer* is reduced to bare life: insofar as his exclusion makes him the mere object of power, he is once again included in the discourses of power. For Agamben, the turn to biopolitics means that *homo sacer,* from a position on the margin, becomes the central object of power as bare life becomes the focus of government.

It is this logic of the juxtaposition of sovereign power and *homo sacer* that, for Agamben, was at work in the Bush administration. On the one hand, there are the detainees of Guantánamo. Labelled unlawful combatants, they are *homines sacri* – outside the law – or, as Agamben puts it, they are subject only to raw power while having no legal existence (Agamben, 2004). On the other hand, there is George W. Bush's position of not having to answer for alleged human rights violations when it came to such prisoners. He is the figure of the sovereign who, just like *homo sacer*, is outside of the law. *Homo sacer* is a nonperson under the law; the sovereign transcends the law.

Here the echo of Zimbardo's experiment cannot but strike us. First of all the prisoners are the included/excluded and are put into this position via the psychological discourse, incarnated by the guards who are supposed to bring them in the 'required *psychological* state' (Zimbardo, 2007a, p. 55, emphasis added). Furthermore the central issue of the Stanford Prison experiment is precisely the power of psychology to reveal the 'crucible of human behavior.' Zimbardo claims to lay life bare as it is – in Agamben's terms, 'pure life, without any mediation.' Is this not the ultimate reason why psychology serves Guantánamo and other extraterritorial black sites so well? The psy-sciences are the tools that remove the mediation; they deliver the technologies to reduce someone to bare life. Consider how Agamben argues for the camp as the central trope of biopolitics:

> Insofar as its inhabitants were stripped of every political status and wholly reduced to bare life, the camp was also the most absolute biopolitical space ever to have been realized, in which power confronts nothing but pure life, without any mediation.
>
> (Agamben, 1998, p. 171)

While Agamben focuses on the implications of medical discourses, Guantánamo reveals the central role of psychology as delivering the tools to strip down the subject and reduce him or her to bare life. Military interrogators not only had access to the medical records of detainees but also to psychological data, such as comments by psychologists on conditions such as phobias (see Slevin and Stephens, 2004). This psychologisation effects a de-politicisation: from political subject, the detainee is reduced to an individualised psychological subject. Moreover, regardless of whether one understands the purpose of this psychologised torture as to make the person disclose information, to simply humiliate him or her, or to scare other detainees or the wider population, it is clear that the effect is actually desubjectifying, depersonalising, if not, de-psychologising.

However, the notion of *homo sacer* poses a few problems. As Agamben attempts to come to an understanding of the current *aporia* of democracy, his main argument is that we are all potentially *homines sacri*. Here two things remain unclear. First, there is the question concerning the way in which we are all potentially *homines sacri* – as most examples given by Agamben (and his commentators) concern *homo sacer* as a peripheral figure and do not address the fact that everyone is, or can become, *homo sacer*. Second, it is not clear how exactly we should conceive sovereignty in the new global order. If the Guantánamo detainee can be connected in a straightforward way to the American president, it remains unclear how, distinct from this, we should think of sovereignty in the case of all of us being potentially *homines sacri*. Maybe Lacan's notion of the discourse of the university can help, as it shows how knowledge itself can take the place of the agent in a discourse or, in Agamben's terms, the place of the sovereign. Academia – particularly psychological discourse – has come to play an increasingly important role in processes of power. Consider how the psy-complex more and more often poses as the sovereign, transcending the law and politics, claiming jurisdiction concerning suburban riots, political scandals, paedophilia cases (see the case of Marc Dutroux in Belgium), terrorist attacks et cetera. The psy-perspective supposedly transcends all contradictions, ideological divisions, and societal ruptures, enabling the psy-expert to partake in the decisions and – without any democratic legitimating – to set policies. Lacan, in his comments on the events of May 1968 (if we make abstraction of their clearly provocative and controversial character) made the interesting remark that there, structurally spoken, we were witnessing a hegemonic shift from the master discourse to the discourse of the university (see Lacan, 2006). Psychological discourse's central role in this shift must be discerned. That is, we are all potentially *homines sacri* insofar as we become the object of the expert, caretaking, psychologising discourse that produces and expropriates our subjectivity. Today our subjectivity and social relations are monitored, controlled, and managed as we find psy-workers everywhere from kindergartens, through the workplace, right up to retirement homes. The new sovereign wears Academic clothes?

The desubjectifying, depersonalising, and hence de-psychologising stance of torture in the end is also the main dynamic of the psy-complex. With Milgram and Zimbardo we already saw how psychology constitutes itself in a de-subjectivisation and, thus, a de-psychologisation of the subject. Processes of psychologisation are always processes of de-psychologisation. Just think of how psychological explanations in contemporary mainstream psychology make way for biological and neurological paradigms, laying bare our brain. It is hard, then, to dismiss Cameron's CIA-funded 'psychic driving' experiments – the erasing of a person's memory using electroshocks, chemicals, sensory deprivation, and the consequent attempt to rebuild the psyche – as a mere anomaly of psychological science (Cameron, 1956).[10] The experiment can be regarded as paradigmatic of a discourse in its entanglement with power. Psychology seems to take a central role as a discourse and praxis in the late modern biopolitical production of bare life, the included/excluded, psychologised/de-psychologised, politicised/depoliticised *homo sacer*. It is due to the privileged place of this matrix in late modern politics that psychology was the last man standing in the black sites of US intelligence.

Conclusion: psychology/psychologisation, the blind spot of science

When president Obama promised a quick shutdown of Guantánamo – up till now an unfulfilled promise – Zimbardo expressed his hope that the APA will have learned its lesson and that the APA ethical guidelines will become the standard not only for its members but for psychologists around the world (Zimbardo, 2007b, p. 73). Recall however Levant's summarisation of his APA-presidency in terms of 'making psychology a household word' (Levant, 2007), and how it can be understood as being foremost realised by psychologists in service of US intelligence spreading psychology worldwide.

Levant subtitled the conclusion of his presidential address 'The Stage Is Set' – a theatrical metaphor that once again suggests that the core business of the mainstream discourse of psychology concerns the scripting of subjectivity.

With this global spreading of the psy-scripts we have reached in this chapter a first appreciation of what psychologisation means in these times of globalisation. It shall not have remained unnoticed that, having set out in this chapter from the perspective of psychologisation within the field of science, I have gradually been led to the field of politics. This can be understood as follows: the psy-sciences promise the ultimate meta-perspective, since everything in this world passes over subjectivity, psychology eventually cannot but vindicate the definite vantage point. This is why the psy-sciences claim a central place in the late modern forms of biopolitical sovereignty. This becomes particularly clear in the already mentioned APA document 'Combating Terrorism Responses from the Behavioral Sciences.' The document presents so-called vignettes that present a problem connected to societal issues after 9/11, provides examples of relevant research, and then proposes implications and applications for counterterrorism. The text abounds with expressions such as 'humans are,' 'the human language is,' and 'what is known of human behaviour.' Does this not suggest a definitive position *beyond* the human, one that looks at humanity as though peering into a human zoo? Furthermore, when this knowledge, allegedly in a second movement, is *given away* to the human zoo this means we as the subjects are pulled out of the zoo and elevated to the same Archimedean vantage point to look upon ourselves. However, it would be a mistake to think that only by bringing knowledge back down to earth can the process of psychologisation start. Milgram and Zimbardo have showed us that this supposedly a priori gathering of knowledge itself is already based on the paradigm of psychologisation. Both experiments are based on a prior scripting of not only the scene but also the psychological subject within it. *Look, this is what you are* prompts you to look at yourself as a *psychologoid*. With *oh really, is this what I am* the subject responds by taking up the position of the proto-scientist and joins the ranks of the psy-scientists. In this double movement of psychologisation psychology asserts itself as a science. Consider for example how Milgram applauds the transformation of his test-subjects:

> In the interview, Mr Braverman summarises the experiment with impressive fluency and intelligence. He feels the experiment may have been designed also to 'test the effects on the teacher of being in an essentially sadistic role, as well as the reactions of a student to a learning situation that was authoritative, rigid and punitive'.

(Milgram, 1974, p. 53)

Braverman has become the scientist-apprentice adopting a scientific and psychologising view on his own behaviour and thoughts. As the experimenter asks the typical psychologising questions, Braverman does not fail to answer him in the expected format: 'There was I. I'm a nice person, I think, hurting somebody, and caught up in what seemed a mad situation . . . and in the interest of science, one goes through with it' (Milgram, 1974, pp. 53–54). *There was I*: this is the gaze of psychology in action. It is not surprising that in a questionnaire one year after the experiment Braverman fully engages in the psycho-babble:

> What appalled me was that I could possess this capacity for obedience and compliance to a central idea, i.e., the value of a memory experiment even after it became clear that adherence to this value was at the expense of violation of another value, i.e., don't hurt someone who is helpless and not hurting you.
>
> . . . I hope I deal more effectively with any future conflicts of values I encounter.
>
> (Milgram, 1974, p. 54)

Milgram's post-experimental question 'What in your opinion is the most effective way of strengthening resistance to inhumane authority?' (Milgram, 1974, p. 52) calls the subjects into the psychology class. But the specificity of psychologisation is that you cannot simply send them back to *outside* naive life again: having adopted a reflexive view, there is no way back. The draft into psychology hails the subject irreversibly into the ranks of the (proto)-psychologists. Braverman will never confront a value conflict anymore as a naive person; he has become too much psychologist for this.

However, if everyone is drawn onto the side of psychology, are the cages of the human zoo then not empty? This would be good news, as we could then emancipate ourselves from this gaze that only offers us (pre)psychological reflections and spectres of the human. A postmodern meta-reflexive gaze that sees us as *zoon psychologicon* would be one way out. But this may not be enough, for what Guantánamo and Abu Ghraib have shown us is that our Western psychologised gaze is based on the Real of the effective and existing cages of the *homines sacri*. Hegemonic discourses feed on real people and natural objects. If we fail to confront the Real of this horror of psychological torture, we will soon find ourselves at the next stage, which will no doubt be neuro-torture. Žižek has already alluded to 'the direct stimulating of the brain centers for pain' (Žižek, 2003b, p. 76). This new Manhattan Project of the mind is most likely already up and running in the laboratories.

At least this chapter has showed that psychologisation is far from being the mere unhappy overflow or the inappropriate colonisation of the sciences by psychology. To the initial question of this chapter – what are the sciences for psychology and what is psychology for the sciences – I have, drawing upon Milgram and Zimbardo, argued for a double answer. On the one hand, the experiments of Milgram and Zimbardo enable us to get a grip on how psychology is inextricably linked to psychologisation. In its vocation to assert itself as a science psychology's main paradigm is that of psychologisation. The discipline of psychology hails its subjects into the psychological gaze by beholding the human its alleged real psychological essence. On the other hand, these seminal experiments testify how psychology in its attempt to be the cornerstone of the sciences, in all the latters' historical vicissitudes, structurally is drawn to a perverted position. Trying to amend the alleged harsh objectivity and rationality of the sciences by putting forward the human factor and emotionality, psychology, instead of a safety net for subjectivity, turns out to be the very discourse and praxis of de-subjectivation. The contemporary theodicy paradox, why does Academia engender suffering and wickedness, is thus embodied by the psy-sciences, as they constitute the structural blind spot of the modern sciences.

Here it shall already be clear that the imposition of the psychological gaze inevitably has decisive effects on culture. It is not a coincidence that Milgram and Zimbardo have contributed in an important and significant manner to the psychologisation of culture. Part of the cultural success of for example Milgram's experiment is due to the fact that the deception is also used in the dissemination of the experiment. Almost invariably the Milgram experiment is introduced in courses and in the media only revealing in the end that 'no-one was actually shocked.' This produces the interpellation *what would you have done?* which is a powerful catalyst to set in motion the psychologisation process. This invitation to look at yourself from the psy-perspective, eventually also drives the Zimbardo experiment, as it necessarily implies the interpellation: *what would you have done in the role of guard?* It is then most significant that when today such experiments would not in any way pass the ethical committee, we are bombarded with the formats of Milgram and Zimbardo via popular culture. As Jenny Diski writes, these days nothing prevents similar 'experiments' (*Big Brother, Castaway*, etc.) 'being carried out repeatedly for our fascination and entertainment on reality TV shows' (Diski, 2004). This is what we will turn to in the next chapter, as we will explore psychologisation in and of culture via the phenomenon of psychotainment.

Notes

1 Note that this Ian Parker (in the book referred to as 'I. Parker') is a British writer living in New York, and is not to be confused with his namesake the psychologist Ian Parker, editor of this book, in this book referred to as 'Ian Parker')

2 In his book *The Lucifer Effect* Zimbardo amply discusses the Milgram experiment, noting also his personal acquaintanceship with Stanley Milgram (Zimbardo, 2007a, p. 518).

3 Jacques Lacan distinguishes four discourses: the discourse of the master, the university, the hysteric, and the analyst (Lacan, 2006). The discourse of the hysteric is the discourse of fundamental dividedness (the Freudian *Spaltung*): for example, the patient bringing his or her symptom into the social as a question. The addressee of the hysteric is the discourse of the master, where the master, for example the doctor, produces knowledge as the (structurally failing) answer to the symptom of the hysteric. The shift in the university discourse is that the gathered scientific knowledge stands in the place of the actor. There, the so-called 'master-signifier' is denied or hidden. The knowledge presents itself as plain and neutral, disavowing the performative gesture of the production of knowledge. In the discourse of the analyst it is not knowledge which is put to work. Within the transference the analyst assumes the place of the object of desire of the analysand, which is to say he or she keeps this place empty in order to make it possible for the analysand to know about his or her desire.

4 Note that not only did the group of guards comprise volunteers, but the role of warden was played by an undergraduate research assistant while Zimbardo himself took the role of superintendent.

5 When I asked Dave Eshleman if he was interested in psychology at that time and knew of the Milgram experiment he replied: 'I had no special interest in psychology when I participated in the experiment. I was majoring in music at the time. I had heard of Milgram's experiment but it had no influence on me during the experiment' (personal correspondence).

6 Concerning the role of Academia in the cruelty of the Stanford Prison Experiment, we should perhaps consider the fact that the degrading hooding, an image returning in the Abu Ghraib photographs, was the experimenters' idea, not the guards. It was their solution to the problem of how to lead the prisoners to the toilets, which were outside the confines of the prison yard, without breaking the sense of an enclosed environment.

7 In this way it is not important whether or not Milgram's research was financed by the CIA, as McCoy suggests (McCoy, 2006). It is clearly part of military intelligence design and thus shows a de facto involvement and entanglement of psychology with the military.

8 The sceptical reader, of course, will argue that this is where I myself engage in psychologising Zimbardo through the lens of Lacanian psychoanalysis. However, my argument is not rooted in an individual psychology. I do not hold Zimbardo himself to be a pervert; rather, I argue that Zimbardo is laying bare a potentially perverse dispositif, namely, that psychology assigns discursive positions according to the structural framework of perversion. For more on the potential structural similarities between psychological discourse and perversion, see: (De Vos, 2011b).

9 Of course, there is no doubt that the ordered use of psychology was also prevalent in Abu Ghraib.

10 For a compelling account of the abhorrence of this experiment see Naomi Klein's story of Gail Kastner, a woman who went through the psychic driving ordeal only to be left completely physically and subjectively broken: 'They tried to erase and remake me. But it didn't work' (Klein, 2007, p. 26).

3 Psychologisation and culture

As this chapter deals with the overflow of psychology into culture, a preliminary question concerning contemporary culture has to be asked: are we not overdoing the argument that culture has become psychologised? Sure, it is emotional, it stresses the individual, reduces the social to interpersonal relations, and its compelling call to reflection weighs heavily on everyday life. But is not the most important and primal observation to make that today culture above all has come under the reign of the image and the virtual? In contemporary image culture we have long since superseded the era of 'let us illustrate this with an image'. Today the image prevails, the captions are secondary, and if possible, left out completely. Concerning moving images – games, movies, television, video – the moving is becoming faster and faster. The rhythm of the image transitions is almost nearing that limit where the human eye fails to notice them. When for example a goal is scored in a soccer game, the electronic billboards behind the goal use that opportunity to fire as many as ads as possible. Faster, and always more and more imperatively are we compelled to face the visual (arte)facts. Television stations for example often interrupt their programming to bring us *breaking news* of events as they happen right here, right now. Images of an earthquake with enough points on the Richter scale are transmitted immediately to your living room, kitchen, and bedroom, or simply directly to your mobile phone, wherever you are. To escape this growing directness and invasiveness of the image we can only zap through the channels at an increasing speed nearing or even overtaking today's montage rhythm, or else, take recourse to programming on demand via the cable or the internet. Maybe this is why the 24-hour news channels are ceding ground to internet media: the constant stream of images via the cable is pushing us a bit too close to reality.

However, is it really the case that the image has brought us closer to reality and the world's current affairs? One can easily argue for the opposite: images shield us off from reality. The screen provides a safe distance between the viewer and the world. Furthermore, images zap themselves away at a brisk pace. In the television news, each item wipes the screen clean. As such, this paradigm transcends the newscast and concerns the very core of broadcasting: one image swallows the other. The transitions are almost imperceptible: a fundraising ad for the post-earthquake cholera in Haiti for example, is followed almost without a hitch by the trailer of the survival soap *Survivor*, presenting us the 'celebs' (in the 2010 Dutch version) who will compete with each other in the various challenges that await them. I spoke of a transition *almost* without a hitch, because it might be possible that in the storm of images, suddenly something sticks out. For, one might be struck with how images of surviving harsh circumstances and deprivation are first the trigger to donate money and only a few minutes later it is the subject of entertainment. But that is not the end of the obscenities, because, as the *Survival* trailer abounds with bare chests of the male celebs and the suggestive bikinis of their female protagonists, one might suddenly bounce back to the Haiti fundraising ad. For in fundraising ads nudity equally is not shunned: the Haiti TV-add of the Belgian NGO Haiti Lavi opens for example with an image of a naked child and features several women with torn clothes, almost or completely revealing their breasts.[1] In image culture the gaze is manipulated, guided and fed: this is something every pickpocket knows: you have to steer the gaze.

However, in opposition to image culture as a powerful tool of commerce and the hegemonic forces to manage public opinion, do not precisely the new technological evolutions open up a space for resistance and emancipation? Think of internet-television and the so-called Web 2.0, the social and interactive internet where everybody can post content and develop the digital environment. New digital recording methods and devices seem in this way to empower the user and to allow him or her to escape the framework of the hegemonic production of images and its coercive guidance of the gaze. You take the images yourself, it is from your laptop that the alternative news website is filled; it is you manipulating the joystick, you, gesticulating in front of the Wii. Have we not become ourselves iconoclastic masters of the image storm? However, against this one can argue that even if we are ourselves part of the image production, this does not mean we escape the image, image creation and its technology.[2] The hegemony of the image might in this way become even stronger in our own hands. Image culture and its logic clearly transcend the subject-object opposition: even when engaging in a seemingly subjective agentic position one remains the object of it.

All this could prompt us to seek psychological explanations of the reign of the image in modern and especially late-modern culture. However, as I shall argue in the first section of this chapter, it might be more interesting to understand image culture as always already psychologised itself. The prime instance of this psycho-image culture which I will discuss amply is *psychotainment* (e.g. reality TV, celebrity culture and other instances of psychologised entertainment). The understanding of cultural critics such as Walter Benjamin and Jean Baudrillard of how imaging technology affects subjectivity will prove very useful here. In the second part of the chapter *psychotainment* is juxtaposed with Daniel Dennett's philosophy of consciousness. It will be argued that Dennett's concepts such as 'cerebral celebrity' and 'fame in brain' are typical examples of how a seemingly hardcore naturalised conception of the human subject always risks being haunted by the psychologised image culture. In the last section our close reading of image culture shall not only help us understand the psychologisation in and of culture, it will also allow us to see how today's neurological turn is actually far removed from a radical materialism.

Image culture and its grounding in psychology

The reign of image culture

Would it be fruitful to turn to the psychology of the gaze and the psychology of the image to get a firmer grip on how subjectivity in our times is so intertwined with the image and became a digital and virtual issue? We could for example take a look at how the image plays a role in the constitution of gender and identity, or how with a child the mental imagery of its surroundings develops, or how colours are related to emotions. Quite rapidly we would be led to the neurological aspects as we would be considering the functions of the visual cortex; how for example object representations are formed and recognition comes about, how tunnel vision occurs in situations of fear, or how visual illusions can be explained. Most probably we would be looking into brain-research involving brain imaging: or literally, the image rendering of what happens in our brain. CT-scans, colourful MRI-plates, elaborate schemes of the dorsal and ventral pathways of visual stimuli, all these would serve to visualise the neuropsychology of the image. But are we here not back where we started? Trying to get a grip on the meaning of the visual for the subject we seem to be unable to escape the reign of the image. There we are threatened to be trapped in a hall of mirrors, or in a more present-day imagery, in the infinite redoubling of the black hole of the lens as the camera is pointed to the monitor screening its own output.

The fact that the psy-sciences are easily drawn into image culture – e.g. the use of one-way screens, cameras and monitors in experimental and therapeutic settings – should come as no surprise; psychology wants to *show* us who we are. Moreover, this objectifying of the human being necessarily entails the construction of a point outside, or even beyond the human, from where the scientific gaze is cast upon the sublunary. Not only have the sciences interchanged God's *point of view* with that of Academia, they furthermore invite each of us to adopt that gaze. *Look, this is what you are*, and you are shown a view of your muscles, your internal organs, and at last your skeleton, prefiguring the dead human already slumbering inside your body. *Ecce Homo*, behold the man, in modernity is issued from the sciences: the human subject can no longer ground his being in God. Is it not here that the modern subject takes its recourse to the image which in its apparent fullness has to remediate the lack of ontology? This is why we are so fascinated by the colourful Andy Warhol-like brain scans: at last we can envision not only our thinking but even the very core of our being. Psychology, seeking to be the universal science of subjectivity and thus the cornerstone of the modern objectifying sciences, is therefore inextricably bound to the dimension of the image. The only problem however is that we have to deny the circularity and paradoxical reflexivity involved. For, modern image culture is a self-enclosed system and does not allow a position from outside it to peer into it. The space of the external god-viewer is forever vacant; science eventually cannot take up this position. The (neuro)psy-sciences and their image gallery of the human as he really is can only give the illusion of a full ontological closure. Eventually at a given point we will get the gaze turned back at us: as the scientist turns the monitor to us, summoning us to look, we will see our own puzzled gaze. This would be the image of a person, MRI scanned, while looking at the monitor portraying the very results. It would be the very repetition of that other iconic image: Vesalius' skeleton holding a skull in its hand and contemplating it from all sides. The disconnectedness and the deep sadness with which Vesalius sketched the skeleton cannot but strike the eye, it shows us how in modernity subjectivity has no external ground than its own gaze questioning itself.

But we have to take yet another step, the fact that modern subjectivity is structurally intertwined with the image means that, not only, psychology itself is deeply immersed in image culture, but that the reverse equally holds true. That is: modern image culture itself is thoroughly psychologised, and this fact might be central to understand contemporary subjectivity. Consider for example the *emoticons* on social network sites such as *Facebook* and how closely these are connected to the mainstream psychology of emotions. Or think how games address exactly those skills and areas of development and depict the human being as being very similar to the subject depicted by mainstream developmental, cognitive or evolutionary psychology. So if theorists from the psy-sciences seek support in gaming and other similar sources to prove their points, one should ask if this is not a case of tautology. What goes into the sack must come out of it: the image industry always already relies heavily on the imagery of the psy-sciences. And does not the same hold true for advertising? Of course psy-scientists can interpret commercial messages as exemplary of their theory, for the psy-theories are already informing the production of the imagery. Images do not come of out of the blue – out of some unmediated human nature – but are mediated, in the same way as they are not screened in a vacuum, but in a mediated environment. And those mediations, I claim, are closely connected to psychology and, hence, to psychologisation processes. This is what we will take a look at – the imagery of the gaze is indeed coercive – in this chapter on culture and psychologisation, as the link between the two has to be understood in the sphere of the gaze and the image.

Modern subjectivity and the law of psychology

In human interaction, we are told, visualising or showing something is crucial. Just think about the naturalising explanations of social behaviour – be it in media popularisations or be it in more sophisticated academic versions – in terms of males showing their virility and females displaying that they are ready to mate. However, what immediately transcends this biologistic approach is that in culture, showing is far more complicated if one asks for whose gaze some behaviour or some kind of artefact is meant. Remember how Walter Benjamin observed that in Homer's time, man was an object of contemplation for the Olympic gods (Benjamin, 2008, p. 42). Slavoj Žižek refers in this respect to the gigantic Aztec figures of animals and humans only to be seen from a point of view high up in the sky, and to the sculptures on Roman aqueducts unobservable for the human gaze from the ground (Žižek, 2002a, p. 225). These examples already show that in a cultured environment craftsmanship and technology are central in the human's economy of the gaze. It is via artefacts that the human is able to address a gaze other than its own or that of its neighbour. Via technology a gaze beyond the human, beyond the life-world is constructed. It is exactly this which according to Walter Benjamin underwent a decisive change in modernity, as humankind entered 'the Age of Mechanical Reproduction'. Benjamin's central insight here is to approach the impact of the modern sciences and technology on subjectivity via the sphere of the image and its reproduction. He starts his famous essay of 1936 with trying to understand the advent of the new technology of recording moving images. For Benjamin, the switch from theatre to film has to be understood in terms of where the illusion and the suspension of disbelief takes place. In theatre the spectator knows the work of illusion in the end is done by himself, from a well-located position; i.e. the seat in the auditorium. In film, however, the creation of the illusion resides in the technique itself: it is the filming, the cutting and editing which create the reality-illusion. This results in a shift in position. For Benjamin, the spectator's pupil is coinciding with that of the camera (Benjamin, 2008, p. 34).

This shift in locus of the spectator's gaze results also in a discursive shift. This is the shift to the new language of the lens (the semiotics of the camera), which for Benjamin also potentially leads to an altered position of the human within the social. Regarding the latter, it is well-known that Benjamin (rather unreservedly) welcomed the emancipatory potential of the medium of film, in that he believed that it could free man from the prison of tradition and open up the world. Film makes this possible because the 'multiple fragments' which are shot with the camera are assembled 'under a new law':

> Whereas it is a commonplace that, for example, we have some idea what is involved in the act of walking (if only in general terms), we have no idea at all what happens during the split second when a person actually takes a step. We are familiar with the movement of picking up a cigarette lighter or a spoon, but know almost nothing of what really goes on between hand and metal, and still less how this varies with different moods. This is where the camera comes into play, with all its resources for swooping and rising, disrupting and isolating, stretching or compressing a sequence, enlarging or reducing an object. It is through the camera that we first discover the optical unconscious, just as we discover the instinctual unconscious through psychoanalysis.
>
> (Benjamin, 2008, p. 37)

Thus for Benjamin the language of the camera opens up a whole field connected to the explanatory framework of psychology or, more particularly, psychoanalysis. Or perhaps we can push Benjamin's analysis a bit further and contend that the 'new law' under which the multiple fragmented reality of the camera is brought together is precisely psychological theory itself. This would then mean that, for example, a close-up of Humphrey Bogart reaching for his lighter and lighting his cigarette evokes thoughts, associations, emotions, in short, a total new imagery, which is actually unthinkable without psychology and, for historical reasons, in the first instance, without psychoanalytic theories. So, to make my point clear, the language and the semiotics of the camera are not to be understood as merely opening up the psychological domain but, rather, they both presuppose and engender the imagery of psychoanalysis and psychology.

It is in this way that we can understand Benjamin's claim that film introduces a way of bringing together the dispersed world of the metropolis. As Taylor and Harris argue, it was Benjamin's aim to understand media technology as serving to acclimatise people to the everyday shocks of heavily technologised city-life (Taylor and Harris, 2008, p. 25). If film made modern life meaningful and coherent, is the psychological discourse not the decisive paradigm here, allowing a bringing together of the dispersed social world?

Film, in this way, testifies that modernity needed a psychology. Psychological theories can thus be situated on the same plane as the modern technological art forms. But importantly, the technical paradigm of psychology is that it not only provides signifiers to account for the emerging modern subjectivity, it also defines the position from which man can assess himself and the world; namely, via a psychologising gaze. In this way we could understand psychology too as a potential way to emancipate man from old traditionalist ways of being with oneself, the other, the world. However, on the other hand, does psychology not also narrow subjective space as it reduces the subject to the psychologised man, to the *homo psychologicus* as the subject is depicted? As such, it is clear that, in the work of integration and bringing together the dispersed world of the metropolis, the semiotics of media technologies and the semiotics of psychological theories are fundamentally intertwined. Image culture solicits a psychology and the latter itself is fundamentally based on images and the imagery. Both share the presupposition of an external vantage point, a point from where the camera and the academic gaze are cast upon the human being and the world. This is why image culture is inevitably itself thoroughly psychologised. As reality TV today is showing these dynamics even more clearly, it is an exemplary case to understand the role of psychology/psychologisation in late-modern culture.

Reality TV: scripted by psychology

Jean Baudrillard describes reality TV as operating in an enclosed space where an experimental zone of privilege is recreated, 'the equivalent of an initiatory space where the laws of open society are abolished' (Baudrillard, 2005, p. 191). Reality TV thus seems to create experimental spaces in which man can free himself from the prison of traditions, to put it in Benjamin's terms. But do we not also recognise in these zones of privilege the experimental settings of social psychology of, for example, Stanley Milgram and Philip Zimbardo? In both experiments the laws of society are indeed abolished, but only to be replaced, as we have seen in the previous chapter, by psychology. Not only can both highly dramatised experiments be criticised for their auto-referential enactment of the psychological explanatory framework, both experiments also resulted in a de-politicised, psychologised view on the use of violence in intelligence and detainment settings.

Reality TV often resembles these social psychology experiments (e.g. *Big Brother*, *Survivor*), not only in the settings they use, but also in the underlying logic: it's all about psychology. Moreover, one can easily discern the shift of Milgram to Zimbardo in the shift within the formats of reality TV. If in the early forms of reality TV such as *Candid Camera* the use of deception and hidden cameras were central, in later forms these two aspects were to a great extent left behind. In the basic format of *Big Brother* for example there is no deception and every participant knows where the cameras are. The latter is considered not to be an impediment to view the emerging personality traits of each contestant and their emotional engagements with each other as genuine and unmediated. What we see we believe to be the manifestations of the personal psychology of the participants and of social psychological mechanisms. This is similar to Zimbardo's experiment as it too claimed to lay bare in a direct way the real human being.

However, against this claim of the unmediated production of real life, it suffices to point to the fact that in *Big Brother* the participants, the Big Brother figure and the audience to a great extent make use of the terminology of the psy-sciences. That the central issues are *self-realisation, self-actualisation* and *taking one's place in the social hierarchy* is the shared psy-script of all involved parties.[3] But in the same way as in Milgram and Zimbardo the mediation of psychology is so omnipresent that it is negated, also in reality TV the mediation of the psychological script is ignored. If Zimbardo argued that by living the part eight hours a day, Eshleman had begun 'internalising his character' (Zarembo, 2004), this is quasi verbatim repeated by Ruth Wrigley, UK's executive producer of *Big Brother*: 'nobody can keep up an act all the time in front of the cameras – the world was going to see them as they really were' (quoted in Ritchie, 2000, p. 26). But maybe both are right on a particular point: that is, not in their claim that eventually true psychology emerges, but in the fact that we cease to see the mediation (of script and camera). This is the illusion Benjamin already pointed at concerning the medium of film. He stresses the fact that in film editing the physicality of the extraneous accessories such as 'the camera, the lighting units, the technical crew' disappears creating the illusion of an 'equipment-free' reality (Benjamin, 2003, p. 263). This apparent disappearance of mediation is not only at work in reality TV, which encourages us to disregard the necessary intrusion of technology and purports to show us *life as it is*, but it can also be discerned in the broader phenomena of psychologisation. While in almost every sphere of social life one is accustomed to adopting a psychologising discourse in order to explain and deal with what is going on between people, this strongly mediated approach to human reality is nevertheless experienced as the *real psychology* of man, *equipment free*.

However, is this critique not a bit outdated? Does it not disregard how in contemporary camera semiotics, instead of concealing the heavy technology and the camera-mediatedness of reality, this process is rather laid bare? Think for example how, in true post-modern style, during a press-conference the cameras often show other cameras and the journalists at work. Or how a DVD gives us beside the film also the bloopers, or how *The Making of . . .* itself can become a full feature film. Post-modern media seemingly unveil and deconstruct their own production process. But then the question of course is, is this deconstructivistic stance really changing the perspective? For is not the most poignant feature of our times that the seeming opposites of the veiled and the unveiled can unproblematically co-exist? Slavoj Žižek argues, in this respect, that the formula of fetishist disavowal *I know very well, but still . . .* is a central paradigm discernable in a whole range of ideological and cultural stances (Žižek, 1989, p. 18). Thus, the meta-perspective of *The Making of,* or of the camera showing other cameras in a press-conference, does not fundamentally affect the structure of the scene. Neither the original movie nor the press conference lose their original seriousness or credibility. On the contrary: the deconstruction only strengthens the language of the image, for the simple reason that the meta-perspective is, as such, part of the very structure: the camera always already takes that position. In the meta-perspective McLuhan's adagio that *the medium is the message* (McLuhan, 2006) therefore gets fully realised. The deconstruction of the medium is the message. For Boorstin, building upon McLuhan's idea that the media necessarily represent themselves, one cannot talk of the media as mediatising or representing an inviolate, prior 'event': they are an integral, co-productive term in all that 'passes through' them (Boorstin as glossed by Taylor and Harris, 2008, pp. 94–95). This is also clear in psychotainment, mainstream psychology is one of the media: the psychological discourse is the co-producer of life as it is, and then of course the question becomes: should not this be generalised to the psy-praxis in general?

But let us for the moment restrict ourselves to the contention that reality TV equals psycho-TV. This is obvious in examples such as educational TV programmes as *Supernanny* or *The House of Tiny Tearaways*, in talk-shows in the vein of Dr Phil or make-over programmes such as *The Swan*, in which for example psychologists exclude pathological cases of *Body Dismorphic Disorder* (Egginton, 2007, p. 225). But beyond these obvious examples there is a proliferation of other formats such as gamedocs, dating programmes and even talent contests which regularly tap directly or indirectly into the psychological discourse and the therapeutic register. *Big Brother*, *Blind Date*, *Britain's Got Talent* (remember Susan Boyle) . . . all of these are instances of reality TV's claim to *lay bare the human condition* (as claims the motto of Zone Reality, a UK TV channel showing only reality programming).

That claim however has been criticised by Philip Zimbardo. Zimbardo argues that reality programmes such as *Survivor* promote 'the worst aspects of human behavior and the wrong human values' (cited in Mason, 2001). Nevertheless, for Zimbardo, the public's 'voyeuristic tendency' can be helpful in bringing 'more valuable and real psychology' to the public. Regarding this *real psychology,* Zimbardo sees reality TV as the logical format through which to educate the public: 'The reason reality TV is so popular is because to observe human behavior is fascinating . . . I spend my whole life doing this' (Mason, 2001).

Do we not have here yet another version of *bring in the good psychologists*? As Betsy Mason put it, it is the psychologist who puts *the real* into reality (Mason, 2001). However, should we not question Zimbardo's celebration of the voyeuristic tendency of humanity? Zimbardo misses the point that, if this reflexive loop is indeed an essential part of the psychic dimension, this would render *The Human Zoo* – the name of the TV programme to which Zimbardo himself contributed – completely empty. There would be nobody in the cages. As said in the previous chapter, having adopted the psychologising gaze at everyday life, everybody would have joined the psychologists. This would lead to the Platonic conclusion that the screen of reality TV is actually empty, we are merely looking at the theoretical spectres of mainstream psychological theory. Should we then opt for a psychology of Zimbardo's psychological voyeur? This, would, of course only result in another tour on the merry-go-round of reflexivity: a psychology of the psychologists can always be topped by yet another meta-psychology.

Should we then, take yet another step and deconstruct the watcher himself, and disrobe him from his supposed substance? Here Daniel Dennett's philosophy of consciousness might be of interest. For, just as we asserted that the proper conclusion regarding Zimbardo's claim for a reflexive loop in regard to reality TV is that the screen ends up empty, so Daniel Dennett makes a similar but inverse claim in his philosophical approach of consciousness, declaring the position of the *viewer* to be empty. Perhaps Dennett's choice for the neurosciences as the departure point of his theory could even save us from the hegemony of psychologised image culture. The question of course will be if Dennett will not be in the end overtaken by the very thing he tries to escape.

The empty stage and the empty theatre: the case of Daniel Dennett's 'cerebral celebrity'

From reality TV's empty stage to Dennett's empty theatre

In his well-known book *Consciousness Explained* Daniel Dennett tries to account for the emergence of consciousness. As the neurosciences proceeded in tracing back subjective experiences to objective material phenomena, the riddle of consciousness and hence of subjectivity indeed became only more and more compelling. If, as the notorious Libet experiment shows, our brain makes decisions well before we consciously decide to take an action, then, according to many scholars, this seriously questions our notion of free will and the notion of subjectivity itself (see Dennett, 1991). However, as I argued in the first chapter, this is not a new issue, as this is exactly what modernity brought us. Insofar as the sciences are objectifying, they pose exactly the question of the subject, and, in this way precisely engender the modern subject in all its problematical dimensions. Today, it is neuroscience that revives the paradox of subjectivity in all its paradoxicality. Being able to show that the impetus to an action starts well before we are aware of it, the neurosciences produce a subject in its zero-level, reduced to objective data.

Dennett addresses the issue of the receding subject via the enigma of consciousness. He firmly rejects the idea of a unified agent/subject. For Dennett consciousness is no *Cartesian theatre* presuming some central agent in the brain integrating all incoming data. Due to our heritage of Cartesian dualism, he argues, we misunderstand consciousness in the imagery of some sort of control room in the brain where the homunculus (the little man in the brain) watches a theatre or a screen on which all sensory data are projected. In opposition to this, Dennett, drawing upon the neurosciences, evolutionary biology and cognitive science proposes his 'Multiple Drafts Model' which leaves the 'central experiencer' behind and puts forward the self-organising functioning of the network. For Dennett there is no theatre and thus no viewer: neural processing occurs in different places in the brain, there is no need for a central audience or agent (Dennett, 1991). Consciousness then for Dennett can be understood as a *competition in fame*:

> Instead of switching media or going somewhere in order to become conscious, heretofore unconscious contents, staying right where they are, can achieve something *rather like* fame in competition with other fame-seeking (or just potentially fame-*finding*) contents. And, according to this view, that is what consciousness is.
>
> (Dennett, 2001, p. 224)

Dennett contends that 'consciousness is cerebral celebrity': those contents succeeding to persevere become conscious; they monopolise resources long enough to achieve certain effects on for example memory or the control of behaviour (Dennett, 1993, p. 929).

However, do Dennett's concepts of 'fame in the brain' and 'cerebral celebrity' (Dennett, 2001, p. 225) – the use of which metaphors he neither justifies nor elaborates upon – not simply take us back to today's image culture and its intertwining with processes of psychologisation? If Zimbardo got stuck in an unacknowledged paradoxical loop between voyeurism and real psychology, does the same thing not occur with Dennett? Slavoj Žižek has already criticised Dennett's *cerebral celebrity* for not being able to account for the very stage on which celebrity appears (Žižek, 2006b). Using metaphors from the media and *celebrity culture*, Dennett surprisingly enough reopens the imagery of the screen and the audience. It can be argued further that Dennett suspects that somewhere something is returning to haunt the debate, but the question is whether he can truly grasp what this is about:

> A neuroscientific theory of consciousness must be a theory of the Subject of consciousness, one that analyzes this imagined central Executive into component parts, none of which can itself be a proper Subject. The apparent properties of consciousness that only make sense as features enjoyed by the Subject must thus also be decomposed and distributed, and this inevitably creates a pressure on the imagination of the theorist. No sooner do such properties get functionalistically analyzed into complex dispositional traits distributed in space and time in the brain, than their ghosts come knocking on the door, demanding entrance disguised as qualia, or phenomenality or the imaginable difference between us and zombies. One of the hardest tasks thus facing those who would explain consciousness is recognising when some feature has already been explained (in sketch, in outline) and hence does not need to be explained again.
>
> (Dennett, 2001, p. 236)

However, will Dennett's *vade retro* suffice to keep the Cartesian spectres at bay? Denouncing something as a folk psychological apparition is one thing, understanding the why of its tenacity is another thing. It is exactly here, one can claim, that Dennett is overtaken by his own spectres, his paradoxical recourse to the metaphor of celebrity is thus to be seen as a *return of the repressed*, to put it in the language of psychoanalysis which Dennett never tires of labelling as obsolete. At least, the popping up of the metaphor of celebrity and its connection to the screen deserves to be scrutinised, as it might be that with it something hidden in Dennett's theoretical edifice – and something problematic in the current mainstream assessments of the neurosciences as such – comes out into the open.

Dennett's misappropriation of the Cartesian Theatre

A first problematic point is that in his coining of the phrase *Cartesian theatre*, Dennett misses how the metaphor of the theatre is used by Descartes himself. The metaphor of the theatre appears in a crucial passage of Descartes' *Discours de la Méthode*. There Descartes explains that in searching for truth, he suspended all certainties, judgements and the opinions of others, and, whilst adopting a provisory code of morals, he embarked on a journey:

> And inasmuch as I hoped to be able to reach my goal better by conversing with men than by staying shut up any longer in the stove-heated room

where I had all these thoughts, the winter was not yet over when I set out again on my travels. And in all the nine years that followed I did nothing but wander here and there in the world, trying to be more a spectator than an actor in all the comedies that are played out there; and reflecting particularly in each matter on what might render it suspect and give us occasion for erring, I meanwhile rooted out from my mind all the errors that had previously been able to slip into it.

(Descartes, 1996 [1637], p. 16)

So the metaphor of the theatre is to be related in the first place to Descartes' step back, his withdrawal from a direct engagement with the world. His *epoché*, the bracketing of all worldly certainties and convictions, transforms the world into a theatre, turning himself into a spectator. William Egginton already described the decisive shift from the mediaeval spectacle to the modern theatre as constitutive for the modern forms of interpersonal relations and self-consciousness. The mediaeval spectacle is about *representing*, it is only in modern theatre that *acting* comes in, as the actor 'can represent a character only insofar as he or she already has an imaginary conception of him or herself, as long as he or she is therefore a character' (Egginton, 2003, p. 73). Acting thus presupposes the modern condition of looking upon oneself from a point outside of the scene. Egginton therefore speaks of 'theatricality' putting forward this concept as the true marker of modern subjectivity (Egginton, 2003). With Descartes it is clear that this historical turn cannot be cut loose from the advent of the modern sciences. For, if the Cartesian stance can be regarded as the cradle of modern science, it is the Cartesian theatre which defines the position of both the academic and the modern subject. Descartes *res cogitans* shows how the objectivations of science on the one hand presupposes an external objectified position to seek the truth, and on the other hand invites the lay person to adopt the very same position. *According to scientific research* . . . pulls you into the dark theatre and its plush theatre seating.

Is Dennett's critique on the imagery of the homunculus in the control room hence not a denunciation of the scheme of modernity? If we return to Eggington's analysis of the advent of modern theatre it is furthermore clear that with theatre, necessarily, psychology comes in. As Egginton contends, actors became 'students of human nature' (Egginton, 2003, p. 102). This becoming scholars of the human is of course the tell-tale sign of psy-chologisation. In modernity *real life*, showed and staged by the sciences of human nature, is watched by an audience sharing this vantage point. Psychologisation is the stance of *Isn't this called . . . in psychology?* by which the so called layman partakes in the scientific gaze of the expert looking at the images projected on the screen. This means that Dennett's rejection of the homunculus as *folk psychology*, disregards the fact that this so-called *folk psychology* is directly informed by science. It is only with modern science, in its re-working of the classic idea of the human as a sensible being (connected to the world via its senses), that the idea of the homunculus in the brain sees light. Dennett's critique of the attribution of metaphorical eyes to the brain overlooks the fact that it is only through science's interest in the structure and function of the sense organs that this idea arose (see research by the end of the seventeenth and the beginning of the nineteenth century (Vidal, 2009, p. 14)). Via science's claim that we see with our brain, the eyes moved up to the brain in so-called folk psychology. Descartes' retreat into the obscurity of the theatre is, in this way, the very trope of the scientific view of how man experiences the world. It is Dennett's missed encounter with Descartes, I claim, which prepares him for his hasty use of the concept of fame and celebrity, disregarding the fact that celebrity as such presupposes the stage or, rather, the screen: or, the return of what he rejects with the Cartesian theatre.

Cerebral celebrity: Dennett overtaken by fiction and missing materiality

Jodi Dean writes that celebrities in the public eye appear as 'the only persons who can act' (Dean, 2002, p. 124). While everyday people are held back by so many social and cultural constraints, celebrities are seen as free, as having the luxury to just be themselves. Of course everybody knows that the celebrity personality is managed, that celebrities in their being what they are only follow scripts, carefully planned or not. But here again, despite that fact, we still act as if we believe in the authenticity of celebrity. Even if we know that the 'je ne sais quoi' is fabricated, we still are tempted to see this aura when the celebrities walk over the red carpet. This is what celebrity culture shares with reality TV: everyone is aware of the manipulations and machinations but one still thinks to see at least a glimpse of the real authentic thing. The fact that everyone moreover knows that being a celebrity often boils down to *being known for being known* (phrase attributed to Daniel Boorstin), is no impediment for celebrity culture, it is for many the very hope of getting access to celebrity.

It is clear that here one would be led quickly into a psychological under-standing of celebrity culture. For, as David P. Marshall contends, celebrity culture is closely related to 'the intensification of the concerns of the personal and the psychologisation of greater areas of life' (Marshall, 1997, p. 59). Hence, the temptation to resist is to understand today's celebrity culture itself along psychologising lines. It is this deadlock which Christopher Lasch in his otherwise very interesting book *The Culture of Narcissism* could not always avoid: 'Apparently free from family ties and institutional constraints, the narcissist can only overcome his insecurity by seeing his "grandiose self" reflected in the attentions of others, or by attaching himself to those who radiate celebrity, power, and charisma' (Lasch, 1978, p. 10). Is not the problem of this that Lasch, exactly in his critique of therapeutic culture, eventually bounces back in psychologisation? He tries to understand the narcissistic pathological quest for identity on the basis of an implicit conception of the proper *authentic* psychological constellation. Consider how Lasch, criticising late-modern culture's 'second nature' for its ironic, pseudo-analytic self-awareness, recourses to the psychoanalyst Heinz Kohut in order to promote a more direct and authentic engagement with the world:

> Those who feel secure in the ego's ability to control the id, according to Kohut, take pleasure in occasionally suspending the secondary process (for example, in sleep or in sexual activity), since they know they can regain it when they wish to.
>
> (Lasch, 1978, p. 97)

The paradox of this advice to skip the Cartesian reflex is that it boils down to the promotion of some kind of *acephalous* subject engaging in a supposed authentic way of just being itself and enjoying life as it is (De Vos, 2010a).

With Lasch's subject, which does not have to be conscious of its engagement in the so-called primary processes, are we not back with Dennett who claims that a lot of important mental processes take place outside of consciousness? Here of course, a new dualism slowly takes form, distinguishing between a kind of parallel reality, where the real material processes are supposed to take place, as opposed to the fiction of consciousness. As such, from a psychoanalytical point of view one could endorse this putting forward *of another scene*. However, the problem with Lasch is that he considers that realm accessible; while the problem with Dennett is that he cannot grasp the true materiality of it. In his use of the celebrity metaphor, Dennett is overtaken be the fiction he rejects.

If Dennett misses the link between fiction and materiality, we should search for a materialist understanding of celebrity culture avoiding the psychologising paradoxes. Here Brian Moeran's suggestion that celebrities form a crucial part of the 'name economy' might be interesting:

> They are 'household names' whose reputations seemingly join together producers and consumers by means of the products (commodities, cultural productions) with which they are associated. They also give commodities personalities by means of celebrity endorsements in

advertising and PR activities, and operate as brand names for the organisation of production and consumption.

(Moeran, 2003, p. 301)

Marshall, in the same vein, considers the celebrity as a commodity
possessing, in its humanness and familiarity, an affective link to the meaning
that is bestowed on consumer objects (Marshall, as cited in Taylor and Harris,
2008, p. 133). It is these, what I would call, *psycho-economics* of post-
Fordism, to which I shall return in the next chapter. But the central point here
is that, along the lines of Benjamin's argument about film, the card-board
psychology of celebrities – with their accidental psychological disturbances
of ADHD, anorexia and the like, all too recognisable by the broad public –
thus transforms a dispersed, antagonistic and fragmented social sphere in
these globalised times into a meaningful and homogenised public space, or
rather, an ersatz public space, the virtuality of a commodified community.
Dennett's casual recourse to the metaphor of celebrity in this way becomes
highly problematic. Recall also Žižek pointing to the remarkable similarity
between Dennetts's conceptualisation of the brain – as a pandemonium of
local agents lacking a central Self – with today's decentralised capitalism
(Žižek, 2006b, p. 263). In this way Dennett's concept of cerebral celebrity
teaches us something of psychologisation in times of globalisation. On the one
hand, in late-modernity both the central state and the central brain agency are
no longer relevant conceptualisations. On the other hand, in a virtual unified
space, a screen still has to be presupposed to contain the fallen angels and the
demons. Reality TV is the ersatz for the public sphere, the celebrities on that
scene replace the subject. Dennett's paradoxical move of denouncing the
theatre and bringing in the screen via the back door has to be taken seriously.

Maybe the wager of an emancipatory project would be that in order to de-
psychologise the subject, one has to opt for a truly radical materialism. A
final tour through psycho-image culture, addressing the virtual dimension of
it, will allow us to make that argument.

De-psychologising subjectivity

Psycho-technology and the screen of virtual reality

If Benjamin observed how photography and film thoroughly altered
something in man's being with himself and the world, is this not only today
coming to full blossom with digital technology in which the screen opens up
a virtual space? Just consider the fact that today we seem to drift from screen
to screen. Imagine the scenario of the child who, when called to come to the
car to visit the grandparents, detaches him- or herself with great difficulty

from the Play Station only to be sat in front of an LCD screen attached to the front seat to watch a DVD and, then, on arriving, after a quick kiss to grandma and grandpa, he or she is sat in front of the television to watch the cartoon network (a Game Boy comes in handy to cover the transitions and to ensure the continuity of the virtual life world).[4] Perhaps the omnipresence of the screen (in cars, sports arenas, concert halls, at the dentist . . .) ensures that we do not notice its mediation anymore. Is this not at work in Dennett's denouncing of the brain as a screen? Does he, for example, not overlook the fact that in today's brain sciences the brain itself is an image on a screen? What is generally ignored is the fact that imaging technology *constructs* the brain: the use of colours, resolution and image enhancing techniques are ultimately, as Francisco Vidal writes, connected to 'a chain of decisions about the processing of numeral data' (Vidal, 2009, p. 27). Are we not too rapidly inclined, or, simply led to see the brain charts as equipment-free, to use Benjamin terms? We are prompted to forget the physicality and complexity of the computers and mediating theories which produce the images which are supposed to reveal us our true Inner Self on the screen.

This turning of the inside to the outside is furthermore one of the central tropes in virtual environments. Just consider how parents post pictures and videos of their newborns on the internet – sometimes even the birth itself is put online. The screen seems to have become a pivotal point for a changed distribution between the public and the private. In the traditional bourgeois education of the so-called Fordist times, parenting was a private practice. The public sphere was foremost the place where the results of education were supposed to become visible. This public field was thus a kind of a stage where the educators and educated became the actors playing according to rather strict conventions. In today's parenting the distinction between public/private has not so much lost its meaning due to the private being increasingly invaded by the public (through, for example, the so called psy-complex) but, rather, through the public becoming flooded by the private in a very particular way. That is to say, through the public becoming a screen rather than a stage. In post-Fordist times the actual practice of parenting is made visible to the gaze of everyone. This is where the private space comes to be folded over into the public. Via photos and videos posted on websites or blogs, in internet forums and chat rooms our intimacy becomes, to use a Lacanian neologism, *extimacy*.

It is here that we also can situate reality TV as it is part of this pulling of intimacy out into the public. In reality TV this often leads to a proliferation of screens. Think of how in so-called *parenting TV* the Supernanny and the like never, or rarely, intervenes *en vivo*. Comments are made and advice is given while watching, together with the parent(s), a monitor showing footage (edited of course) shot by a whole battery of hidden or unhidden cameras. When the expert does intervene directly, she or he does it in *real time*, meaning that the parent is connected via a radio device with the expert who is operating from some kind of control room watching the screen. Do we here not find, most strikingly, the imagery Dennett so vigorously denies? What Dennett denounces thus seems to be a central trope of how in reality TV subjectivity takes form: we take a seat next to the expert or we are electronically connected to the control room of Knowledge, in both cases the real thing of life is situated on the virtual screen.

This should prompt us to leave behind the mere metaphoric use of the screen and engage with the materiality and the technology of the screen and its relation to subjectivity. In this respect Christopher Lasch made a pertinent remark on how electronic images change the way in which we experience the actions of others and of ourselves:

> Modern life is so thoroughly mediated by electronic images that we cannot help responding to others as if their actions – and our own – were being recorded and simultaneously transmitted to an unseen audience or stored up for close scrutiny at some later time.
>
> (Lasch, 1978, p. 47)

However, in order to grasp this claim, we should try to understand how man's mediated existence with himself, the others and the world has gone through some major shifts. Let us start with the simple assertion that in pre-technological times, the rule was that if I can see you or, better, if I can see your eyes, then you can see mine. On the human, bodily level the gaze was reciprocal. In this constellation the human gaze was set against the gaze of God coming from a totally different and inaccessible space. The first shift came with the advent of modern technology: to use Foucault's example, Bentham's panoptical tower was so constructed that the human eyes of the guards were concealed and reciprocity was put out of play. Foucault's central insight is that this made the gaze turn inwards: the fact that one knows that he or she is potentially watched over every single second, leads to the incorporation of that constant controlling gaze. This internalisation can easily be understood as the beginning of the psychologisation processes in modernity. The gaze incorporated here was not God's (a perspective unfathomable for the human) but, rather, the gaze of the disciplinary powers from which man came to look upon himself.

The second shift occurred with, in Benjamin's terms, the advent of *the age of reproduction*. As technology made recording and playback of the gaze possible, something fundamentally changed. And this is best understood as a shift in the possibilities of relating or reporting something. Prior to the emergence of recording technologies the gaze of the other/Other could only be repeated discursively; playback was symbolically mediated. In these times one could only be confronted with *a story* about oneself. Thus, immediate experience, the cutting-edge present, was mediated by imagining what others (which include oneself) would *tell*. More concisely, the experience of the present was tied to an imaginary voice in one's head giving comments on what was happening: the present equalled instant relating. God was, in this perspective, the ultimate horizon, the big Other supposed to contain the totality of all the stories. With the advent of recording technology however, repetition and reporting left the paradigm of the story behind and came under the reign of the image. Especially with film, the past became not only relatable but also now repeatable, opening in the present a window to the past.[5] With this, living in the present became a case of imagining being *seen* by the Other, or as Lasch wrote, by an unseen audience. However, if in pre-technological times the imaginary public was oneself, the neighbour and the traditional authorities, does in times of mechanical reproduction the privileged spectator in the public not become a particular version of the Self, that is, the Self as the gaze? For one of the most enigmatic aspects of recording technology is that it made it possible to see oneself as oneself. In playback I literally watch myself; this means that in my actions I always imagine and presuppose my own future gaze. In this way the Self, as the pure gaze, becomes the primordial spectator.

However, one can argue that this auto-reflexivity was only fully realised with a third technological shift. The simultaneity, which Lasch mentioned was only effected with advanced electronics which made possible that playback, is not for close scrutiny at some later time, but can be added in *real time* to the present. The photo roll does not need to be developed; the monitor directly shows the recordings. This advanced technology, perfected by the progressive digitalisation, makes the incorporation of the auto-gaze possible in the here and now, meaning that one can look at oneself in real time: in one's actions one already looks at the screen capturing the events. In this respect the photographer Hana Jakrlova produced some very enigmatic pictures in a series called Big Sister with pictures of men engaged in sexual activity in a brothel while these men were watching a video monitor screening the very act (http://www.hanajakrlovaphoto.com/). These images were, furthermore, broadcast in real time via a website. Thus, with the internet not only the watcher became everyone and everyone becomes watched, moreover, the internet becomes the place where watching and being watched become interchangeable. Other and Self collide and are cut loose from tradition and the former figures of authority. The Other came to equal the mass, with which we are united within a virtual space where the private and the public meet each other as two ends of a continuum in a folded space.

Late-modern subjectivity is screen subjectivity. The screen is the cross-road, the only constant factor within the zapping and skipping through

Facebook and Twitter, life-blogs and live-blogs. It is thus not a surprise that in late-modern subjectivity the tropes of reality TV and celebrity culture return. For, the basic principle of celebrity – making oneself seen, accessible and available to others on the screen (Dean, 2002, p. 121) – is also the essence of today's blogging and social network sites: we create our own fan-sites and becomes our own paparazzi. Or, as Baudrillard puts is, what is important today is to resemble oneself, to find oneself everywhere, 'to be on all movie screens at once' (Baudrillard, 1988, p. 41). Today we are not so much actors on a stage; we are celebrities on the screen. In the format of celebrity, we make ourselves seen, accessible to others and thus to ourselves.

It is in this way that we can understand that today's hyper-surveillance is not threatening to but, rather, constitutive of subjectivity. Here it is interesting to note that, as Karen Lury for example argues, parenting programmes such as *The House of Tiny Tearaways* are similar to the hard reality TV shows like *Big Brother* insofar as every spot of the *Tiny Tearaways* house is camera-covered (Lury, 2009, p. 493). As is well known, the crux of the Foucaultian *panopticon* is that the cruel horror is not the certain knowledge of being watched, but rather the uncertainty of never knowing if or when one is being watched. Ian Buchanan contends that in reality shows such as *Survivor*, this anxiety is relieved the minute one knows we are being watched all the time and, with this, the anxiety shifts from an anxiety of being watched to an anxiety that we might *not* be watched (Buchanan, 2001). Drawing on Žižek, Buchanan argues that the fear is that the Big Other is not up to this task, that it might be an imposter, and he recalls Frederic Jameson's idea that paranoia is a form of narcissism, entailing the secret fear that no-one is watching after all (Buchanan, 2001). Is this not why critiques of academisation and psychologisation often meet with so much resistance, as they threaten the ideal image of Academia as the ultimate Big Brother in whose gaze we actually feel secure? The critique of the Life Sciences, therefore, is not easily accepted as it undermines this reassuring gaze of Academia. In this way Elizabeth Roudinesco may have missed something when she claimed that 'nothing is more destructive for a subject than to be reduced to his or her physico-chemical system' (Roudinesco, 2001, p. 127). Could we not assert the opposite, that we want to be psychologised, we want to be reduced to neurobiology, we long for the Big Brother to *screen* us? Again, this is why a critique of the psy-sciences is often so threatening; it would condemn us to our own and the others' unmediated presence! There has to be a Big Other of science, there has to be a psychology which can guarantee a distance. As this imagery of the central Audience in the Control Room today is omnipresent, Dennett misses a crucial point. The end of the subject, as we know it, should be understood along other lines.

The end of the subject as we know it: aestheticising 'death as it is'

Should we not drop the whole concept of subjectivity, which seems to be only an empty shell or, rather, an empty screen whose content is but a random procession of bits and bytes? Is Dennett's claim that neuroscience means the end of man as we knew him not appropriate here? *Fame in the brain* as the obituary of the Ego? However, in the same way as Francis Fukuyama missed the historicity of his claim that history had come to an end, those who proclaim the end of the subject might miss what is truly at stake in modernity, namely a zero-level of subjectivity. Dennett's celebrity metaphor is in this way to the point, as it suggests that the end of man is not only to be seen on the brain monitor, it will surely be (or is already being) televised. The motto of reality TV, life as it is, is in this way misleading, reality TV, as it reveals us a zero-level of subjectivity, is about death.

Thus perhaps we should reverse the idea of Chung Chin-Yi who, drawing upon Baudrillard, writes that the reality show *Big Brother* turns our existential banality and the boredom of our own lives into a spectacle (Chin-Yi, 2007, p. 33). For, one can argue, ultimately this existential banality and boredom is not ours, but that of the psychological beings we watch. In the phoniness of both psychologised celebrity culture and *celebriticised* subjectivity we deal with prototypes of the human being, *terrible real people*, to borrow Frank Vande Veire's term with which he describes soap stars (Vande Veire, 2008). With their genuine and simple quest for love, passion, success and happiness, celebrities are so real, so *psychological*, that they become phony. Which reminds us of how, for Adorno, the psychological as such is tantamount to the dimension of fictitiousness and phoniness (Adorno, 1991). If the celebrity, that uncanny lookalike of the human, that endlessly reproduced image of the *homo psychologicus*, still has an aura, it is one of alienated and fake authenticity, the aura of psychology. But does this not mean that the true subjective position lies outside of psychology? Watching, for example, the phony characters of reality TV as they are informed directly and indirectly by the scripts of psychology, we find ourselves in a meta-position. And this meta-position is ultimately not the homunculus which Dennett denounced, but the zero-level of psychology, the empty position left behind in the emergence of modern subjectivity. Maybe it is exactly this uncanny, even horrific, point of non-subjectivity which Dennett tries to escape with what I should like to call his naive materialism. It is here, in this zero-level of psychology and subjectivity, that a more radical materialism can be conceived. We shall return to this in our conclusion. But let us first return to Walter Benjamin to assess how this zero-level of subjectivity, this end of the subject, is being aestheticised. 'Humankind, which once, in Homer, was an object of contemplation for the Olympian gods, has now become one for itself. Its self-alienation has reached the point where it can experience its own annihilation as a supreme aesthetic pleasure' (Benjamin, 2008, p. 42). Is this not a most concise definition of reality TV and psychotainment? Just think of the personal and social breakdowns teeming in *Survivor*, *Supernanny*, *Dr Phil* and other reality shows, aestheticised for our pleasure. For Benjamin, self-alienation is connected to the technological developments of modernity which fundamentally changed the human experience qua experience. It brought about the waning of experience as such. The First World War was decisive in this respect. Benjamin observes how soldiers came back from the war 'grown silent, not richer' (Benjamin, 2002, p. 144). Their battlefield experience was cut off by tactical warfare, in the same way as economic experience was numbed by inflation, and moral experience was evaporated through power mechanisms (Benjamin, 2002). Giorgi Agamben restates this most aptly as the 'expropriation of experience' implicit in the founding project of modern science. This expropriation, Agamben writes, is effected by the conflating of knowledge and experience in one single agent:

> For the great revolution in modern science was less a matter of opposing experience to authority (the *argumentum ex re* against the *argumentum ex verbo*, which are not in fact irreconcilable) than of referring knowledge and experience to a single subject, which is none other than their conjunction at an abstract Archimedean point: the Cartesian cogito, consciousness.
>
> (Agamben, 1993b, p. 19)

For Agamben modern man's average day contains virtually nothing that can be translated into experience and this makes everyday existence intolerable. Not that there are no more experiences, there still are, but they are enacted outside the individual who merely observes them (Agamben, 1993b, p. 14). Here we find again, not surprisingly of course, the Cartesian theatre as the very trope of the impossibility of reconciling experience with knowledge. Also, for Agamben, technology is decisive here, as he gives the example of how the majority of the tourists who visit El Patio de los Leones in the Alhambra have no wish to experience one of the great wonders of the world, preferring instead that the camera should experience it for them (Agamben, 1993b, p. 15). To which we can add that if analogue technology still required you to look through the lens to make sure that the focus was right – in this way the lens was a filter or a buffer – with digital technology you can let the device itself do all the looking and the focusing. According to Agamben, we should not simply deplore this state of affairs, but take note of it, as in it there may be a grain of wisdom and a 'germinating seed of future experience' might be found (Agamben, 1993b, p. 15). Maybe Agamben has a point: in a botanical garden in Marrakech I once saw a Japanese tourist pointing her digital video camera at the exquisite plants while she herself was chatting away with her companion unbothered with the comments of the guide which were being transmitted wirelessly via a radio device as she had her earphones unplugged. So perhaps, in the radical acceptance of the expropriation of experience, something emancipatory is to be found. In the case of the Japanese tourist, she succeeded in letting the electronic device obey the injunction to experience the visit in the appropriate way. Via the device, she could open up the space for something else. When contemporary ideology, commerce and psychology tell us, or command us, to enjoy and to fully experience life, this is a way of not accepting these lures, of refusing to enjoy.

But, as with Benjamin's optimism, we should ask how much weight we can give to the emancipatory potential of Agamben's stance? Agamben repeats his claim regarding the emancipatory possibilities when discussing Guy Debord's *The Society of the Spectacle*. For Agamben, the spectacle being the ultimate expropriation of the experience, harbours 'a positive possibility' that can be used against the spectacle (Agamben, 1993a, p. 80). But can we be that sure of the emancipatory potential of the spectacle? Is it not that late-capitalism itself is always capable of incorporating even the experience of the zero-level of subjectivity into the spectacle itself? This is exactly what the power of reality TV as psychotainment is about. It has the ability to transform virtually everything into something which can be digested and enjoyed.[6] And here the most central tool to hammer down the indictment to fully experience life and make it an object of enjoyment is exactly the psychologising discourse which is omnipresent in the media. Just consider the total grip of questions such as 'why won't you tell us what you feel right now, please share your emotions with us . . .' Those questions, originating from therapeutic settings and passing over into psychotainment, have now returned to evade all other spheres from professional to private life. Mainstream psychological discourse, posing as the mediator between experience and knowledge, cannot but repeat the alienation and this is not easy to counter.[7]

Benjamin's insight was precisely to point to the aestheticisation of this alienation. Psychotainment aestheticises the experience of man's own destruction and self-alienation. Is Dennett then not also, in his turn, caught in a kind of aestheticisation? His public lectures are filled with all kinds of amusing optical experiments with drawings designed to prove to the audience how funny, ingenious and interesting the wiring of our brain is. As he shows how the brain plays tricks with us, are we not supposed to enjoy the end of the autonomous subject and the denouncement of the free will? Is, in addition, this aestheticisation of the brain not particularly discernable in the full colour brain scans with which we are bombarded through all sorts of media? Looking like yet another variation on Andy Warhol's Marilyn Monroe prints, these pop-art brain charts seem to portray the brain as a celebrity. From the aestheticisation of the beautiful brain it is just a small step to other forms of aestheticisation of the human condition. Just consider the so-called quality TV documentary where, in opposition to ordinary reality TV, producers refrain from showing grand emotions and shun the easy effects of close-ups and other editing techniques. Such documentaries on cancer, dementia, or social problems in all their serenity often result in an equally alienating aestheticisation, using arty black and white footage, minimalist soundtracks (or no music at all) in order to celebrate the human resilience and the beauty of real everyday life. Whether in the black and white of the quality documentary or the full colour palette of reality TV, this aestheticisation and celebration of the human condition should be seen as a kind of vulture-like feeding on what Benjamin calls self-alienation and man's own destruction. This morbid dimension of contemporary media can, furthermore, be connected to another of Benjamin's theses. In trying to grasp the transition from the pre-modern epic story to the modern novel he writes in *The Storyteller*:

> (T)he reader of a novel actually does look for human beings from whom he derives the 'meaning of life.' Therefore he must, no matter what, know in advance that he will share their experience of death: if need be their figurative death – the end of the novel – but preferably their actual one.
> (Benjamin, 2002, p. 156)

As we have seen, regarding reality TV, the meaning of life is what the psychologist, with his/her *real psychology,* brings to the programme. The morbid character of this may be discernable in the omnipresent trope of elimination. This phenomenon could be explained as a Darwinian survival of the fittest or in terms of the rat-race of capitalism but maybe Benjamin's insight is more useful here. In the elimination, the spectator hovers ghost-like over the consecutive deaths of the competitors. The motto of reality TV, *life as it is,* can thus be replaced by *death as it is.* But it is important to see that the trope of elimination is in the end meant to lead to the denial of death, as the ghoulish spectacle of elimination culminates in the survival of the One, the Ego. In this victorious moment the ultimate meaning of life is supposed to be revealed. The winner receives not only the pot of gold but also celebrity status, at least in this week's Pleiades of fame. But is not the radical conclusion to be made that, despite the glorious moment of the Ego, the subject as such is dead, only it does not know it? It can only try to grasp its death in its aesthetisations via the spectacle and enact its resurrection in a pseudo-event. Maybe this is also what Dennett tries to get at. The modern Cartesian subject, with all its paradoxes, cannot but be a still-born child. Dennett clearly fails, however, to grasp the Freudian insight that man cannot represent his own death and this is why, in the end, Dennett cannot fully bury the little homunculus and his little theatre: he fails to keep the zombies (those who are dead but do not know it) at bay. Dennett's alternative route to understand subjectivity in terms of fame and of celebrity cannot but connect his theory with the alienating sphere of the aesteticised spectacle.

Conclusion: a plea for a radical materialism

While Dennett rightfully understood that the conception of the subject-homunculus as an unified agent of the brain is untenable, he cannot account for the zero-level of subjectivity this entails. His recourse to the celebrity-metaphor thus connects him to the society of the spectacle in which psychotainment features the deadly Ego as the ultimate commodity in late-capitalism. In this way, in deconstructing the Cartesian theatre, Dennett is still looking for a meaningful entity: the human subject as defined by its brainware and by the evolutionary history of his species. But, as our reading of Dennett's 'cerebral celebrity' has shown, it turns out that the object of the gaze of the neuro-scientific discourse is the zombie-like spectre of the human, virtual meat. Can this still be called a materialistic view of man? Here Cathérine Malabou is absolutely right in asking for a far more radical materialism: 'The only philosophical issue is today the elaboration of a new materialism which precisely refuses to envisage any, even the smallest, separation not only between brain and thought, but also between brain and the unconscious' (Žižek, 2008a, p. 26). One way to understand this, is to propose above all a correlation between the subject and the screen. As Taylor and Harris write, drawing upon Baudrillard, in late-modern media there 'is no longer a scene or stage of action that we view from a distance' (Taylor and Harris, 2008, p. 169). The radical truth of the collapse of the Cartesian theatre is that this disappearance of the Cartesian subject has left something behind, an empty space, a zero-level of subjectivity. This is then the spectre haunting neurology and the brain sciences (as well as their companions in psychology advocating a de-psychologised neuro-bio-psychology), a spectre which they try to contain by positing a positivised neuro-psychological entity which is fully itself. The neuro-scientific discourse hence is always at risk to glide into a psychologising discourse. In this way Dennett, in his refusal of a radical materialism, might in the end be a psychologist, a (neuro)psychologiser. It is the gaze of the latter, the neuro-psychological gaze, which everyday man via today's hegemonies is called upon to adopt. Seated in today's unacknow-ledged neo-Cartesian theatre, the late-modern subject watches *life as it is,* whether this comes in the form of a reality or celebrity show or in the form of colourful braincharts.

Maybe the first to effect such an escape from radical materialism was Julien Offay de La Mettrie who I mentioned in the first chapter. Remember how La Mettrie tried to do away with Cartesian dualism by denying the *res cogitans* any substance as such. For La Mettrie, man is a machine; thinking, willing and feeling are but bodily reactions and functions (La Mettrie, 1996 [1747]). But drawing the *cogito* into the *res extensa* cannot be achieved without a remainder. As Marc De Kesel argues, La Mettrie's operation (and with it, the operation of the whole of modern science) of stripping the subject of all of its contents, leaves behind an emptied, non-substantial space where once the subject was (De Kesel, 2008). This is the empty chair of Dennett's theatre and the empty cage of Zimbardo's Human Zoo. Where we flee from this radical abyss of subjectivity, we also flee from radical materialism. Consider how La Mettrie's attempt to defy the *skandalon* of the zero-level of subjectivity led him to devise a hedonism based on a naturalised scientific discourse, advancing a natural, unified *voluptuous* subject (De Vos, 2011b). It is in this tradition that we find Daniel Dennett. In his recourse to metaphors of fame and celebrity, he is eventually overtaken by Cartesian spectres. Here, at the crossroads of the imaginary screen of the brain, cognitivism meets psy-chotainment:

> The task of all media and information today is to produce this real, this extra real (interviews, live coverage, movies, TV-truth, etc.). There is too much of it, we fall into obscenity and pornography. As in pornography, a kind of zoom takes us too near the real, which never existed and only ever came into view *at a certain distance*.
>
> (Baudrillard, 1983, p. 83)

This extra real today is evident both in reality TV and in brainscans. If reality TV can be labelled as *psychoporn*, as it claims to show us life as it really is, starring psychological man stripped of the unnecessary introductory romantic stories, then what Dennett is offering is *brainporn*, showing us the mind as an unveiled genital.

The obscenities this chapter started out with are thus structural: image culture and the psy-sciences pretend to show us the bare state of things, the naked *homo psychologicus*. A critique of psychologisation of culture should thus not envision to rescue Everyday Life: the idea of a real, de-psychologised and authentic everyday life is precisely the core of the imagery of psychology. This should remind us the 1960s slogan *reality is for those who cannot support the dream*. As Slavoj Žižek points out, this is of course to be understood within the Freudian dream logic: we escape into a dream to avoid a deadlock in our real life, but there, encountering in the dream the true horror, we have to escape literally from the dream back into reality (Žižek, 2006c). This is the Lacanian real, the zero-level of subjectivity, which a radical materialism should confront. The political echoes this phrase might evoke are justified. Just consider Adorno's argument on how in the enlightened world, mythology has entered into the profane. Being cleansed of the demons, reality itself assumes 'the numinous character which the ancient world attributed to demons':

> Under the title of brute facts, the social injustice from which they proceed is now as assuredly sacred a preserve as the medicine man was sacrosanct by reason of the protection of his gods . . . Through the countless agencies of mass production and its culture the conventionalized modes of behavior are impressed on the individual as the only natural, respectable and rational ones.
>
> (Adorno and Horkheimer, 1989 [1944], p. 28).

This *Realpolitik* of the psy and behavioural sciences, today coming more and more in the form of neuropolitics, is the subject of the next chapter, psychologisation and politics.

Notes

1　See: http://www.youtube.com/watch?v=aDTtftKc9eY
2　As for example Marc De Kesel contends, contesting the virtuality of the internet has to be done on the net (De Kesel, 2010).
3　For how the audience of *Big Brother* reverts to psychological terminology see Lothar Mikos (2004), and how this is reinforced by the discourse of the show's producers and the critics pro and con, see Ernest Mathijs and Wouter Hessels (2004).
4　Of course children do still play outside all day long with no single screen in sight. However, we should be aware that even in that case the hegemonic framework might be that of the screen and of virtuality. Compare this with my generation, the television generation, who not only returned at night to the TV-set but who while playing outside often re-enacted the popular TV-series or imagined that its adventures were televised.
5　A painting could never realise this: the canvas in this way tells stories; it does not show how things really are or were.
6　If Boorstin argues that television is the site of the artificially generated pseudo-event (Boorstin, 1992 [1961]), then it is clear that in reality TV it is the psychology which has to provide the spectacle and the pseudo-event. Just consider how in the soap *Survivor* the assignments that the participants have to fulfil are often nothing more than trying to remain standing on a wooden beam. The spectacle has to come from the psychology.

7   One could even argue that this entails that psychology, in terms of Jean Baudrillard (2007), is the praxis of the *simulacrum* of man. Just like the Irish pub theme bars in other countries as such exceed by far what an Irish pub actually is (Taylor and Harris, 2008, p. 210), psychology depicts a man which as such also does not exist. But the problem with simulacra is that they create a compelling model: as the Irish pub theme bar returns or better turns to Ireland itself to shape the bars (Taylor and Harris, 2008, p. 222, n. 2)!

4   Psychologisation and politics

The devastating January 2010 earthquake in Haiti, day three: a humanitarian NGO has started to provide children with pencils and paper to let them come to terms with their bereavement and fears. In humanitarian aid the psychosocial dimension has become essential. For the Red Cross, to take one example, psychological support is not a speciality but is integrated into all activities; even first aiders are trained to 'treat the wounded, not only the wound' (IFRC, 2001, p. 8). Beyond the food, shelter and bandages, the surplus of the wound, the human, is taken care of.

This psychosocial dimension takes centre stage in the 'developed' Western countries too. The 'imploring eyes' of the African Child are the obvious example of how potential donors are interpellated as subjective-emotional beings. However, at another level subjectivity seems to be the end-goal and not only the means to make people donate. Already in 1993 Moore remarked how in charity the 'feelgood factor' had come to replace compassion (cited in Burman, 1994). Consider for example the yearly Red Cross fundraising campaign *Music For Life* – in Flanders also called *Het Glazen House* (*The Glass House*) – run by the Flemish radio station Studio Brussels (similar to *Serious Request* of the Dutch radio station 3FM). Three popular DJs live for five days in a kind of glass house, mimicking circumstances in the South as they subject themselves to pseudo-starving and live on a limited ration of 'smoothies'. In the square in front of the glass house, a crowd gathers to sing, to dance and to support them. Money is raised by selling music requests. After six days the DJs are led to a stage accompanied by loud cheering and camera flashes. As the TV reporters probe their psycho-emotional status, tears flow. The end goal is thus not only the cardboard cheque unveiled by the selected dignitary but, foremost, it is the production of emotions and good feelings. In other words, the aim is the production of what I would call *the surplus of subjectivity*. In this way, the fundraising event mirrors the rise of the psychosocial in humanitarian aid, with its emphasis on psychological and mental health aspects of the human condition.

To truly grasp this interconnectedness, this chapter will argue that in both cases what we are seeing is the post-Fordist production paradigm at work, understood in accordance with Hardt and Negri (2000) as the direct and the non-material production of subjectivity and social relations. Within globalisation, according to Hardt and Negri, productivity, wealth, and the creation of social surpluses take the form of cooperative interactivity through linguistic, communicational, and affective networks (Hardt and Negri, 2000). The case of humanitarian aid, both at the sites of the beneficiaries and the donors, not only exemplifies this, but also allows us to scrutinise the role of the psy-discourse (the theories and praxis of the subjective and the social) in post-Fordism. An analysis of the rise of psycho-social humanitarian aid can thus serve to comprehend the contemporary close link between psychology/ psychologisation and politics. Just consider how in the media politics became thoroughly personalised and emotionalised. Or how, in these so-called post-political times, psy-matters themselves became an important terrain for politics. It seems the more that decisions that matter are taken by supra-national organisations and enterprises, the more governments confine themselves to the field of human interests. Are you unemployed? See a psychologist and follow a psycho-social enhancement course. *Politics is psychology* here receives a particular twist: politics' action terrain became reduced to psy-matters; the redefining of well-being and welfare. Psychologisation is not only a process, but also an official policy, think about governmental information programmes on, for example, bullying at work, depression or self-realisation.

In this chapter I will first situate the general phenomenon of psychologisation within the move from *biopolitics* (Michel Foucault's concept of the politics of bodies, biologies and life) to what we can call *psycho-politics*. In the second part I shall look at the so-called therapeutic turn in humanitarian aid. The juxtaposition of those two analyses will show us that the psychologised production of subjectivity has a problematic waste-product, insofar as it reduces the human to *bare life*, to *homo sacer*, to use Giorgi Agamben's terms (Agamben, 1998). In this way it will become clear how, as *The Glass House* event already shows, psychology, subjectivity and money are interrelated. These *psycho-economics*, will be explored in the last part of this chapter.

From biopolitics to psycho-politics

Biopolitics and the psy-sciences

With his notion of biopolitics Michel Foucault described the processes in modernity whereby natural life came to be included in the mechanisms and calculations of State power. In modernity, Foucault argues, governing stopped meaning only the managing and controlling of resources and wealth. Rather, the populations and life as a whole became subject to the rule of government. Politics at the beginning of the eighteenth century thus became bio-power, involved in the control and modification of life-processes. Biopolitics concern thus the particular means, mechanisms and devices to effect an all-encompassing 'administration of bodies and the calculated management of life' (Foucault, 1978, p. 140). Foucault's 'technologies of the self' (Foucault, 1988), such as the psy-sciences, have a central role here, as they made it possible for pre-modern discipline to become internalised. Violence or threat of violence issued by a sovereign monarch or ruler was replaced by disciplinary technologies and disciplines, demanding and interpellating the individual subject to discipline 'their own bodies and souls, thoughts, conduct, and way of being' (Foucault, 1988, p. 18). Foucault's analysis of the Panopticon-architecture of prisons is exemplary here: as in Bentham's Panoptical tower the guards were made invisible, this effected an auto-disciplination. Knowing one is, or could be, watched all the time, makes the gaze turn inwards (Foucault, 1979).[1] In a Foucaultian analysis the psy-sciences are central to the modern self-disciplination (see Rose, 1990). We know that we are monitored all the time, as governmental and other agencies, teachers, counsellors, etc. constantly probe our mental health, our happiness, our social relations . . . This leads to the internalising of this psycho-technical gaze: *isn't that called in psychology . . .?*

However, as noted by Agamben, what remains unclear in the Foucaultian analysis is how to understand the precise link between disciplining and self-disciplination. Agamben starts from a gloss of how Foucault discerns these two dimensions of bio-power. On the one hand we have the *political* techniques (the science of the police) with which the State integrates the care of the natural life of individuals and, on the other hand, we have the issue of subjectivisation, the question of how the individual binds himself to both his own identity and consciousness and, at the same time, to an external power. Biopolitics entails both discipline and auto-discipline. According to Agamben, Foucault never succeeded in elucidating the relation between those two aspects of power, despite the fact that he argued that they constitute a genuine political 'double bind'. Agamben – and this is significant from our point of view – asks if psychology would help in developing an understanding of the relation between the two:

(W)hat is the point at which the voluntary servitude of individuals comes into contact with objective power? Can one be content, in such a delicate area, with psychological explanations such as the suggestive notion of a parallelism between external and internal neuroses?

(Agamben, 1998, p. 6)

This, of course, implicitly refers to Sigmund Freud's holding, for example, that religion is the universal obsessional neurosis of humanity (Freud, 1955 [1927]). But Agamben quickly dismisses meta-psychological explanations of the double working of biopower, briefly arguing that phenomena such as the power of the *society of the spectacle* makes it impossible to hold political techniques and subjective technologies apart (Agamben, 1998, p. 6). Thus, Agamben shoves psychology aside, as it only draws parallels and does not allow us to understand the connection. This is where Agamben engages in a rethinking of the concept of biopolitics, revalidating the figure of sovereignty via the introduction of the figure of *homo sacer*, intending thus to theorise the link between techniques of individualisation and totalising procedures.

But maybe Agamben proceeds too quickly here, and threatens to miss the central role of psychology, not as an explanatory framework, but as the prime discipline realising biopolitics. This was precisely Foucault's insight, which, however, he may not have fully pursued to the end. Foucault's idea of the internalisation of the disciplining gaze is a useful and indispensable concept to understand the genealogy of psychologisation. It rightfully deconstructs the power scheme of *sovereign – subordinate*. However, Foucault's 'analytics of power' and its writing off sovereignty (Foucault, 1978, p. 90) might miss some key elements of the paradigm of psychologisation. Thus what I propose, on the one hand, is to follow the Agambian move of reintroducing the figure of the sovereign into biopolitics, the latter somewhat lost by Foucault. But on the other hand we should also hold on to the Foucaultian idea of the central place of the psy-sciences in biopolitics; an issue not fully addressed and even neglected by Agamben.

The sovereignty of Academia

In order to scrutinise the shift from biopolitics to psychopolitics I shall first defy Agamben by asking whether psychology after all is not able to deliver the explanation of modern self-disciplination. For, if we return to the dancing and singing people in front of the glass house, is not the question then whether one can analyse the presumed absence of pre-modern discipline and authority in such phenomena in biopolitical terms or, rather, in terms of mass or crowd psychology? Foucault or Freud? As such the idea of the crowd is rather young: it goes back to the nineteenth century's concerns regarding the rise of the masses. These new phenomena can be connected to the birth of the industrialised metropolis. The masses are the product of the drastic economic and demographic changes brought about by the technological-industrial revolution and rapidly expanding capitalism. A growing urban population was being proletarised and pauperised and its increased number meant that they came to be looked upon in terms of *mass* and *crowd*. The enormous impact of the demographic changes and the uncertainty regarding their consequences, prompted social scientists to get a scientific grip on the phenomenon of the masses. Remember for example Gustav Le Bon's[2] seminal work *The Crowd: A Study of the Popular Mind* (Le Bon, 2002 [1895]).

However, one can argue that the modern crowd is precisely engendered by 'massifying' biopolitics. The mass is thus not a natural issue to be approached by the psy-sciences, rather, it is the outcome of biopolitics as these address, as Foucault puts it, 'a multiplicity of men' forming 'a global mass that is affected by overall processes characteristic of life' (Foucault, 2003, pp. 242–243). In other words, the mass is as such the product of biopolitics, in which the life-sciences play a central role. Must we then conclude that Le Bon's psychology of the masses is not as much descriptive but rather constitutive of the crowd?

We could illustrate this strange and rather bold thesis with a recent example of how the psycho-social explanatory framework seems to function precisely as that which actually structures the crowd. Vanessa Pupavac, speaking of Princess Diana's death, describes how therapeutic forms have taken the place of religious ceremonies as the predominant mode of performing cultural rites (Pupavac, 2004a). Is this not a clear instance of, as we already argued in the previous chapter, the psy-discourse transforming a dispersed and antagonistic social sphere into a meaningful and homogenised public space? This would mean that, as the participants in such psychologised rites are directly familiar with the body of knowledge in play, it is actually the psy-analysis of the crowd which gives form to the crowd. Knowledge of the psy-sciences thus directly produces subjectivity and social relations.

In this way it is remarkable how the public of *The Glass House* events display the signifier 'emotions' so much. So yes, fundraising is about the feelgood factor, but this analysis is also made by the public: 'I saw that the DJs had to swallow, that touched me so much, that much that I had to cry myself' (http://seriousrequest.3fm.nl). The psychology is primordial and situated with the other, it is only from there that the analysis returns to bear on the subject itself, and in this movement the group or the crowd is formed:

> When the documentary on Justin and his brother [who lost both parents from AIDS] was show[n] . . . I saw that the DJs had to swallow, that touched me so much, that much that I had to cry myself . . . a documentary which meant that The Netherlands as a whole had to contemplate the disease of AIDS.
>
> (http://seriousrequest.3fm.nl)

Other examples are the well-known Belgian White Marches. Belgium had its first White March after the paedophilia case of the infamous Dutroux: the poor functioning of the judicial and police systems brought people on the street to demand reforms. After that, other similar occasions lead to white marches which invariably explicitly wanted to transcend politics as they put forward more or less clear and concrete demands. For example, a case of a young man shooting at random at coloured people in the city of Antwerp, led to a protest march. In that instance, the experts all pointed to the collective trauma and the necessity of rituals for collective mourning. But also the arguments of the organisers and the participants put forward in numerous interviews invariably were informed by the same psychological and thera-peutic discourse. As a relative of one of the victims proclaimed: 'This is not a political march, but a march to show our grievance.' In the White March the view of the expert is always already incorporated, the analysis is always already included. Or: the ritual is the collective performance of the analysis.

This might bring us to the limit of the Foucaultian conception of biopolitics, and, by extension, of Hardt and Negri's understanding of biopolitics in post-Fordism. In line with the Foucaultian departure from sovereignty Hardt and Negri discern in late-capitalist times a direct and unmediated production of subjectivity and social relations. As only now is production able to transcend the framework of state and of capital, Hardt and Negri attribute to this an emancipatory potential. Post-Fordist production is said to open up the perspective of a direct democracy bypassing the old forms of representation. Hardt and Negri define this direct global democracy as 'Becoming-Prince', or, 'the multitude learning the art of self-rule and inventing lasting democratic forms of social organization' (Hardt and Negri, 2009, p. 8). The example of the White March however contests this: the production of subjectivity and social relations are neither direct nor unmediated: the psychological discourse, stemming from the mainstream, hegemonic psy-apparatus, is the mediator here: defining both the content (the signifiers) and the discursive positions in play. This is how we should understand that biopolitics became *psycho*-politics. In contrast to classic Foucaultian understanding, where every political analysis risks ending up in the adagio *power is everywhere* (and the subject nowhere), one should again try to discern the sovereignty in place.[3] As I already argued in the first chapter, *Academia* and especially the psy-complex, even if it is a dispersed and heterogeneous network, are here the primordial agents to be scrutinised. It is in this way that we might understand Jacques Lacan's response to the 1968 anti-structuralist Parisian graffiti 'Structures do not walk on the streets!', stating that the events of May 1968 did show that structures walk on the streets. Lacan was very sceptical to the events in Paris, remember his famous statement: 'The revolutionary aspiration has only a single possible outcome – of ending up as the master's discourse . . . What you aspire to as revolutionaries is a master. You will get one'

(Lacan, 2006, p. 207). Lacan's interpretation was above all that the so-called *discourse of the master*, would be merely replaced by the *discourse of the university*.[4] Even if this might be regarded as a sweeping and reductionist interpretation, there might be a grain of truth in it, as the May 1968 events at least testified that something was shifting regarding authority. Or, in the words of Slavoj Žižek: it is no coincidence that the May 1968 revolt was located at the universities; it signalled a shift to new forms of domination in which the scientific discourse legitimises the relations of domination (Žižek, 2004a, p. 505). In this way one could venture to say that the truth of *structures walking in the street* is shown in events such as the White March: It is *academic structures* walking on the street.[5] The participants assume the academic position: being beyond politics, they are merely neutrally and objectively pleading for everybody's well-being. They are convinced they march the streets for the things that really matter in life, as if they have an objectified knowledge of it. Maybe this is the shared fantasy of Academia, of the White March protesters, and of Hardt and Negri: that there is an access to unmediated and direct life, life as it is. Immanuel Kant may have shown that *Das Ding* remains inaccessible, the hunger to get a glimpse of it or to feel connected to it, nevertheless has not left us.

Hunger for the real

To explore this hunger for the real and its place in psycho-biopolitics, let us turn here to the social scientist Michael Walzer and his comments on events similar to those of the recent so-called *Arab Spring* of North Africa and the Middle East, namely the people on the streets in the communist countries in the late 1980s. In his book *Thick and Thin. Moral Argument at Home and Abroad*, Walzer tries to account for two kinds of moral principles: the *thin* ones, which are universally valid, and *thick* ones, maximalist principles which only apply within a given culture. Commenting on television images showing people marching in the streets of Prague in the year of 1989, Walzer recalls protesters carrying signs saying 'Truth' and 'Justice'. He writes that he immediately recognised what the signs meant and instantly endorsed the values being defended. He asks:

> How could I penetrate so quickly and join so unreservedly in the language game or the power play of a distant demonstration? The marchers shared a culture with which I was largely unfamiliar; they were responding to an experience I had never had. And yet, I could have walked comfortably in their midst. I could carry the same signs.
>
> (Walzer, 1994, p. 12)

The issue is how to understand Walzer's almost joyfully celebrated claim of universality. The first remarkable thing is that his sympathy above all is directed to his *own* feelings, as he seems to be surprised by his being human after all. He seems to revel in the idea that, if circumstances were different, he too would walk on the streets as a true citizen. Nevertheless, this is only one side of the picture: almost immediately Walzer interrupts his reveries and defies the post-modern thinkers he mistrusts: 'Is there any recent account, any post-modernist account, of political language that can explain this understanding and acknowledgement?' (Walzer, 1994). From the real world back to Academia. The academic movement resembles that of a creature, probing the outer-world with its tentacles only to quickly withdraw them and contemplatively devour the sampled reality. Challenging post-modern relativism Walzer returns to the academic debate and thus himself in a way *deconstructs* his alleged authentic feelings and being connected to the real world. His nostalgia as such confirms that (post)modernity is thoroughly marked by an ever returning reflexive distance. Are not both movements, the push to reality and the return to the academic pondering on it, the primal axes of (post)modern reflexivity? Modernity made us all academic subjects who regard ourselves through the academic gaze; academia became post-modern man's habitat. As science never satisfies the modern subject in his quest for a positive ontological ground, modern man must leave academia to rehumanise himself through eruptive excursions to a supposedly real outer world. After which we retreat to our *alma mater*.

What Walzer as such testifies of is that the point of departure is a de-subjectivised, de-psychologised subject. The modern subject has no content, it is an empty box. The problematic link between disciplination and self-disciplination might here find a solution. The disciplination concerns primordially the recruitment of the modern subject into the ranks of the psychologists and thus eventually equals to auto-disciplination. This is also where psychologisation at its turn, equals de-psychologisation: for the modern subject the authentic human psychological being is situated outside of itself. It watches itself – and looks upon the watcher once again – from a point outside of itself, beyond subjectivity and beyond psychology.

Psychology in a way thus realises what Adorno already saw emerging in the rise of fascism in the 1930s; namely a de-psychologised subject as effect of administrated modern life. For Adorno the modern subject came under the sway of the logic of techno-rationality instead of the Oedipal father figure who was responsible for the psychological profile of pre-modern man (see for example Adorno, 1991, p. 140). As argued, this de-psychologisation is exactly effected by the technology of the psy-sciences themselves. Interpellating the subject to assume the scientific–psychological gaze, the psy-sciences push the subject to assume a position outside of the human sphere. Adorno points to the fact that here the dimension of fiction enters the social field, in a somewhat enigmatic passage on fascist propaganda, he writes:

> It is probably the suspicion of this fictitiousness of their own 'group psychology' which makes fascist crowds so merciless and unapproach-able. If they would stop to reason for a second, the whole performance would go to pieces, and they would be left to panic.
>
> (Adorno, 1991, p. 132)

This passage can be understood together with what Adorno writes on the same page: When the leaders become conscious of mass psychology and take it into their own hands, it ceases to exist in a certain sense' (Adorno, 1991, p. 132).

We could understand this as follows: from the moment at which psy-chology becomes a discipline its subject matter ceases to exist. If the word is the murder of the thing, psychology is the dead of the psychological: the subject who takes the psy-position has to acknowledge that from that moment on any supposed naive and direct psychology ceases to exist. The modern subject is, so to say, *outwith psychology*. However, this also fuels a desire to reclaim the lost psychological authenticity. The modern subject knows that it is not real, that it is nothing but theory and psychology, and this propels it into a passionate but always enacted stance of re-joining a mythical real. The *psychological crowd* is thus always at risk of engaging in a blind, merciless acting out of its own group psychology.

Walzer's account already revealed that there the image of the People arises: his fascination with the television images of people marching in the streets therefore lays bare a fantasy of the people at last united by a righteous cause, being the enactment of the escape from the constraints of (post)modern academicised life. Does this then not risk coming close to the proto-fascist fascination with natural man and natural life, man and life as they really are? Beyond Academia seems to lead to a beyond politics. This quest for the real and the authentic is furthermore the key of many mainstream psycho-social action programmes as these often come in terms of *repairing the social fabric*, or, the *creation of spaces for dialogue and encounter*. The illusion that a return to the real, down to earth, unspoiled, pastoral life is possible, comes uncannily close to the organicist-corporatist metaphors promising us a return to the alleged authentic way of life we seem to have lost.

It is these two stances, de-psychologisation and de-politicisation which are at stake in the case of the therapeutic turn in humanitarian aid. I shall address this in the next section, where I will argue that psycho-social humanitarian aid has to be understood as the paradigm of the post-Fordist psycho-political economy.

(De)psychologisation and (de) politicisation: the case of psychological humanitarian aid

The crisis in humanitarianism in the 1990s and the therapeutic turn

The psychotherapeutic turn in humanitarian aid is commonly situated in the 1990s. Vanessa Pupavac, for example, contends that trauma eclipsed hunger in the 1990s as the issue most flagged by international aid agencies (Pupavac, 2004b). The first time *Médicins Sans Frontières* (MSF), for example, involved psychiatrists and psychologists was in Armenia after the December 1988 earthquake. In subsequent MSF-projects in Palestine, mental health became one of the primary activities (Médecins sans Frontières, 2006). For social anthropologist Didier Fassin (administrator of MSF in 1999–2001) the Israeli–Palestinian conflict was the first time in history that a humanitarian crisis was described in terms of subjectivity:

> Where previously the language evoked in defending oppressed peoples was that of revolution, current usage favors the vocabulary of psychology to sensitize the world to their misfortune. Yesterday we denounced imperialist domination; today we reveal its psychic traces. Not so long ago we glorified the resistance of populations; we henceforth scrutinize the resilience of individuals.
>
> (Fassin, 2008, p. 532)

Pupavac understands this psychosocial turn in relation to the crisis in which humanitarianism found itself in the 1990s. The critique that aid undermines local economies, feeds the villains and fuels conflicts led to 'a demoralized humanitarianism and a demoralized humanitarian aid worker' (Pupavac, 2004a, p. 497). The psychosocial turn can be understood as a response to the crisis in humanitarianism as it attempted to 'bring back the human in the face of the bureaucratization of aid, foregrounding how people and communities personally experience disaster or conflict' (Pupavac, 2004a, p. 497).

Mark Duffield in turn looks at the crisis in humanitarianism from a Foucaultian-Agambian perspective. According to Duffield, biopolitics, the taking care of the health of populations, has become a global issue wherein global governance is 'power over the life of populations conceived as existing globally rather than nationally or territorially' (Duffield, 2004, p. 6). Humanitarian aid is hence de facto entangled with biopolitics. Drawing on Agamben, Duffield contends that the claimed neutrality of humanitarian projects could no longer be maintained as a comforting shield, but actually draws NGOs into biopolitics: 'The insistence that humanitarianism is "neutral" and separate from politics, means that humanitarians can only grasp human life as bare life. By excluding the political, humanitarianism reproduces the isolation of bare life and hence the basis of sovereignty itself' (Duffield, 2004, p. 13). Duffield concludes, quoting Agamben, that despite the best intentions, humanitarians maintain 'a secret solidarity with the very powers they ought to fight' (Agamben, 1998). This radical interconnectedness and interpenetration of the new security terrain is at the heart of the crisis of humanitarianism (Duffield, 2004, p. 16). Direct territorial control based on juridical and bureaucratic authority is replaced by mutable and networked management and regulation of economic, political and social processes: "People in the South are no longer ordered what to do – they are now expected to do it *willingly* themselves" (emphasis original) (Duffield, 2001, p. 34).

If Duffield does not really explain why globalisation led to the psycho-therapeutic turn we can easily amend this: *psycho-politics* is obviously the best way to accomplish the reformulated biopolitical goals. Placing the focus on self-reliance and sustainable development, the psycho-social dimension and thus psycho-social techniques necessarily enter the scene.

Pupavac furthermore links this psychosocial turn in the South to the psychologisation of the North. The fall of the Berlin Wall and the consequent demise of ideological alternatives as the origin of this position, in conjunction with increasing social atomisation led to a therapeutising of public discourse which blurred the political with the therapeutic (Pupavac, 2004b). Pupavac shows how the Western pathologisation of war, for example, is rooted in the wider psychologisation affecting the West itself. Lacking strong convictions themselves, Pupavac writes, donor countries find it difficult to imagine people believing in causes worth fighting for and thus declare populations at war as dysfunctional (Pupavac, 2004a).

However, what is still lacking in this psycho-biopolitical analysis is the *psycho-economical* factor. For can one not say that the psychologising of the South implies an export of psychological resources in order to realise a surplus? A surplus which is then cashed in the form of for example the feelgood factor in fundraising events. The crucial point here will be to grapple with how subjectivity came to play a central role in late-capitalist modes of production. But before we can engage fully in a psycho-economical critique of psychologisation, we have first to flesh out two central and interrelated paradoxes of the psychologisation of humanitarian aid. The first paradox stems from the fact that one cannot *not* psychologise. The second from the fact that psychology and psychologisation are but two sides of one coin, this is the paradox of psycho-education.

(De)psychologisation: how you cannot not psychologise and psycho-education

The first thing to notice is that the therapeutic turn, with its stress on trauma, did not solve the crisis in humanitarianism, with manifold critiques of psychologisation and therapeutisation emerging very quickly. Derek Summerfield, for example, argued in 1997 that 'the globalisation of western psychological concepts and practices risks perpetuating the colonial status of the non-western mind' (Summerfield, 1997, p. 1568). Defenders of the trauma approach counter-argued that psychologists and psychiatrists are dealing with universal realities. Sound science and evidence-based research (e.g. on the Post Traumatic Stress Syndrome) are posited as transcending all cultural and anthropological differences (e.g. de Vries, 1998). But the remarkable thing is that when Summerfield answers this by arguing for the historicity of diagnoses such as PTSD, he takes recourse to signifiers such as *suffering, distress, problem-solving*, etc. (Summerfield, 1998), apparently assuming the validity of universal categories. His carefully chosen terms from everyday life (*misery, distress . . .*) betray the resolve to evade psychological language but they risk postulating a similar kind of universalisation. In every critique of the psychologisation of humanitarian aid, this danger of falling into yet another mode of psychologisation is always immanent. Summerfield, for example, eventually ends his critique of the neo-colonial mindset with which he characterises the discourse of trauma with a plea for a 'wiser and truer use of the term psychology'. Or, get the bad psychologists out and bring the good ones in.[6] Similarly, Dag Nordanger argues against the 'western trauma discourse' and advocates the acknowledgement of 'local folk psychology' (Nordanger, 2007). For Pupavac the critique of trauma relief needs to acknowledge that the trauma programmes themselves raise issues; we could even say that the trauma programmes are themselves *traumatic* for those subjected to them:

> The very intrusion into the personal sphere may inadvertently corrode the sense of intimacy necessary for cohesive family and community bonds, which are so important in mediating and overcoming trauma. Since stress and anger can be a spur to action, psycho-social intervention may disempower people in the long-term.
>
> (Pupavac, 2002, pp. 3–4)

That is to say, through the critique, Pupavac cannot help but slip into psychological discourse, drawing as it does on the same language as the psychotherapeutic programmes themselves. Pupavac cannot help but consider therapeutic governance to be detrimental to a population's *mental health* (Pupavac, 2004b).

Even a return to the human rights approach to opposing therapeutic governance does not seem to be able to evade the paradox of therapeutising.

Inger Agger, for example, endorses the opposition to therapeutic discourse from psychologists and psychiatrists in exile from the military dictatorships in Chile and Argentina and supports their claim that people do not suffer from mental illness or PTSD, but that they are 'suffering from the dictatorship' (Agger and Jensen, 1996, p. 70). However, not only do signifiers such as 'treatment,' 'coping strategies' and 'healing' still pop up in Agger's discourse but, moreover, the only shift proposed seems to be a turn from psychotherapy to socio-therapy. Here Agger endorses the Red Cross's policy of making a 'shift from a trauma approach to a community-based approach,' focusing 'on healing through already existing cultural and spiritual belief systems' (Agger, 2002, p. 17). But what is gained by trading the psycho-engineer for the socio-engineer who promotes 'natural support networks' and 'coping strategies'? Ultimately, what we can discern here is the same Olympian vantage as we saw at work with Michael Walzer. It is from a point beyond contingent everyday life from which the academically informed promote the cultural approach as the least traumatic and the most beneficial. Eventually, this allegedly more sophisticated access to the universal and 'real' problems, paradoxically boils down to bypassing all socio-cultural dimensions. Are we not back here with the psycho-social action programmes aiming to repair the social fabric and their risk to be caught in the organicist-corporatist fantasy to return to the unspoiled, pastoral authenticity of social life?

Consider for example Agger's plea to build on 'local cultural resources such as traditions, and human resources such as traditional healers, elders, women's groups, teachers, and key people within religious communities' (Agger, 2002, p. 18). She cites Wessels for whom it is sadly often local people themselves who view their own approaches as inferior, believing that the modern, Western methods are better: 'This deeply ingrained sense of inferiority is one of the worst residues of colonialism and is itself a major form of psychological damage' (Wessells, 1999, p. 276). However, to put it bluntly, is not this *let them have their dances and voodoo-rituals* the ultimate residue of colonialism as it places us, sophisticated Westerners, once again in the superior position of being able to judge? Wessells and others end up taking the ultimate meta-perspective, a meta-psychologising one, where they criticise the locals' inferiority complex and assume to assess the real psychological damage caused by their breaking with traditions. Here the question to ask is whether this ethnographic God's eye view, which places 'culture at the centre in any type of psychosocial assistance' (Agger, 2002, p. 18), risks endorsing precisely the oppressive conservative currents evident in local societies (the traditional healers, the religious communities . . .)? Is it perhaps the case that they feel that the more progressive and truly political movements will not be the ideal partners? Here of course the deadlocks rapidly present themselves. What if these traditional 'local cultural agencies' turn out to repress women, children and homosexuals?

I will return to these problematic political entanglements below, but first I will turn to the second paradox of psychologisation evident in psycho-social humanitarian aid, the paradox of psychologisation as psycho-education. This is where the fact that one cannot *not* psychologise, is linked to what seems to be the very opposite: the total impossibility of psychologising and psychology itself. For, as it has already become clear in this book, processes of psychologisation are already, paradoxically, de-psychologising. Just consider how the hegemony of neuro-organic models have turned the psychological into a non-category in both the theories and the praxes of mainstream psychology. For mainstream psychology, the psyche is but the function of chemical substances and brain waves. In this way, psychologists themselves, wittingly or not, promote de-psychologisation. But even where there is more distance towards the neurochemical perspective – where there are, for example, attempts to account for the psychological in terms of cognition or behavioural and evolutionary patterns – even there it is hard to discern a true subjective or properly psychic dimension. Is psychology as a science not by definition bound to end up with the human being's reduction to an automaton governed by forces from which it itself is exempt? Hailed to adopt the scientific–psychological gaze, the psychologised subject sees itself reduced to either neuronal or behavioural laws and remains in the end de-subjectivised and, thus, also de-psychologised. Psychology moreover appears unable to account for this paradox of non-subjectivity. This is why the critiques of psychology are, more often than not, paralysed by the same deadlock. In their attempts to safeguard the dimension of subjectivity, they are bound to end up in the same psychologising/de-psychologising stance that they criticise.

This is where psycho-education comes in. For, the fact that the psychological and subjective dimension is a central problematic in today's scientific field is nowhere as evident as it is in the idea of 'psychological first-aid' in trauma relief. Definitions of what this 'psychological first-aid' would mean, rarely get much further than the idea of getting people to talk. Psychological first-aid encompasses foremost forms of help or support which can hardly really be called psychological at all, such as providing information and securing basic needs.[7] Here it is clear that the fact that the psychological is effectively a non-category turns psychological aid into a logical impossibility. The most common attempt to evade and negate this impasse, it could be argued, is by turning psychological aid into psycho-education. Consider for example how Jones et al. plead that 'large-scale community outreach and psycho-education about post-disaster reactions should be included among public health interventions to promote calming' (Jones et al., 2007). So while the wound can be treated directly, the treatment of the wounded has to pass through knowledge-distribution and education. This is also the main tenet in a Red Cross 'good practices' report:

> The Colombian Red Cross set up a radio programme following a natural disaster to teach people about the psychological aspects of disasters. This method proved useful in terms of disseminating information related to the disaster, developing understanding, and reaching out to target groups. In general, teaching survivors to understand the psychological mechanisms behind their worries and difficulties helps them to cope with their feelings.
>
> (IFRC, 2001, p. 6)

The radical conclusion is that, while psychological first aid is a logical impossibility, it turns to the practice of teaching psychological theories to the target population. Foucault's self-disciplination passes over the induction of the subject into the sovereign discipline of the psy-sciences. The beneficiaries of psycho-social aid have to assume the dual position of both being the object and the subject of psychology: *Look at yourself as we the psychologists do*. This is effected variously through the use of audio-visual media as well as the distribution of what are referred to as *patients' leaflets*. In the following quotation from such a leaflet it is clear that what is expected from the survivor is a *theoretical* understanding; the internalisation of the psychological theory is supposed to be healing:

> A talking treatment called cognitive behaviour therapy can help people who have PTSD. This kind of therapy is a short, practical treatment. It focuses on helping you understand your thoughts and feelings, and find practical ways of coping with them. You'll probably be offered around 10 sessions lasting an hour or so, with more sessions if you need them.
>
> (BMJ, 2010, p. 2)

Psychological first-aid thus manifests, remarkably, as the administration of psychology itself. In this way certain characteristics of psychosocial aid can be understood as the typical strategies for attaining educational compliance. The Red Cross guidelines for psychosocial humanitarian aid at times even read like a propaganda manual, complete with *newspeak*. It is, for example, recommended to sometimes call a psychosocial centre an *information centre*, as was done in Macedonia where people felt resistance against the psycho-social discourse (IFRC, 2001, p. 7). Where a Danish project in Bosnia and Herzegovina served food to the children during workshops, the report, rather bluntly, states: '[e]ating highly nutritional food together forms part of the children's social activities' (IFRC, 2001, pp. 40–41). The ghost of Pavlov seems to hover here. Pleasurable activities such as excursions and expressive activities such as singing, dancing, and drawing are also seen as ideal vehicles for the psycho-educational programme. This *sing, dance, draw, cope and enjoy*-discourse – which is not only reserved for children but also implemented with adults – is extremely patronising, reducing, as it does, the subjective as well as the social to a de-politicised, schoolified, if not outright infantilised, issue.

The politics of psycho-social humanitarianism: you cannot not de-politicise

Psychosocial humanitarian aid is about handling and manipulating subjectivity via the establishment of the compelling model of psycho-education. A surgeon or a physiotherapist primarily implements techniques or uses chemical substances to influence bodily processes. The patient can be completely oblivious to the theory behind these practices. This scheme cannot be transferred to psychology, as there the techniques are invariably applied by introducing the patient to the background knowledge. Psychology seems thus to work via psychologisation. A trauma-patient has to be briefed; *you have experienced a shocking event and these are your symptoms*. In this way, together with the appropriate signifiers, normative models of subjectivity are introduced. This psycho-educational praxis results, as Erica Burman puts is, in a technology of emotional regulation 'that normalises and circumscribes emotional expression in the very act of 'giving voice' to it' (Burman, 2006, p. 325). Help thus manifests as the administration of normalising theories. The American Psychological Association, for example, describes the task of the psychologist at the site of a disaster as to help survivors to 'understand how common what they're [sic] feeling is, whether it's anger, sadness or other strong emotions,' and to 'educate people that it is normal for disaster survivors to have an array of common reactions' (APA, 2010). Central to psycho-education is, therefore, the transfer of what the academic perspective deems common, the norm.

To understand the political meaning of this, the imposition of a rather limited set of normativising and normalising signifiers is one thing. The second, probably most important factor is the shift in discursive positions effected by this induction. As aid becomes education, the beneficiaries are put in the position of pupils. They have to adopt an academic gaze with regard to themselves and their situation. It is perhaps this that authors like Didier Fassin miss when they argue that the psycho-social discourse in humanitarian aid only produces a 'particular form of subjectivation' through which the beneficiaries can also exist politically (Fassin, 2008). This misses the fact that psychologisation is not just another set of signifiers which the oppressed can creatively use to seek subjectivation and politicisation.[8] It is clear that any creative and political attempt to escape psychologising discourse will be easily re-inscribed in the psycho-social hegemonic framework. Every political stance will be re-translated in terms of, for example, trauma and coping mechanisms. It is here, in this virtual and never-ending appropriation of subjectivity that the psychological discourse decisively reassigns the positions; the particular forms of subjectivation will inevitably be forced into the pre-formatted discursive frame of psycho-education. The model of 'what you experience' is strongly interpellative: even where 'psychological distress' is granted culture-specific dimensions, this is only so against the background of a presupposed universal dimension. In being asked to behold oneself as the universal psychological human being, the subjective and political dimension Fassin wants to safeguard will again and again be appropriated by the theoretical and academic perspective.

Are we thus to conclude unequivocally that psychologisation serves a de-politicisation? Maybe things are a bit more complex. In the same way as psychologisation equals de-psychologisation, politicisation and de-politicisation are defining each other. The question then becomes to understand how both couples are interconnected. Let us first reconsider the idea that psychologisation equals de-psychologisation. This is discernable in the trauma approach which pathologises war itself. Postulating *cycles of violence*, war is explained as resulting from earlier, undealt with traumas. Without the right treatment, the victims of war remain vengeful because of their 'traumatisation' (Summerfield, 2002, p. 1105). Therapy can then be said to actually prompt the victim to overcome the psychology of traumatisation. That is to say, the psycho-educational approach aims to pull someone out of his/her own psychology, drawing him or her into the observational position of the psychological gaze. Becoming your own psychologist enables you to control your own psychology, enables you to de-psychologise. What the pathologisation of war shows us is that it is exactly where it compromises the psychological-subjective dimension that war and violence are de-politicised. Psychologisation is de-politicisation insofar as it de-psychologises.

But of course, de-politicisation cannot but, in itself, be a political stance. This brings us back to Duffield's argument that it was in the crisis of humanitarianism that the politicisation of humanitarian assistance came to the surface (Duffield, 1997, p. 531). For Duffield, globalisation led to, on the one hand, complex forms of economic and political integration within the main bloc areas, and on the other hand, ethnocentric or fundamentalist assertions or breakdowns outside the borders of the main bloc. It was in those crisis regions that, in contrast to former direct inter-governmental aid, humanitarian assistance became the West's favoured response (Duffield, 1997). This led to an increased role for Western NGOs and allowed aid policy 'to reassert a form of sovereignty within the crisis regions' (Duffield, 1997, p. 532). This means that there are two levels of politicisation to be discerned. First, there is the politicisation of the NGOs which have become subcontractors within the machine of the donor governments. Duffield points, in this respect, to the dependence of NGOs on military protection and logistics (transport or large-scale commodity handling). Secondly, humanitarian aid is also involved in politicisation on the level of the so-called failed or weak states themselves. As Duffield notes, relief aid agencies have to secure a negotiated access to conflict zones and this involves gaining the consent of warring parties or sectarian political entities (Duffield, 1997, p. 534). The most important *political* effect of this double bind politicisation of humanitarian aid is of course the de-politicisation of the field and with the beneficiaries. As Duffield puts it succinctly, what happens at the borders of the main bloc is only seen as a temporary phase in the transition towards liberal democracy, and not as the emergence of new types of 'socio- political formation adapted to exist on the margins of the global economy' (Duffield, 1997, p. 529).

One can now argue that the psychologisation of humanitarianism serves precisely to legitimate the twofold politicisation of humanitarian assistance. If, for example, humanitarianism has traded the perspective of long-term development for a focus on relief in war zones, then it is the psycho-social discourse which provides the scientific support for this political shift. Signifiers such as *development* or *underdevelopment, exploitation, social and economic convergence* become obsolete and are replaced with psycho-social concepts such as *capacity building, empowerment,* and *resilience.* On the other hand, when it comes to the politicisation of aid on the local level, with NGOs seeking partnership with warring parties or sectarian political entities, the psychosocial discourse again serves to cover over the NGOs problematic political stance. Take, for example, Nordanger's plea for a 'deep respect for the subjective elements of psychosocial coping and the contextual limits within which these elements operate' (Nordanger, 2007, p. 560). Concerning Tigray in Ethiopia, he advocates cooperation with the clergy and does so through mobilising a particularly psychologising argument:

Based on spiritual power alone, the church would not be able to preserve its authority in the long run if its guidance were not meaningful in people's perception. Most probably, people themselves preserve and reinforce the power of the church and other discursive authorities, as these authorities give credence to coping strategies, which under the socio-economic conditions may seem to be the only viable option.

(Nordanger, 2007, p. 559)

Faced with the choice of which side to take, Nordanger makes his decision on the basis of an essentialist psychology. His argument is that from a psychosocial point of view (invoking the idea of coping strategies) the support of the existing clerical power structures is to be preferred. The coalition between NGOs and local power bases is legitimated from a meta-psychological discourse. Claiming jurisdiction over what is local and genuine – and paradoxically articulating this in terms of the alleged universal categories of the psy-sciences – humanitarian aid is again thoroughly politicised. But again, this politicisation entails a de-politicisation in the field, as humanitarian aid, especially in its psycho-social turn, impedes and neutralises the politicisation of local people and groups.[9]

The conclusion is that the psycho-social turn of humanitarian aid, redoubling psychologisation and de-psychologisation, serves as the foundation of a humanitarianism which is thoroughly politicised in exactly the same movement through which it de-politicises. What remains to be done however, is to place these paradoxical dynamics of (de)psychologisation and (de)politicisation within a critique of biopolitical economy, or better, within a psychopolitical economy. The psychologisation of humanitarianism, that is, can show us how we can understand that subjectivity has taken centre stage in late-capitalist modes of production.

De-psychologising economy

The psycho-economics of psycho-social humanitarianism: skimming the battlefield and ghouling the disaster zone

To understand the bio-political strategies and techniques of psycho-social humanitarianism let us take a closer look at an example, a peace education project for primary school children in Croatia. What we see here is a standard psycho-educational approach through which normativising/normalising psychological theory is introduced. It aims to get teachers and students to talk about 'experiences of loss, separation and grief', 'normalising and validating' the 'emotional reactions and possible symptoms like flashbacks' *Woodside* et al., 1999). In the project's manual it is easy to detect the structure of psychologisation at work. For example, each group session starts with what one might call an academic interpellation:

> What we will be doing today: Observing our behaviour when we feel gloomy, angry or furious; we are going to practise some techniques to manage our rage and to get rid of our feeling of anxiety and aggression.
> (Uzelac, 1997)

This kind of introduction, repeated in each session, immediately prompts the children to adopt the position of observer, the position, that is, of the academic psychologist. This is then followed by some kind of activity, for example, role-play, drawing, singing, etc., after which each session is concluded by a final round up: what have we learned?

> How did you feel doing this exercise? How did you feel when somebody invited you into the group or pushed you away from the group? How do you think a person feels when he doesn't belong . . . and was thrown out of the group by everybody? At the end let's explain why people gather in groups, why they form groups. Life needs to be secure and predictable. People like to be part of a group so that they can feel wanted and needed. What do you think, what other reasons are there?
>
> (Uzelac, 1997)

Here the model is Stanley Milgram's *now that you know, how do you feel?*[10] Now you know how people as psychological beings (are supposed to) think and feel, how do you – looking at yourself as a psychological being – think and feel? Doubtless the children will, more or less, comply and deliver the signifiers which have been introduced. In this way the psycho-educational stance is the self-fulfilling prophesy par excellence. But what is more important here is that psycho-social techniques, via this (re)production of psychology, aim at the production of subjectivity. *What have we learned today* is a very mandatory interpellation to produce a surplus of psychological feelings and cognitions which is then considered to be the very human condition laid bare: throbbing and pulsating psychological life. Questions such as *how did you feel doing this exercise?* are thus very coercive in their forcing the subject to offer his or her subjectivity to the therapist in charge of collecting these surplus-values.

The conclusion which forces itself here is that we should consider the therapist as the ultimate late-modern capitalist. The exploitation of the South suddenly emerges in a totally different light, as humanitarian aid appears as the very paradigm of psycho-political economics. To understand this let us return to Pupavac's idea that the modern Western subject in this supposed post-ideological era lacks strong convictions and is subjected to social atomisation and caught up in a therapeutisation of the public discourse (Pupavac, 2004b). For Pupavac this late-modern condition is, furthermore, responsible for the typical Hobbesian imagery of ubiquitous war and conflict through which the West pictures the South:

> The notion of a continuum of violence underlying the rationale of psycho-social programmes overlooks how individuals in violent situations con-

tinue to evaluate what violence they consider acceptable or unacceptable. Effectively, the psycho-social model resurrects the Hobbesian spectre of war of all against all as the perpetuation of abuse of all against all.

(Pupavac, 2002, p. 12)

Haunted by the Hobbesian imagery, the West considers conflicts in the third or fourth world as reflecting the natural struggle for power. We think to see a life that due to conflicts and precarious material circumstances is so close to death that is seems so intense. Families on the run, children and elders being carried . . . images far removed from our own atomised social sphere. We see life as it is, survival of the fittest, resilience, altruism, . . . we know the psycho-evolutionary mechanisms! The function of this fantasy is double. To begin with, via the naturalising and psychologising, we remove the sting out of conflicts and disasters in the South, that is, we remove their embedment in the broader global political and economic framework. Second, the fantasy serves to satisfy our hunger for the real thing. In the same way as the Prague protester sets in motion Walzer's reveries of joining the street, the breaking news for the South compels us to ask ourselves: *what would we do in such circumstances? What would it mean to* really *live?* The non-Western other eventually has to function as the ontological closure: the guarantee for our own being. This is why the West looking upon the South, imagines to see the human condition laid bare, the human being stripped of its thin layer of cultural varnish. In others words, the West, de-politicised, de-ideologised and thus seemingly bereft of subjectivity, seeks authentic, pulsating life elsewhere. The psychologising of humanitarian aid testifies to the hole in our own psychology and our attempt to re-psychologise. The psychological gaze, launched inevitably from a point outside, a point beyond psychology, eventually attempts to produce psychology and subjectivity with the object of our interest, the object of our care.

The new humanitarian worker does not dispense food packets but, rather, knowledge, knowledge which pretends to cover the field of being, the very ontological sphere. Formerly the beneficiary only had to receive food and shelter. Albeit in a limited way, he/she was still free to think and say what he/she wanted. The contemporary psycho-social approach is, in contrast, much more total. The receiver has to produce the right emotions, feelings and cognitions, collected by the third-party enabler of empowerment. If the old humanitarian worker could find job satisfaction out of certain paternalism, the new humanitarian claims the unselfish and professional position of being the mere servant of a body of knowledge, dealing with the universals of humankind. But one should always be suspicious when the third-party position of mere enabler is claimed, for then the question becomes, what drives and what fuels the servant psy-worker if not the production of emotions, the blossoming of resilience, the coming to terms with trauma, the letting go of racial prejudices, the beautiful tears? The image which imposes itself here is that of the humanitarian worker skimming the battlefields and ghouling the disaster zone for subjectivity; the one who gathers the broken people and brings them together in a tent to subject them to some therapeutic programme through which psychology can be reproduced. It is a rather distressing image in which, as Duffield calls them, 'the best of people – the idealists, the rebels and the driven' (Duffield, 2004), while trying to escape the straitjacket of Western de-ideologised life, become caught up in, to use Agamben's phrase, the production of bare life. It is thus that they maintain 'a secret solidarity with the very powers they ought to fight' (Agamben, 1998).

To summarise: Duffield's borderlands thus have a quite specific function for the late-modern West; they feed the imagery of the other space, the non-liberal, non-democratic zone where warlords reign, where illegal trade runs rampant and any moment a tribal conflict can explode into a chaotic dispersed war. The borderlands function as a heart of darkness, offering a glimpse of the human being as it really is, beyond the thin layer of civilisation; the fantasmatic *homo psychologicus* driven by a rather simple interplay of genes and Darwinian principles, topped by some old cultural-religious idiosyncrasies (themselves nothing more than residues of phylogenetics). This brings to mind Freud's aforementioned comment to Jung: 'Little do they know we are bringing the plague.' The crucial difference today is that it is the psychosocial worker him or herself, on board a military C-130, who is ignorant, unaware that he or she is carrying the plague, through his or her psycho-social and neutral professionalism. Or as Slavoj Žižek claims, the refusal of any higher Causes in the so-called post-ideological era is the biopolitical move at its sharpest. As we consider the ultimate goal of our lives as life itself, this stance cannot do anything other than become caught up in the production of *homo sacer*, 'the dispensable object of the expert caretaking knowledge' (Žižek, 2003a). The psy-worker, convinced he or she is merely tapping into scientifically proven universals, reduces the other to bare life, to *homo sacer*.

The Hobbesian spectre of the war of all against all not only invokes how the fantasies of Academia are the basis for the biopolitical technologies of global governance, but it also suggests that if one tries to understand the contemporary Leviathan one should no longer look for the social contract which constitutes the State, but for the *learning contract* which establishes the sovereignty of Academia. As said earlier, the new sovereign wears Academic clothes and enrols everyone in the psy-class. When empowerment, resilience and other signifiers from the academic psy-complex become the credo of humanitarian aid, aid becomes power, and this reveals how Academia comes to play the central role in the biopolitical and psycho-political economy. The psychosocial turn in humanitarian aid, if not directly propelled by university departments or universitarian experts, is thoroughly and fundamentally academic in its structure. Not only does Academia deliver the rationale (the fantasies of the *homo psychologicus*) and assign the positions (turning everyone into a pupil of psychology) but it also economises and capitalises the surplus-value of subjectivity.

The Multitude has Academia as its sovereign

The psycho-social turn in humanitarianism reveals the structure of what Hardt and Negri call the biopolitical economy. Just as Hardt and Negri argue that there is no longer an outside to the logics of biopower, so we can argue that there is no longer an outside to psychology. As a totalising discourse, *psycho-biopower* is able to devour everything and spit it back out as psychology. However, globalisation does not effect a complete homogenisation. According to Hardt and Negri, there are still determinate and concrete places of exploitation to be discerned. They argue that we 'need to understand exploitation on the basis of the specific sites where it is located and specific forms in which it is organized' (Hardt and Negri, 2004, p. 102). If one can regard psychologisation as a central and *specific form of exploitation*, then the *specific sites* are Duffield's borderlands. The psychologisation of the West is founded on a psychologisation of its wastelands. That is where psycho-social humanitarian aid is caught up in the exploitation of subjectivity in a (de)psychologising/(de)politicising matrix.

This allows me to reformulate my critique on Hardt and Negri's other central thesis; namely the idea of immaterial production. While Hardt and Negri rather unproblematically welcome the post-Fordist direct production of subjectivity and social relations – considering it an opportunity for direct and absolute democracy – our critique on psycho-social humanitarian aid forces us to question this rather optimistic view. Their basic idea is that post-Fordist production is no longer aimed at the production of material goods but, rather, at the production of relationships and ultimately social life itself (Hardt and Negri, 2004, p. 109). Moreover, this production is no longer exclusively owned by those who possess capital. Rather, for the first time in the history of capitalism, traditional ownership is bypassed by the *multitude*, producing communication, affective relationships and knowledge which 'can directly expand the realm of what we share in common' (Hardt and Negri, 2004, p. 114). Discerning here a road to absolute democracy beyond any form of representation, Hardt and Negri take their distance from Agamben's gloomier analysis and his thesis of a more structural *aporia* in modern democracy. In particular, they reject Agamben's analysis in which Western democracy is underpinned by the close structural bond between sovereignty and the production of bare life. Hence they refute Agamben's central example of the Nazi-camp as the paradigmatic site of production of bare life and *homo sacer*. For Hardt and Negri the motif of the camp embodies precisely the attempt to 'destroy the enormous power that naked life could become and to expunge the form in which the new powers of productive cooperation of the multitude are accumulated' (Hardt and Negri, 2000, p. 384). Uncoupling bare life and sovereignty, Hardt and Negri claim that the production of social cooperation is 'no longer the result of the investment of capital but rather an autonomous power, the *a priori* of every act of production' (Hardt and Negri, 2000, p. 366). The direct production of subjectivity and social relations is, from Hardt and Negri's perspective, something with takes place outside the traditional capitalist scheme of creating surplus value through investment.

But does not our analysis of psycho-social humanitarian aid contradict this? For today's humanitarian camps reveal that the blossoming of subjectivity is not a spontaneous process, it is the result of a production process in which a surplus is created via the investment of academic psychology. Given the clearly de-psychologising and de-politicising effects, contra Hardt and Negri, we do, thus, still end up with *homo sacer*. Naked life is not raised up to the 'dignity of productive power' as Hardt and Negri would have it (Hardt and Negri, 2000, p. 366). Rather it is the result of the expropriating inclusive/exclusive discourse of psychosocial humanitarian aid which reduces humanity to the disposable object of expert care. If Hardt and Negri claim that in the new global order there is no outside, they miss the fact that this is only realised by an Agambian *inclusive exclusion* of bare life. There psycho-social humanitarian aid reveals itself as one of the central *modi operandi* in the encapsulation, in an envagination-like movement, of the outside borderlands which it then capitalises on by putting bare life into a sterile culture.

However, we should also attempt to surpass the limits of Agamben's analysis upon which we have already touched in chapter two dealing with the involvement of psychologists in torture. To rehearse the twofold problem with Agamben: when he reintroduces sovereignty in biopolitics coupling it to the figure of *homo sacer*, he claims that in these late-capitalist times we are all potentially *homines sacri*. The first problem concerns how to understand that we are all potentially *homines sacri* – Agamben and his commentators foremost address *homo sacer* as a peripheral figure. The second problem is how exactly we should conceive sovereignty if everyone is considered as *homines sacri*. My analysis of psycho-social humanitarian aid addresses both these issues. To begin with the question of sovereignty, instead of Hardt and Negri's multitude bypassing any representation or sovereignty, we found Academia as the instance of sovereignty involved in the production/ appropriation of subjectivity. Perhaps we can put it this way; if feudal society had its king and modern democracy its state and representative democracy, then the multitude has Academia as its sovereign. It is, furthermore, exactly here that we are all potentially *homines sacri*, insofar as we become the object of the expert, caretaking, psychologising discourse, producing and expropriating subjectivity. Post-Fordism is not about the simple and direct production of subjectivity and social relations, today our subjectivity and social relations are monitored, controlled and managed as we find psy-workers everywhere, from kindergartens, through the workplace, right up to retirement homes.

However it is crucial not to see this as a secondary process: it is not that the psy-discourse enters the scene only afterwards to skim off the spontaneous production of the multitude. For this would presuppose a primordial unmediated field, maybe accessible to another, better psychology. The economy of this fantasy has become clear in our closer look at the psychosocial turn in humanitarian aid. The supposedly spontaneous production of social relations and subjectivity in the West cannot avoid being mirrored by a blunt psychologisation and an alienating production of subjectivity at the borders and in the folds of the Empire.

Of course one could object here that in my critique on Academia and its, as I claim, rather disastrous Olympian point of view, I do have my own vantage point. But to be clear, there is nothing wrong with taking a meta-perspective, in fact, I have done nothing but search for such a position in this book. It only becomes problematic if a return is considered possible, in other words, if the illusion is held that the insight obtained from the vantage point is useful for the terrain itself. This is what the psy does: educating the youngsters in the theory of puberty, for example, they are sent back to life, at least, that is what the psy thinks. Should it not be thoroughly questioned what the effect is of inducing the psychological gaze? For having left the class, the knowledge on the identity crisis and the sexual experimenting will chime in every encounter the youngster has with those fields. I repeat, there is nothing wrong with the meta-perspective as such, only one should realise that once one has claimed a vantage point, one is moving on a totally different terrain, one has entered, so to speak, another world. In contrast, the foundational myth of psychology is that such a return is possible. Moreover, our journey through the phenomena of psychologisation has shown that it is precisely here, where the psy-sciences try to flesh out the *homo psychologicus* that they produce naked life and the *homo sacer*. It is this figure of *homo sacer* which compels us to take a partisan stance and use this stance furthermore as a vantage point to raise one's voice and denounce certain practices. Here, at the site of the structural violence of psychology, we have to oppose the hidden political double bind of psychology with a clear and open political and partisan engagement.

Psychology, subjectivity and money

Here, at the end of this chapter, we might perhaps be able to understand how in late-modernity psychology, subjectivity and money became interrelated. As such it has been observed that in general aid is very much about money: a vast industry has grown up around humanitarian aid as money is (re)routed to the private sector or multinational corporations that the NGOs rely on.[11] One can argue that the psychosocial turn still shows another aspect of this: as it reveals that in these post-Fordist times subjectivity itself has become a vital commodity to make profit on. In this way, the analysis of psycho-social aid skimming the battlefields and ghouling the disaster zones allows us to understand anew Walter Benjamin's assertion that humanity came to view its own destruction as a spectacle (Benjamin, 2008). Destruction at the borders of the Empire is what is supposed to unearth real and pulsating bare life, which has become the ultimate commodity in late-modernity. Benjamin's thesis means that the human being assumes a kind of extra-human observational position from which to contemplate humanity. Psychologisation is, then, today's hegemonic discourse which serves both as a tool to lay bare real life and to allow us to take the outsider position. To understand the importance of the psychological in the spectacle, it suffices to look at psychotainment, with which I dealt in chapter three. In reality TV the psychosocial plays a central role in the mediated production of subjectivity. Just recall *Survivor*, in which, cynically, the hunger-trope is a central catalyst to produce the – pre-formatted of course – subjectivities and Hobbesian social relations, a spectacle culminating in the pot of gold awaiting the participant who has proved to be the most complete and ingenious *psychologoid*. To understand this conflation of subjectivity, psychology and money, let us turn to Guy Debord:

> The spectacle is the other side of money: it is the general abstract equivalent of all commodities. Money dominated society as the representation of general equivalence, namely, of the exchangeability of different goods whose uses could not be compared. The spectacle is the developed modern complement of money where the totality of the commodity world appears as a whole, as a general equivalence for what the entire society can be and can do. The spectacle is the money which one only looks at, because in the spectacle the totality of use is already exchanged for the totality of abstract representation. The spectacle is not only the servant of pseudo-use, it is already in itself the pseudo-use of life.
>
> (Debord, 1994, p. 33)

One is tempted here to replace *spectacle* with *psychology*. Psy-experts themselves often testify as to how psychology and money are interrelated, arguing, for example, that psycho-social programmes contribute to the nation's *emotional wealth* and *social capital*. In her analysis on the idea of emotional intelligence Burman thus rightfully contends that, emotions have become 'a vital commodity' in, for example, the context of elections (Burman, 2009). The analysis of psychosocial humanitarian aid suggests that the radical conclusion to make is that subjectivity has become the *ultimate* commodity, with psychology as the other side of money. In psychosocial humanitarian aid, psychology reveals itself as, to put it in Debord's terms, the pseudo-use of life: *how did you feel doing this exercise?*

Psychology aims at restoring the experience of the totality of the world, aims at making society a totality once again. Psychology thus makes it possible to capitalise, to make profit at the very borders, at the waste-heaps of capitalism itself. Also, in the Marxist sense, psychology and money can be conflated, for psychology can be seen as a medium of exchange which permits a false equivalence between incommensurate objects. Furthermore, if anything can function as the framework for the commodity to be the congealing of social relations, then it is psychology. Psychology is the ultimate commodification, blurring out the social and economic contexts. This ossification of the social is realised by a whole array of psy-approaches, their seemingly wide theoretical difference withers away as we see that they all result in the objectification and the turning of subjectivity in a thingness, be it genes, neurotransmitters, evolutionary patterns, emotions, skills, brain areas, childhood traumas, cognitions, rapid eye movements . . . each is a commodity in the psycho-political economy.

The equation of psychology and money allows us to make one final step; namely, to understand how the Academy became the bank within this psycho-political economy. In Fordist times, the worker offered his or her labour-time to the market. Labour-time was a commodity which could be bought and sold on the marketplace. Thus, whilst working in a specific place for a given time, someone's labour-time could be sold/resold numerous times on the stock market. In post-Fordism, labour-time has traded its hegemonic place with subjectivity – or, put differently, labour-time takes the form of subjectivity. While in Fordist times it is the bank which functions as the virtual gathering place of all value, now it is the Academy. In the new global order the human being (not only the labourer as such) offers its subjectivity on the market (or it is expropriated from it in other ways), where it becomes a commodity, not on the stock market, but in the market of the spectacle. If in industrialist times the market could not function without the bank, today the economics of subjectivity cannot function without Academia. The difference is that in Fordist times the labourer was forced to bring his labour time to the market due to material dependency, in that he or she lacked access to or ownership of the means of production. In contrast, today it is important that everyone has access to the means of production and that is where everybody is subjected to the psycho-educational discourse. In Fordism everybody had to become a client of the bank – so that consumer behaviour could be regulated – now everybody has to be engaged in life-long-learning – so that the production of subjectivity can be regulated. While capitalism was the first mode of social organisation to capitalise on the capacity to produce, late-capitalism is the sophistication of this: it is ultimately the capitalisation of the very capacity to be.

The fact that the fund-raising event *Music For Life* with which this chapter started out is also referred to as *The Glass House* is significant. To begin with, the link with psychotainment shows such as *Big Brother* is immediately clear; *The Glass House* offers us the spectacle of subjectivity. The gimmick of starvation, as the DJs have to survive on smoothies, carries echoes of the psychotainment show *Survivor*. *The Glass House* gives us a glimpse of bare subjectivity, bare life. Not only does donating money restore the balance of this access to another's subjectivity but, moreover, the cheering we do, the songs we sing, the good feelings we produce, all of this adds to the spectacle of emotions and subjectivity being economised and capitalised. However, the signifier 'glass house' is peculiar in yet another albeit coincidental way. The event was located for two years in Ghent: in the same city-quarter, just two streets away from the event, the red-light district of the town centres around a street called the 'glass alley'. Not only is it a typical nineteenth century street covered with a glass ceiling but, moreover, the 'glass' also refers to the practice of window prostitution. Does this not reveal some of the obscenity involved in the fundraising event? The glass house of the fundraising event shows us the bare psychologised subject with its emotions laid out in the open and for sale. Here humanitarianism turns out to be not only about disaster pornography (as coined by Omaar and de Waal, 1993)[12] but is also revealed as subjectivity-porn and psycho-porn, to be added to the other obscenities of psychology we have stumbled on in this book.

Notes

1 See also Chapter 3.
2 See also Chapter 2.
3 Maybe this will also allow us to regain a notion of the subject other than the Foucaultian subject. In Žižek's terms: the subject is not the result of the objectivisations of science as Foucault would have it, in contrast, the subject is the 'indivisible remainder' of that operation, (Žižek, 1989)
4 See also Chapter 2 and the move to the discourse of the university initiated by Stanley Milgram and confirmed in the experiment of Philip Zimbardo.

5 This is why, looking at all those people dressed in white, one could get the impression of seeing the white uniforms of the scientific, medical, or psychiatric staff of a hospital in the streets.

6 See Chapter 2 on the position of the APA-psychologists against torture.

7 'Psychological first aid: whether among the general population or among aid workers, acute distress following exposure to traumatic stressors is best managed following the principles of psychological first aid. This entails basic, non-intrusive pragmatic care with a focus on listening but not forcing talk; assessing needs and ensuring that basic needs are met; encouraging but not forcing company from significant others; and protecting from further harm.' (The Sphere Project, 2004, p. 293)

8 The central claim of this book is thus that psychology is not just about terms which, along with material from other discourses, can freely be used and serve whatever self-construal. Rather, when psychology enters the framework the discursive and hence the subjective positions are decisively altered. That also means that even if many NGOs operate under a strong religious if not fundamentalist flag, one can easily discern a psychological and therapeutic scheme as the organising undertow. As I argued earlier, fundamentalism should be regarded as a truly modern stance (see my argument in the introductory chapter concerning the structural similarity of the Islamic fundamentalist with the Western *homo psychologicus*). The, of course healthy, Popperian reflex to look for falsifying evidence to my claim of a pan-psychologisation should not overlook that my approach aims to be a structural one, wanting to analyse the paradigmatic and hegemonic position of the psy-discourse in (late)modernity.

9 As Palmary and Nunez argue, a political engagement with the South is often invalidated with the 'home-grown' demand which often boils down to favouring the local elites which can hardly make a meaningful claim to local context (Palmary and Nunez, 2009).

10 See Chapter 2.

11 As the press text of Linda Polman's book *The Crisis Caravan* (2010) goes: 'a cavalcade of organizations – some 37,000 – compete for a share of the $160 billion annual prize, with "fact-inflation" sometimes ramping up disaster coverage to draw in more funds.'

12 Remember the description in Chapter 4 of charity TV commercials following the Haiti earthquake which did not shun nudity.

13 (Agamben, 2002a, p. 142)

5   Psychologisation in times of globalisation

In this last chapter I want to scrutinise where the analysis that psychology is inseparably linked to psychologisation has brought us. Maybe the first thing to make clear is that I did not as such refuse to provide another psychology beyond psychologisation, but, rather, that this search for another psychology gradually has become obsolete. At least, I hope that the question of the psychology of the *homo psychologicus* has been, to put it in the words of Adorno, lit up momentarily only to be consumed at the same time (Adorno, 1977, p. 120). But here two questions must be answered: first, can the outcome, this zero-level of subjectivity boiling down to a zero-level of psychology, really be said to have a universal status, and, second, can this analysis claim much use?

First, concerning the universality, it shall be clear that in the end my argument of the zero-level of psychology is connected to the psychoanalytic view on the human as the subject of language. That is, insofar as the human is a speaking subject, it should be thought of from an empty agential position. Just consider how Lacan defines the subject precisely starting from the signifier: 'a signifier represents the subject for another signifier'. This entails that the subject should be regarded as an empty point in the chain of signifiers. Having itself no substantiality as such, its emptiness nevertheless conditions the possibility of the discourse and hence of the social bond. What I have called the zero-level of psychology is nothing but the modern reworking of this human condition. As the modern subject is the subject of the sciences, it is fundamentally marked by psychology, which as I mentioned in the first chapter, according to Husserl sought to become 'the universal science of the subjective' (Husserl, 1970, p. 112). In this way I do claim psychologisation as universal and as touching upon humanity despite the geographical and cultural differences: with globalisation the modern condition indeed is globalised. Although, if anything late-modernity shows us, it is the existing side by side of often opposing currents, modern and traditional, exemplified in the religious fundamentalist active on Twitter and Facebook. Hence, we should not be lured by the phenomenological level of traditionalism or fundamentalism and seek for the underlying hegemonic modern structure. Remember Žižek's comment on Chakrabarty's example of the Indian software specialist remaining faithful to local religious traditions, Žižek asks: 'What if, in today's global civilization, we are more universal than we think and it's our own particular identity which is a fragile ideological fantasy?' (Žižek, 2010a, p. 285).

Similarly, what if our idea that we are more than or different from what the psy-sciences reduce us to – believing that we can creatively construct ourselves using different repertoires, or imagining a non-Western subjectivity untouched by psychologisation – what if this is precisely repeating the basic phantasm propelling academic psychology? The phantasm that there is a full substantial and unmediated subject propels psychology/psychologisation and denies the universality of the zero-level of psychology.

This brings us to the second question, is this analysis of the zero-level of psychology of much use? Maybe one should be cautious with theories which, not only tend to a kind of celebration (celebrating the multitude, diversity, the beauty of human resilience, the beauty of the brain, etc.), but which are also easily used and implemented. Consider, for example, how the Deleuzian concepts of 'smooth' and 'striated' space were explicitly used by Israeli military experts to devise the combat strategy in Nablus in 2002. The strategy was to see the city as a 'smooth space' and to alter its syntax: instead of using streets and alleys, the troops moved horizontally through walls and vertically through holes blasted in ceilings and floors (Weizman, 2006).

The claimed for *non-usability* of my critique of psychology is, however, not meant to be without effect. One could even say that it envisions something very much similar to what psychology/psychologisation itself results in. For, is not one of the paradoxical effects of psychologisation that once one is drafted into the psychology class there is no turning back? Once, as in the example already given, an adolescent is told that puberty is about coming to terms with sexuality, authority and personality, this knowledge will resonate in every encounter he or she has in these fields. Or, to give another example, once a parent takes cognisance of developmental psychology, this knowledge will irreversibly shape the way he or she interacts with their child. In both cases, the subject can in no way return to a *before psychology*. Being brought into psychology, the psychologising gaze cannot be warded off: the way of looking at oneself, the other and the world is decisively altered. What I envision with my critique of psychology is the same. The argument that *psychology is psychologisation* is meant to resonate in each of your encounters with psychology. The radical ambition of this book is that the reader will never look upon psychology and psychologists in the same way.

Hence, the question of this closing chapter is, if I am allowed this little twist of Milgram's question, *now that you know* that psychology equals psychologisation, *how do you feel*? To allow the draining of the emotions, I will in this chapter first address the relation of psychology/psychologisation to the logic of representation, in order to rehearse and to sharpen the key themes of this book. This will enable me, in the second section, to restate the question how psychologisation is related to globalisation? In the last section I will then make a final tour around the zero-level of psychology, where, as a sort of *deus ex machina*, I will bring in *das Ewig Weibliche* (the eternal feminine) in order to provide, not in a full closure of the book, but, rather, in a seal meant to block off any possible simple return to psychology.

Now you know too *much*, how do you feel?

The logic of representation

When the ex-king of Bhutan, Jigme Y. Thinley, became Prime Minister he promoted the term *Gross National Happiness* (GNH) in order to modernise Bhutan without losing the traditional culture and without endangering the well-being of the population. As the main concerns of the GNH, the Bhutan administration identified psychological well-being, health, education, good governance, living standards, community vitality, and ecological diversity (ABC News, 2008). However, one could ask, is this holistic, and clearly psychologising, approach an effective strategy against the negative effects of globalisation or is it, in contrast, the very Trojan horse which will bring in all the evils of uprooting capitalism and neo-liberalism? It is the latter, critics have argued, that is the case. Thinley most tellingly contends, for example, that happiness is not really the task of government: 'It is largely up to individuals to find happiness' (Makino, 2009). GNH thus seems just another vehicle for individualistic and neo-liberal policies, safeguarding, as argued in the report of the Norwegian Refugee Council, above all the values and identity of the Buddhist elite (Norwegian Refugee Council, 2008). According to the report, GNH – effectively promoted and welcomed in the West – is moreover a strategy for covering up the violations of human rights in this 'media-created Shangri-La' (Norwegian Refugee Council, 2008, p. 2). The psychologising of the personal and the social clearly plays a central role in creating this myth of Bhutan as an exotic land of happiness.

We should in the same way be wary of, for example, the idea of introducing 'emotional intelligence' (*EQ*) in schools in order to safeguard education from 'relentless technicisation and instrumentalisation', as already criticised by Erica Burman (Burman, 2009, p. 137). For, is it not exactly via this scientifically informed psychologising discourse on emotional intelligence that technicisation and instrumentalisation is realised? Just consider how psychologising discourses are very technical and use a de-subjectivising instrumentarium of standardised tests, surveys and evidence-based psycho-educational methods. A similar battery of surveys and quantitative research methods were, by the way, employed in Bhutan: GNH Bhutan officials conducted a poll of around 1,000 people to drawn up a list of parameters for being happy (ABC News, 2008). In this way, the psychologising recourse to well-being or emotions is not to be misunderstood as the wrong solution to tendencies (globalisation and instrumentalisation) endangering an allegedly authentic everyday life unspoiled by psychology. Rather, they are the very means of implementing globalisation and instrumentalisation.

The conclusion here is that the authenticity which both the discourses of GNH and emotional intelligence want to safeguard vis-à-vis the threat of too much globalisation, cannot be the point of departure for a true critique of psychologisation; in their very conceptualisation of what needs to be rescued, they realise the threat. Hence, departing from these psychologisations, the issue to scrutinise closer is how subjectivity relates to processes of objectivation and the discourses and praxes of science, technology and economy. Let us approach this via the so-called issue of *the logic of representation* and its central question where the *surplus* or the *excess* should be situated: at the site of representation or at the site of reality, or, more appropriate for our purposes, at the site of objectivity or at the site of subjectivity. These are the two options.

In the first option the objectifying representations are considered insufficient to fully cover or to fully contain the site of reality and the human. This supposes an excess of reality over representation, the idea that science, for example, cannot, or cannot yet, fully account for the realm of the ontological. This is the stance of anti-philosophy, which puts forward the excess of the pre-conceptual, the excess of production over representation. What is of interest to us is that this *too much* is rapidly situated at the site of the emotional, the personal and the intersubjective. Furthermore, assigning this terrain to the psy-sciences immediately engenders a few paradoxes. The most crucial paradox is that it would make of the psy-sciences the praxis of both the preservation and the expropriation of the *too much of subjectivity*. For, objectifying the excess of the subjective over science would eventually again drain the subjective. The only way to circumvent this paradox would be to put forward a kind of eco-psychology dedicated to reducing the psychological footprint of the psy-scientists. It is, as such, clear that in such a stance there is some super-expert who oversees the whole terrain to decide, for example, how much psychology is allowed to be administered in the terrain itself so as not to contaminate the authentic life-world. One can observe, moreover, that, where the excess of subjectivity is claimed, the meta-expertise is the attempt to devise a technology of mastery, control involved in and power over the excess of subjectivity. Suffice it to look how, for example, the emotional turn in education rapidly leads to, as Burman points out, the attempt to pin emotions down to neuro-chemical variables (Burman, 2009) so as to contain subjectivity, if not with chemical substances, then with psycho-education. Also Bhutan's GNH policies eventually boil down to reducing individual and social excesses of subjectivity to hard scientific data in order to gain control and power. After all, the GNH survey and its propaganda served the King's command 'One nation, one people', attempting to contain the social antagonisms as these manifested themselves ethnically (Norwegian Refugee Council, 2008, p. 2). GNH boils down to a psychologised discourse aimed at unifying the people, turning them into one controlled nation. The choice in the logic of representation to situate the excess at the side of reality puts forward a *too much life* which then per definition becomes the stake of biopolitical strategies.

In this book I choose the other option, of situating the excess at the site of our understanding and at the site of representation. Subjectivity is then not so much that which resists objectivations, rather it is the paradoxical effect of too much objectivation and representation. Or, in the words of Giorgio Agamben, what does it mean to be subject to desubjectivation?[1] Subjectivity is thus the paradoxical shadow of the very surplus of science. Just consider that the desubjectivising 'this is what you are' (*brain scans reveal . . . , psychological research proves . . .*) not only presupposes but actually produces a departure point for the installed gaze. *Look, this is what you are* posits you at a place beyond what you are. The *too much* on the side of science thus results in the instalment of this extra, but actually empty, agential point from where the modern being looks upon itself and the world. Modern subjectivity is the construction of a point from where the human being looks at the brain scans and the psycho-neurological homunculus/golem depicted by the neuro-psy-sciences. The produced surplus is thus, paradoxically, without content as such. The departure point of modern subjectivity is a zero-level of subjectivity, a zero level of psychology.[2] This zero-level of psychology allows us to approach anew the question *why do need so much psychology?*

Why do we need so much psychology? Revisited

The discipline of psychology already answers this question: as it starts from the premise that there is too much of the psychological at the site of the human, hence the need for a psychology. This is where claims are made that the psy-sciences are not (yet) able to fully chart and fully manage the human and the (neuro)psychological. Fred Wertz for example argues that 'science in general and psychology in particular do not eliminate or eradicate the dirty, diseased and troubled element of human life,' hence the horror (Wertz, 1994). Psychology as a scientific discipline is thus declared as (yet) insufficient to grasp the (too much of) psychology of the human. This, I claim, should be unhesitatingly reversed: instead of a too much (the dirty, the diseased) of human life, there is a too much at the site of science, hence the horror; the horror of a zero-level of subjectivity. The dirty element is as such not to be found in the *too much* of the human psyche, but rather in the *too much* of representation. It is this *too much* of representation at the site of the sciences, but also at the site of culture or politics as the previous chapters have shown us, which the psy-disciplines try to confront. Psychology is the other name for the excess of representation, the excess of science, culture and politics. One might even venture to say that psychology is the very symptom of the surplus, as it tries to give form (and to contain) the excess of the scientific, the cultural and the political over the human. But, as we know from symptomatology, a primordial symptom always structurally fails in its solving of the subjective deadlock, and thus leads to secondary symptom formations. Hence, as psychology can never completely cover the problematic excess of the sciences and techo-rationality, psychologisation as the secondary symptom enters the scene to fix the failed solution. The three phenomena I treated in this book (the involvement of psychologists in torture, psychotainment, and the psycho-social turn in humanitarianism) should thus not be regarded as mere bastard children of a specific discourse. Rather, instead of being mere unfortunate side effects they testify how modern science, culture and politics are structurally haunted by psychology/psychologisation. The too much at the side of representation (science, culture, and politics), channelled into the psy-sciences, is always at the verge of returning and spilling over to science, culture, and politics. It is precisely here that mainstream psychology is caught up in the un-emancipatory, alienating praxes of contemporary globalised biopolitics.

This threatens to certainly be the case in the contemporary neurological turn in the psy-sciences. There the psy-sciences risk finally being fully overtaken by the logic of representation that they pretend to supersede. Claiming a direct access to naked life, neuropsychology becomes the ideal vehicle for late modern biopolitics, consider both the EQ and GNH-issue. But, of course, then the question returns, why, considering the neurological turn, do we still need a psychology? For, rather than signalling the end of (too much) psychology, neurologisation still structurally needs a psychology (and thus effects a psychologisation) so as to operationalise the neurological discourse. The neuro-discourse not only resorts to, relies upon or simply ends up with the signifiers of psychology, it also inevitably mobilises the distribution of discursive positions of psychologisation. Just consider how for example the syndrome of Gilles de la Tourette (TS), Attention Deficit and Hyperactivity Disorder (ADHD), Obsessive-Compulsive Disorder (OCD) and other abbreviated neurological conditions share the fact that they (a) invariably rule out any psychological or subjective factor (b) are not yet (or not yet fully but almost) located in the brain or on the DNA-helix, (c) as they are not diagnosable with laboratory tests, they are to be assessed via typical psychological methods of interviewing and the clinical feel, and (d), they all put forward as a treatment, besides the drugs of course, psycho-education: *look, this is what you suffer from, and these are symptoms*: inviting the patient to look from the expert-position to its own subjective excesses.

In the same way, the gist of mainstream philosophy of the brain/mind is that, in spite of its celebration of the hard substantial essence, it often ends up psychologising the brain. As it fails to deal with the central issue of the logic of representation – the self-relating of a totality to itself, or the fact that representation is part of the presence itself – the short-cut to psychologising is often taken. As I have shown in Chapter three, Daniel Dennett is an exemplary instance here. In his refuting of representation as such, in the end he gets stuck in paradoxes where all kinds of metaphors have to be used only to let the disavowed representation, and thus psychology, in by the backdoor. Even where in the neuro-sciences the paradoxical pseudo-autonomy of the 'illusion'[3] or the subjective is acknowledged, the goal most often remains the establishment of a link between psychic events, illusionary or not, and material processes in the brain. In this attempt to materialise the illusion, Cartesian dualism and its paradoxes still haunt us. The always immanent tautology of, for example, fMRI-research cannot but strike us: psychology informs neurology, neurology informs psychology.

What the tandem psy-sciences/neuro-sciences thus always risks missing is that it is exactly in this tautological parallax-relation between (too much) psyche and matter that the very materiality of subjectivity is to be situated. Thus instead of trying to *MRI-se* and materialise the illusion, one should acknowledge the materiality itself of the illusion. This is how we can understand Žižek's plea for a radical materialism. Drawing upon Marx's *commodity fetishism*, Žižek argues that we do not simply deal with 'subjective illusions' (money, religion, nations . . .), but rather 'objective' illusions; illusions which are inscribed into the facts of social reality (Žižek, 2006b, p. 171). Žižek, glossing Marx, argues that it was the latter's finding that, at the very bottom of the critique of the economic process, one again encounters the theological dimension inscribed in social reality; Marx's well-known 'metaphysical subtleties and theological niceties' (Žižek, 2006b, p. 171). In this way, one can consider the subject as the subtle but, as such, objective illusion between psyche and brain. It is objective in the sense that it determines and grounds our social reality.

Moreover, observing the psychologisation and fetishisation of subjectivity in today's hegemonic discourses in science, culture and politics, one is tempted to alter Marx's claim that the critique of religion is the departure point of all critiques. Today the critique of psychology and psychologisation forces itself as the primal critique. This critique should not envision some ultimate material, finally de-psychologised ground of our social and economic variables, but, rather, it should value the subject in its very paradoxical *material* zero-level of subjectivity. A critique of psychology and psychologisation does not revalorise a true inner life but, rather, the empty subject, as this testifies to the fact that, as Žižek argues, the subject is, for itself, an inaccessible phenomenon.[4]

Once again: it is the psycho-economy

The fact that the *too much* of representation, both engendering and presupposing the materiality of the zero-level of subjectivity, is a politico-economical issue becomes clear where it is bypassed in Hardt and Negri's concept of the multitude. As discussed earlier, Hardt and Negri claim that the hegemonic mode of production in late-capitalism is the immaterial direct production of subjectivity and social relations (Hardt and Negri, 2000). However, as they fail to address the materiality of the zero-level of subjectivity, the alleged direct modes of production they celebrate might be nothing but the very expropriation of subjectivity on which late-capitalism thrives. It is here that Hardt and Negri's idea of the autonomous multi-faceted multitude foregoes the sovereignty involved in today's production of subjectivity. The sovereignty (a dimension Agamben has brought back to the fore of biopolitics) (Agamben, 1998) here is Academia, an area in which the psy-complex plays a leading role. An analysis of late-modern processes of psychologisation shows that the psy-discourses are the backbone of today's capitalisation processes in the form of the production of subjectivity and social relations.

The relation of psychology and capital is hence not only about Big Pharma exploiting today's discontents under globalisation, nor is it just a discourse and praxis of adaption, placing flat stones under the feet of the suffering workers pulling the boats up river (as in the example of Bertholt Brecht in his play *The Measure Taken*). Rather, in a more radical sense, psychologisation realises in late-capitalism the surplus-production as it capitalises on subjectivity. Recall Stanley Milgram's collecting the surplus of subjectivity in the form of psychologised commodities: '*now that you know, how you feel?*' Today's commercials clearly testify that subjectivity is the true commodity. Nike sells assertiveness (*Just Do It!*), L'Oréal self-confidence (*Because You're Worth It*) and Nokia retails social relations (*Connecting*

People). The overt commodity is only the carrier of the real commodity at stake, that is, psychologically produced subjectivity and social relations. In this way, it is clear that Bhutan's GNH policy is not about a cautious and slow progress towards capitalism. Rather, it is an immediate jump to late-capitalism which places psychologised subjectivity at the centre as something on which to capitalise. Similarly, the celebration and promotion of emotions in education, as it is supposed to be the counterweight for today's relentless technicisation, envisions the direct production of subjectivity. In all this, the old capitalist scheme of surplus-production remains very much alive, albeit that the investment of resources here is not primarily of capital as traditionally conceived but, rather, it concerns the investing of psychology and theory into the production units. Or, as in *The Matrix*, the human resources imprisoned in their water-filled cradles are given a virtual *Lebenswelt*, a computer program written with the scripts of psychology, in order to produce subjectivity. Psychology proceeds by psychologisation, by putting the *too much of representation* into the economic process. Milgram's phrase should thus be amended: 'now you know too *much*, how do you feel?'

Hardt and Negri's Deleuzian ontological claim to go beyond representation and claim the possibility of a direct democracy of the multitude is, therefore, highly problematic. The belief in the political emancipatory potential of the multitude and its direct mode of production of subjectivity and social relations bypasses the fact that the multitude cannot itself be ridden with the social and the political. Symptomatic of the celebration of the multitude is the fact that the dimension of conflict within the multitude is not thinkable on a theoretical level. This is where Hardt claims that 'the question of conflict within the multitude is one of those questions better addressed in more practical terms rather than at this rather philosophical level' (Hardt, 2005). For a concise (representational) way of thinking the conflict through on a theoretical level, we can turn briefly to Žižek who argues upon Hegelian grounds that man did not make the leap from nature to culture as such. Rather, this supposed leap had to pass over some wildness, an excess, and a radical un-humanness (Žižek, 2010b). Nature (at least human nature) is not what remains as a domain not fully, or not yet fully, covered by the human, rather, it is the wild excess of representation and humanity itself. The emotional turn in education thus misses the point that education does not deal with nature as such, but with *human nature*, as wildness, as excess, as a radical un-humanness. Hardt thus mistakenly situates the question of conflict within 'more practical terms', while it is clear that the antagonisms are to be situated on the basis of representation, theory, and (too much) knowledge.

Psycho-globalisation

One world, one psychology class

To understand psychology/psychologisation within the logic of representation requires us to consider the contemporary intensification of the phenomena of psychologisation not as something structurally new, but rather as a phenomenon connected with the advent of modernity. As such, the claim is rather simple, if not trivial; modernity gave birth to psychology whose structural shadow of psychologisation only came to full blossom in late-modernity. Psychologisation in these times of globalisation brings to light the fact that modernity was already the birth of the *homo psychologicus*. That is, it is only setting out from today's crisis in the psy-field that one can make sense of the beginnings, as such, of psychology. And, the other way around, only by understanding psychology as a central issue of modernity, can we make sense of today's phenomena of psychologisation.

To assess how psychologisation evolves under globalisation, let us turn for a moment to how the psy-sciences themselves assess these late-modern times. In the sector of parental support for example, one often pleas for more funds arguing that in our times parents no longer have fixed points of reference in their education. In a rapidly changing world, it is argued, the contemporary parent is basically insecure about parenting. Knowledge on education is not transferred easily between generations, let alone that the best-before date of that knowledge expires promptly: one cannot address his or her child in the same ways as one's parents did. As the UK organisation *Family Lives* puts it in their 2011 report, today's parents are 'unprepared and pressurised': '70% of parents, and 78% of grandparents surveyed, believe that being a parent today is a harder job than it was a generation ago' (Family Lives, 2011, p. 1). So the efforts of the government and the educational world to provide everybody with expert-based parenting support and advice seems legitimate. The point of departure is here, that the inadaptedness of today's parent concerns a lack of knowledge which should be tackled offering workshops and courses. The parents are hence provided theory on parenting. This is what we have seen time and time again in this book: there is no other way to do psychology other than by psychologising, by calling the subject into the psychology class. Or, as we read on an official Flemish site on education, parents nowadays increasingly rely on the findings of scientific research to answer their questions on education. Professionals thus offer to parents the 'necessary strategies to manage [their] own feelings', or, 'simple parenting "tools", such as "Act don't React"' and 'techniques to communicate'. It is clear that one can start none too soon with the necessary transfer of knowledge of the psy-sciences. As Family Lives pleads: 'Age appropriate Sex and

Relationships Education (SRE) should be available to all children.' (Family Lives, 2011, p. 71). But how soon is concerning the administration of psy-theories, is nowhere as clear as in the so-called *attainment targets* in education, as they are for example officially formulated by the Flemish Education Department (Roelands and Druine, 2000, p. 79). The three- to six-year-olds are, for example, supposed to be 'able to speak about feelings such as joy, fear, sorrow, and surprise' (Vlaamse Gemeenschap). Pedagogical methods developed for teachers operationalise this in terms of teaching the children 'a more differentiated vocabulary concerning emotions', in order to 'express feelings in a more appropriate way' (Kog et al., 1997). Again, it is important not to miss what exactly this boils downs to: namely, nursery school teachers introduce the toddlers to nothing else but the *Elementary Psychology of Feelings*. What we teach those young children to adopt is the academic gaze. And here Child Psychology is indispensable, not as psychology of the child but exactly as psychology *for* the child. In their introduction to *A Box Full of Feelings* Kog et al. for example claim that working with the four basic feelings 'happiness, fear, anger and sadness' enables children to 'recognize emotions in themselves, accept them, name them and have a more differentiated awareness of them' (Kog et al., 1997).

This schoolification which is at the core of psychologisation is tantamount to globalisation. Just consider post-politics' embrace of the learning discourse. For the political answer to a multitude of problems arising in a globalised context seems to be *everybody becomes a student again*. Unemployed or worried about keeping your job? Engage in lifelong learning: the ultimate answer to our economy's failure to create jobs? Moreover, and this should come as no surprise, in the learning discourse the psy-signifiers rapidly pop up. Take for example the official communications of the European Community: 'Lifelong Learning is a core element . . . central not only to competitiveness and employability but also social inclusion, active citizenship and personal development' (Cited in Contu et al., 2003, p. 942). It has been criticised that the claim of lifelong learning to be an emancipatory project cannot help but result in the opposite. As for example Alessia Contu contends, the learning discourse tends to maintain relations of power and subordination: the positions are defined according to seemingly neutral technical skills and this exactly proscribes the roles that are taken by and ascribed to the citizens/workers (Contu et al., 2003).[5] As said, the social contract seems to have been traded with the learning contract: only insofar as we are in one class we are in one world.

Politicised psychology and the policy of psychologisation

The political processes of globalisation clearly had an important bearing on the theories and the praxes of the psy-sciences. One can for example observe how in the 1990s a managerial or even quasi neoliberal model was introduced in the care and the psy-institutions in many European countries. With the objective of budget control and clearly inspired by the so-called Third Way Politics adopted by the European leftist parties after the fall of the Berlin Wall, official agencies induced the discourse of efficiency and quality control in hospitals, schools, kindergartens, mental health institutions, etc. This resulted in a blurring of the psy discourse and the entrepreneurial discourse: a good manager was considered to use psychology and in psychology phrases popped up such as *manage your anger*, *work on yourself*, and more recently, *invest in your brain*. Far from receiving much resistance this liberalisation and (post)politicisation was widely welcomed: the neoliberal entrepreneurial discourse seemed to furnish the psy and other similar professions with a new and firm foundation. Moreover, the post-political end of the big ideological stories seemed also the end of the big theories in psychology. The clash between psychoanalysis and the humanist theories for example was transcended in the idea that an *evidence-based* praxis had no need of theory. This book has shown that precisely here psychology, in doing away with theory and choosing for a pragmatic, down-to-earth and naturalised vision of the human, definitely took the path of psychologisation.

But perhaps the most important tenet of this neo-liberal politicisation of psychology is that it made psychologisation an official policy of late-modern states. Think for example of the government-induced massive screening programmes for ADHD or autism. If one looks at the broad societal domain, one can easily discern how, in a short period of time, various areas such as education, health care, community life, etc. have all undergone decisive changes due to policies enforcing a psychologising discourse in those fields. Just consider how official policies, of course highly influenced by psy- and related lobbies, redesigned the school in a few decades to become a kind of welfare centre providing a total package of schooling, education, and therapy. As such, this is an argument against the thesis that under globalisation the nation state has lost its impact and relevance. Post-politics can indeed be defined as politics having retreated from its traditional areas, such as economics, leaving this field to the jurisdiction of supra-national organisations and companies. However, it is exactly via a kind of psycho-biopolitics that traditional agencies, such as the state, stay in business, and this is where Academia is the central ally. Post-politics is, for example, concerned with mobbing legislation, diversity and gender issues . . . in short, psycho(social) matters which are not to be decided along political lines, but on the basis of what the experts put forward.

A clear example of how psychologisation is an official policy is the case of Flanders where the government explicitly promotes the Triple P-method (Sanders, 1999), a typical CBT (Cognitive Behavioural Therapy) approach, as the key method for parenting support programmes. Official policy holds that every urbanised area should have its Triple P 'parenting support shop' (sic). In this way the psy-apparatus seems to have become just as omnipresent as the ecclesiastical apparatus was in the past (De Vos, 2006), and, although it may lack its central papal authority, it is nonetheless powered by a strongly uniform and worldwide expanding psychologising discourse. For, as we have seen in the case studies on torture, psychotainment and humanitarian aid, the becoming global of psychologisation is an established fact. Should we hence not rename the psy-complex as the *global (non)governmental-academic psy-complex*, so as to clearly indicate both the scope and the agencies involved? The post-political agenda is to a great extent realised, so it seems, via *soft politics*, dealing with harassment, sexual identity, diversity, mental health . . ., legitimising the implementation of policies not on the basis of political or ideological choices, but on the basis of the academic allegedly neutral and objective expert knowledge. If psychologists themselves consider psychology too important to leave it to the psychologists (hence their mission to enlist everyone in the discourse) maybe we should at least endorse the premise. That is, psychology and its structural dynamics of psychologisation should be a primordial terrain for contemporary ideology critique to understand the essential tenets of globalisation.

Psychologisation in times of globalisation

As such, the fact that the psy-sciences cannot do anything but proceed by exhorting their subjects to join the ranks of the psy-scientists has never been as apparent as in these times of globalisation. If Žižek argues that today's all-pervasive renaturalisation is strictly correlative to the global reflexivisation of our daily lives (Žižek, 2001, p. 10), then this is clearly discernable in processes of psychologisation. The (pop)psychological naturalising adagio of 'get in touch with the real you' – put forward worldwide by educational, entrepreneurial, commercial and other discourses – shows that the road to natural authenticity eventually runs over the path of theory and reflexivity. The psy-sciences proceed here by inducing their subject into the theoretical position. And, as I have shown, where psychology is unable to assess the paradigm of psychologisation as its own founding gesture, it is bound to get caught in the, now globalised, alienating and un-emancipatory praxes of biopolitics. Psychology's blind spot is that it addresses the human being both as the modern subject of the sciences – hailing it to look at itself through the academic gaze – and as the human psychological thing looked upon. The case-studies show how this *human zoo* approach actually turns the *homo psychologicus* into a *homo sacer*, the disposable object of care of biopolitics. In this way the psy-sciences actually realise what they deny: a zero-level of subjectivity. *This is the psychological-neurological-biological thing you are,* in the end constitutes another, albeit weightless agent looking at itself from a zero level of psychology, neurology and biology. Maybe it is precisely here that the link to globalised capitalism comes to the fore, as globalisation can be linked to the production of zero-levels. As Žižek writes:

> What is capitalist globalisation? Capitalism is the first socioeconomic order that detotalises meaning. It is not global at the level of meaning (there is no global 'capitalist worldview,' no 'capitalist civilization' proper – the fundamental lesson of globalization is precisely that capitalism can accommodate itself to all civilizations, from Christian to Hindu and Buddhist); its global dimension can only be formulated at the level of truth-without-meaning, as the 'real' of the global market mechanism.
>
> (Žižek, 2006b, p. 181)

Thus the *real* is not to be found at the level of an everyday life, polluted by globalisation (or by psychologisation). Rather than at the level of a personal or a cultural authenticity, it is at the level of truth-without-meaning. Thus one can argue that the de-totalising, de-ideologising stance of globalisation actually lays bare the zero-level of subjectivity. In processes of globalisation the zero-level of ideology meets the zero-level of psychology: the automaton of globalised economics is the correlate of the human being conceived as an automaton. As said, modernity only gets fully realised in late-modern globalisation.

So we should not fall in the trap of the simple plea for a de-psychologisation or de-academisation of life. In this way psychologisation might be understood in terms of Žižek's conception of *pseudo-concreteness*. Žižek explains that notion pointing to computer operating systems. To counter the growing complexity and opaqueness of computers, Apple was the first to try to recreate an artificial concreteness with a graphic interface: the pseudoconcreteness of icons enables us to relate to the complex environment of the computer (Žižek, 2006a). If the function of psychologisation is to give an artificial concreteness to our complex post-modern world – then the PC-metaphor can show us how to understand this. Pseudo-concreteness is not about, for example, the white male concretising his socio-economical uncertain situation in the fear of the migrant – pretty much as primitive man sees heavenly creatures at work in thunder and lighting. These simplifications overlook the fact that pseudo-concreteness is always a secondary process. The graphic interface Apple invented is a secondary virtualisation allowing us relate to the primary one, namely the growing opaqueness of the PC: evolving from a mere electronic device to a medium of virtual reality. In the same way, it is in light of a primary virtualisation of our habitat in post-modernity – as an essential feature of globalisation – that man loses his grip and seeks pseudo-concreteness. According to Žižek, the key issue of late-capitalism is that the ultimate power and control is no longer in the hands of the firm or individual who owns the means of production; it has become a virtual level in which companies are the shareholders of other companies, and borrow money from the bank and in reality own nothing (Žižek, 2002b). These paradoxes of virtualised capitalism constitute contemporary alienation and lead to attempts to cope with it. The second virtualisation is always an attempt to domesticate the first. The virtuality of Second Life should not be understood as though First Life were the real and authentic one. Likewise, the dissemination of theories on the functioning of the brain, social skills, group dynamics, etc., seems to bring us back a meaningful, manageable life-world: denying the late-modern alienation of globalisation it thrives on the illusion that Real Life lurks just behind the veils of post-modern complexity. And, as already argued, here the line between certain tendencies within mainstream psy-praxis and the populist conservative discourses becomes thin as they share the same envisioning of a lost but regainable authentic, pastoral kind of first life.

Psychologisation in times of globalisation thus inevitably entails the image of a simple, natural-psychological human, in all its neurobiological straightforwardness projected onto the background. In George Orwell's novel *1984* the protagonist Winston Smith ascribes to the 'Proles' (the labourers, those who 'are free as animals') a sordid swarming of life, as they have retained primitive emotions. But what if the 'Proles' were nothing more than illusions created by Big Brother or the Party? In a globalised and totalised world the alienated subject is called upon to envision the 'psychological 'prole' as the point of departure for its outlook upon itself, the others and the world. If this is the truth of psychology in times of globalisation, as we end up with a non-subject, is this not where we should revive the alternatives of psychoanalysis, and feminism?

Psychology/psychologisation, psychoanalysis and *Das Ewig Weibliche*

(The end of) psychology versus the truth of psychoanalysis?

In the 19th century there was a psychology without a soul, in the 20th century there was a psychology without subjectivity, and in the

21st century there may be a psychology without psychology. Indeed, such a development would mean the end of psychology.

(Teo, 2004)

Thomas Teo's summary is very apt, only, he might be mistaken arguing that this development means the end of psychology. Moreover, psychology has always been without psychology, as it per definition creates a subject beyond psychology. Looking at itself as a psychological thing, the subject itself testifies of a zero-level of psychology. In this way one can argue that psychology was always already dead but only did not know it. Are we thus not dealing with a zombie-psychology, which, moreover, always repeats its own death at the site of the subjects it addresses? For, psychology both effects the zero-level of subjectivity with the human, and denies this by resurrecting consequently a fully constituted *homo psychologicus*. *Look* – and this pulls you out of life itself – *this is what you are* – and there your psychological double sees the light.

Milgram's experiment is as shown exemplary here, but looking upon it from still another angle, one sees that the experiment realises a zero-level of subjectivity precisely by emptying out the relation of the subject with its fellow human being of any human qualities. For, is not the effect of Milgram's putting the authority of science central stage that the locus of humanity shifts to the transferential relation of the subject with the scientist or science in general? For at the debriefing *the other* turns out to be nothing more than an actor, a prop on the stage. The only substantial and meaningful relation at the end is the one between the subject and Milgram, the representative of the powerful psy-sciences. Milgram's experiment there is the enactment of the production of psychological man isolated and locked in his relation to Science. But do we here not have a similar logic with psychoanalysis, on which I drew substantially in this book? Is not the psychoanalytic setting the ultimate example of emptying the outer world? As the analysand engages in his soliloquy the others and the world as such become nothing more than the effects of solipsism. If Stam et al. write that in the Milgram experiment the 'subjects' bodies are first abstracted from their social context and then recontextualised in a way that denies their social constitution' (Stam et al., 1998, p. 161), then this critique might also hold for psychoanalysis. Is here, moreover psychoanalysis not, as Žižek puts it, the ultimate method of humiliation?

[I]s not the very aim of the psychoanalytic process to shake the foundations of the analysand's fundamental fantasy, i.e., to bring about the 'subjective destitution' by which the subject acquires a sort of distance toward his fundamental fantasy as the last support of his (symbolic) reality? Is not the psychoanalytic process itself, then, a refined and therefore all the more cruel method of humiliation, of removing the very ground beneath the subject's feet, of forcing him to experience the utter nullity of those 'divine details' around which all his enjoyment is crystallized?

(Žižek, 1991, p. 156)

Of course maybe the crucial point is that psychoanalysis does not, as psychology does, envision a subsequent restitution of man as a psychological being: in contrast to psychology, psychoanalysis pretends not to be the cure to the experience of this subjective destitution, this zero-level of subjectivity. But, one could reply, what does psychoanalysis then offer? Is not psycho-analysis equally impotent in showing alternative ways of emancipation other than the enacted psychologising solution of Milgram? For, if Milgram ends up celebrating the heroic act of disobedience, is this not very close to Žižek's appreciation of the individual act? Ian Parker for example criticises Žižek's romanticising of resistance, while it reduces collective political action to individual heroic 'acts' (Ian Parker, 2004, p. 97). This critique then returns almost literally in Parker's assessment on Milgram: where Parker states that Milgram blocks the road to a valuation of the social: Milgram's message is 'the social is bad for you and others' (Ian Parker, 2007, p. 85). But is not the social, together with subjectivity, a category that has become problematic and paradoxical since the Enlightenment? Both categories are invariably deconstructed and reduced to biological, evolutionary, psychological, or social mechanisms. Academia is the total incorporation of the *Lebenswelt*, alienating both the individual as well as the social. In this way both the individual and the social have irrevocably lost any positive substance outside Academia. Regarding the social, just remember the governmental pro-grammes backed up by Academia aiming to restore the social fabric by creating meeting spaces to provide chances for dialogue and encounter. The social there cannot but come in an academic version.

Perhaps, if psychoanalysis starts from both a zero-level of subjectivity and a zero-level of society, the crucial point becomes then the position one takes vis-à-vis Academia. The mainstream psy-sciences embrace the university discourse unproblematically: claiming to be a full science, the psy-sciences promise reconciliation and academically informed ways to integrate both subjectivity and society. The paradox of this we see emerging with Milgram: puzzled with the Eichmann figure, he says, let us study authority, take the authority of, let us say . . . science. This is, as said, highly problematic because Milgram himself claims to speak from within science. This prevents him from seeing how science itself is implicated in modernity and its deadlocks – of which the Holocaust might be one of the important manifestations. So is not the problem of modernity, coming to light especially in late-Modernity, that Academia has itself become the stand-in for society, depicting a psychological human as the stand-in for the subject? This is what psychoanalysis as a discourse which claims a place (partly) outside of Academia is able perhaps to critique. For psychoanalysis is not a discourse of knowledge, but a discourse of truth. My choice to found a critique of psychologisation in psychoanalysis is precisely grounded in the fact that, at its best, psychoanalysis is the theory and the praxis which connects the truth to the fundamental impossibilities which thwart the crucial human domains of science, culture and politics. Consider again the *skandalons* of psychoanalysis, e.g. the death drive, polymorphous sexuality etc., with which psychoanalysis tries to conceive of those fundamental but in the end ungraspable coordinates of human life: birth, sexuality and death. However, my choice is also done in the full awareness that psychoanalysis is itself marked by this truth, or allow me to put it in Lacanian, by the gap in the Big Other. Moreover, it is precisely there where psychoanalysis, faced with the impossibility of both its theory and praxis, inevitably and necessarily tilts over to the fields of science (e.g. psychoanalytic psychology or neuro-psychoanalysis); of politics (e.g. Freudo-Marxism, Lacanian ideology critique) and of culture (informing and shaping the arts and literature).

But maybe we should still try to make one thing clear, that is that at each of those tilting overs of psychoanalysis, the pivotal point might be *the eternal feminine* that which Sigmund Freud time after time stumbled on, remember Freud saying 'was will das Weib?', or, *what do women want?* (quoted by E. Jones, 1955, p. 468). Just consider the critiques from feminist perspectives on psychoanalysis being a phallocentric psychology or endorsing a patriarchal conception of politics. Perhaps *das Ewig Weibliche* is the eventual *skandalon* of any theory and praxis of the psyche.

The masculine-feminised homo psychologicus

If here, at the end of this book, I resort to a *bring in the Woman*, this brings in mind Zimbardo's experiment, connecting the feminine to psychology in a perhaps paradigmatic way. So let us return to the Stanford Prison Experiment and retake the question of the fantasy scenario that underlies Zimbardo's account of the *crucible of human behaviour*, his claim to stand at the abyss of humanity. Here Zimbardo, keen as he is on romantic imagery – just think about the imagery invoked by the book title *The Lucifer Effect* – might have been inspired by the Faustian mad scientist and the related Gothic theme of unravelling the secrets of life. One of the key issues here is precisely the Feminine. There is some circumstantial evidence to support this idea. If the study can be understood to culminate in an *all's well that ends well* marriage

– remember how the closing down of the experiment was instigated by Zimbardo's wife-to-be – this theme is already redoubled in the experiment itself. At one point the guards stage a mock marriage featuring, most aptly, Frankenstein's monster: 'Why don't you play Frankenstein? 2093, you can be the bride of Frankenstein . . . 7258, you be Frankenstein? I want you to walk over here like Frankenstein, and say that you love 2093' (Zimbardo, 1989 my transcription). Upon which the guard nick-named 'John Wayne' brutally shoves the prisoners together into an embrace, making them say *I love you*. Of course it can be argued that this mock marriage is a mere coincidence and that it would be stretching things too far to connect it to the personal story of Zimbardo. But is not this image of the monster created by science already lurking under the surface of the experiment, only to be brought to light by Eshleman who, as Zarembo reports, immediately sensed that the experiment was meant to bring out 'the evils inherent in a prison-type environment' (Zarembo, 2004)? The mock marriage of Frankenstein's monster seems to presage that Zimbardo's mock prison drama and its enacted encounter with the horrible Real of Humanity could only ever end with the classical solution of bringing in the bride. And are we here not justified in interpreting the bride in the classic manner, as the bourgeois solution and defence against the enigma of the feminine: *was will das Weib?*

As such we should resist the temptation to play down the girlfriend episode, dismissing it as an aspect of Zimbardo's personal drama unhappily interfering with the experiment. On the basis of that assumption one could still claim that Zimbardo's experiment does touch on a real socio-psychological ground beyond the methodological flaws introduced by his personal history.[41] But are these two aspects really separable? We should consider the following anecdote. On Zimbardo's website there is a video of him giving a PowerPoint presentation. When he comes to the Christina Maslach episode and her ultimatum – 'I'm not sure I want to . . . have anything to do with you if this is the real you' (Sundance Channel, 2006) – he remarks, 'The next day I stopped the experiment.' The next slide is of their marriage photo and he comments, '. . . and the next year I was married to her' (Zimbardo, 2008). At this point the whole audience explodes in laughter and applause, as if relieved by the happy end of the horror story: they married and had children. Does this collective emotional release on the part of the audience not show that the conclusion of the Stanford Prison experiment saved more than just Zimbardo's experiment and his career? It saved a whole discourse and a particular approach within the psy-sciences, namely a psychology, blind for its inevitable and structural link with psychologisation, grounding itself in a fantasised encounter with the Real Crucible of Humanity.

But still, how should we understand that it is exactly there that the figure of the Woman takes central stage? Is the zero-level of subjectivity which psychology inevitably touches upon, linked directly to the enigma of the feminine? Just consider how women have always been a main target of psychologisation. Recall Dr Spock and co.'s vast attempts at psychologising and reducing women to mothers, a category under the jurisdiction of the medical discourse and the psy. Moreover, forced to be good mothers, women were furthermore rapidly forced into the position to which psychologisation always leads: the mothers were instructed and trained how to read the psychological signs with their children: they had to become psychology trainees or proto-psychologists, albeit under supervision of the doctor. This primordial link between psychology/psychologisation and femininity might also explain why allegedly feminine qualities and issues prevail in the discourse of mainstream psychology. Consider for example the discourse of emotional intelligence, in which issues such as empathy, relationships, caring, etc. are central. As Ian Parker furthermore remarks, this kind of feminised humanism is often evoked by critics of old experimental paradigm psychology as a fully-fledged alternative paradigm. However, Parker continues, this is where feminism risks sliding into a *feminisation* endorsing the old masculine paradigms:

> Psychology is part of an academic and professional apparatus that increasingly feeds on an image of the subject as feminised, but which still attempts to predict and control the trajectory of that subject through their life course as they engage in the stereotypically masculine activity of growing, thriving, and competing.
>
> (Ian Parker, personal communication, 10 December 2011)

The *skandalon* of the zero-level of subjectivity is warded off by psychology in a particular way: by putting forward a masculine-feminised *homo psychologicus*.

The genealogy of this might be understood starting from how the sciences de-sexualised the view of the world. In most cosmogonies the origin and the existence of the world is connected to the sexual difference. The most well-known example here is that of Yin and Yang, a female and a male principle whose interplay determines everything. Modernity however ceased to see the world as organised via sexual principles. However, does not psychology/psychologisation and its masculine feminisation show that there is something problematic with this scientific desexualisation? Maybe we can understand this by considering the specific position of psychoanalysis on this point. As Žižek explains, the particular stance of psychoanalysis was to re-sexualise the universe but without regressing to a pre-scientific or esoteric discourse (Žižek, 2011). One can argue that Freud was driven to such an attempt as he saw that in modern society the constitution of subjectivity indeed passes over sexuality, a sexuality moreover far removed from a supposedly natural sexuality. Žižek argues however, that it was only with Lacan's grounding psychoanalysis within a theory of language that psychoanalysis could envision sexuality in a pure formal way. For example, language allows us to understand that sexuality structurally tends to spill over to other terrains than the purely sexual one. Žižek calls this a weakness rather than a strength: sexuality cannot realise itself on its own terrain. Žižek makes the quip: if it might be true that the male thinks only about sex, the question is what he is thinking about while doing it. But perhaps the most important point to make is that, as Žižek contends, the decentring of sexuality by psychoanalysis makes that ontology always fail (Žižek, 2011). Something escapes ontology as sexuality is never where you expect it: something non-sexual can become sexual and the sexual can become de-sexualised. The crucial point is then, as Žižek puts it, that the sexual difference is not a binary or natural opposition, let alone a complementary one. The male and the female are two possible positions vis-à-vis a third point, which is according to Žižek, the impasse in ontology brought about by sexuality (Žižek, 2011). It is precisely this radical deconstruction of sexuality, at which psychoanalysis arrived in its attempt to understand modern subjectivity, which mainstream psychology tries to evade. In its characteristic feminisation, psychology puts forward a masculine femininity supposed to make ontology into a whole.

The dog looking at the sick cow

Not long ago the Flemish minister of education pleaded for better sex education. She contended that the fact that there are still girls who blush when the subject is brought up in class means that there are still taboos to be tackled (Jonckheere, 2004). To blush with shame warrants an educational if not therapeutic intervention. Is this not a typical example of a feminisation driven by the masculine fantasy of being in control? It is clearly inspired by mainstream psychology's aim to get rid of every antagonism, be it a scientific, cultural or political one. In the end it even aims at being on top of sexuality as such, seeking to go beyond any shame and to project us a sexuality situated fully in the realm of possibility and adaptation. In other words, this is psychology presenting us impudently *psycho-porn*, the fantasy of a direct, unmediated and unproblematic access to *jouissance*.

A critique of psychologisation, which should be central to contemporary ideology critique, should radically target these obscene gestures of promising a short-cut to ontology. For, as said, psychology is too important to leave it to the psychologists. And again, I would not interpret this as for example

Bernard Baars does, echoing George Miller, that the more widely a scientific approach is understood, the less likely it is to be misused (Baars, 1986, pp. 3–4). The claim of this book, in contrast, is that we are all already fully immersed in psychology: no missionary work is to be done anymore. Time thus to make this fully clear and proclaim an engaged *we, the psychologists*. From that perspective psychology can be looked upon as not carrying some precious and valuable core leading to a full ontology, but rather as fundamentally interchangeable with psychologisation. There psychology becomes the sick cow, that what is wearily – and most probably also with some bashfulness – looked upon by the dog.

Notes

1   Alain Badiou also sets out from an excess of representation over presentation, which he grounds in set theory: the excess of subsets over elements (there are more ways of grouping elements into parts than there are elements of a set) (Badiou, 1988, pp. 113 and 309). This pushes him, as Bosteels puts it, not to the postulating of 'some originary lack for pious ecstasy or postmodern respect for the unpresentable' but to the idea of the possibility of a site where an 'event' can arise, leading to 'subjective fidelity' (Bosteels, 2006, p. 150)
2   These are more or less the words Žižek uses as he describes contemporary neurological research, in my view somewhat too optimistically. (Žižek, 2006b, p. 170)
3   'At it most radical, the Unconscious is the inaccessible phenomenon, not the objective mechanism that regulates my phenomenal experience.' (Žižek, 2006b, p. 171)
4   Contu further remarks that it is very difficult, if not impossible, to be against learning; it is not easy to oppose the values of individual emancipation or social progressivism promoted by the learning discourse. The same holds for psychologisation, how can one oppose a discourse which promises empowerment or self-realisation?
5   For Martha Nussbaum, for example, Zimbardo is far too emotionally involved for the resulting behaviour to be scientifically reliable (Nussbaum, 2007), which suggests that the scientific reliability of psychological research can be realised by restraining the subjective factor.

References

Aalbers, D. (2008) 'APA Approves Measure Banning Psychologists from Interrogations'. Retrieved 24 June, 2008, from http://www.cageprisoners.com/articles.php?id=26476

ABC News (2008) 'Bhutan Tries to Measure Happiness'. Retrieved 1 September, 2010, from http://www.abc.net.au/news/stories/2008/03/24/2197797.htm

Adorno, T. W. (1977) 'The Actuality of Philosophy', *Telos*, 31: 120–133.

Adorno, T. W. (1991) 'Freudian Theory and the Pattern of Fascist Propaganda', in Bernstein, J. M. (ed.), *The Culture Industry: Selected Essays on Mass Culture*, London: Routledge.

Adorno, T. W., and Horkheimer, M. (1989 [1944]) Dialectic of Enlightenment (J. Cumming, trans.), London: Verso.

Adorno, T. W., Levinson, D., Horkheimer, M., and Frenkel-Brunswik, E. (1993 [1950]) *The Authoritarian Personality*, New York: Norton.

Adriaenssens, P. (2006, 4 November) Interview: 'Laat Gerust je Kwetsbaarheid Zien', *De Standaard*.

Adriaenssens, P. (2007, 2 October) Interview: 'Ik Lach Niet met Marokkanen-grappen', *De Morgen*.

Agamben, G. (1993a) *The Coming Community* (M. Hardt, trans.), Minneapolis: University of Minnesota Press.

Agamben, G. (1993b) *Infancy and History* (L. Heron, trans.), London: Verso.

Agamben, G. (1998) *Homo Sacer* (D. Heller-Roazen, trans.), Stanford, CA: Stanford University Press.

Agamben, G. (2002a) *Remnants of Auschwitz*, New York: Zone Books.

Agamben, G. (2002b) 'What is a Paradigm?' Lecture at European Graduate School. Retrieved 27 March 2012, from http://www.egs.edu/faculty/agamben/agamben-what-is-a-paradigm-2002.html

Agamben, G. (2004) Interview with Giorgio Agamben 'Life, A Work of Art Without an Author: The State of Exception, the Administration of Disorder and Private Life', Ulrich Raulff (interviewer), *German Law Journal*, 5(5): 609–614.

Agger, I. (2002) *Therapeutic Approaches to the Treatment of Refugees – A Historical Perspective*. Working paper. Retrieved 27 March 2012, from http://www.oasis-rehab.dk/Sider/Bibliotek/Artikler/Inger%20Agger.pdf, no longer available.

Agger, I., and Jensen, S. B. (1996) *Trauma and Healing Under State Terrorism*, London: Zed Books.

Anthony, D. (1999) 'Pseudoscience and Minority Religions: An Evaluation of the Brainwashing Theories of Jean-Marie Abgrall', *Social Justice Research*, 12(4): 421–456.

APA (2004) 'Combatting Terrorism: Responses From the Behavioral Sciences'. Retrieved 27 March 2012, from http://www.apa.org/ppo/issues/svignetteterror2.html and on old.apa.org/ppo/issues/svignetteterror2.html, now no longer available online.

APA (2010) 'What do Psychologists Do at Disaster Sites?' http://www.apa.org/helpcenter/disaster-site.aspx

Baars, B. J. (1986) *The Cognitive Revolution in Psychology*, New York: The Guilford Press.

Bachner-Melman, R., Gritsenko, I., Nemanov, L., Zohar, A. H., Dina, C., and Ebstein, R. P. (2005) 'Dopaminergic Polymorphisms Associated with Self-Report Measures of Human Altruism: A Fresh Phenotype for the Dopamine D4 Receptor, *Molecular Psychiatry*, 10: 333–335.

Badiou, A. (1988) *L'être et L'événement*, Paris: Seuil.

Banyard, P. (2007) 'Tyranny and the Tyrant. Zimbardo's "The Lucifer Effect" Reviewed', *The Psychologist*, 20(8): 494–495.

Baudrillard, J. (1983) *In the Shadow of the Silent Majorities*, New York: Semiotext(e)

Baudrillard, J. (1988) *The Ecstasy of Communication*, New York: Semiotext(e)

Baudrillard, J. (2005) Conspiracy of Art, New York: Semiotext(e)

Baudrillard, J. (2007) *Simulacra and Simulation* (S. Glaser, trans.), Ann Arbor, MI: University of Michigan Press.

Beck, J. (1999) 'The Adapted Individual', paper presented at the European Conference 'Lifelong Learning – Inside and Outside Schools' 25–27 February 1999, University of Bremen. http://www.davidtinapple.com/illich/1999_conditional_human.PDF

Benjamin, M. (2007) 'The CIA's Torture Teachers', *Salon*, June 21, 2007. Retrieved 27 March 2012, from http://www.salon.com/news/feature/2007/06/21/cia_sere/index.html

Benjamin, W. (2002) *Selected Writings*, vol. 3, 1935–1938 (E. Jephcott, trans. Jennings, Michael, ed.), Cambridge, MA: Belknap Press of Harvard University Press.

Benjamin, W. (2003) *Selected Writings*, vol. 4, 1938–1940 (E. Jephcott, trans. Jennings, Michael, ed.), Cambridge, MA: Belknap Press of Harvard University Press.

Benjamin, W. (2008) *The Work of Art in the Age of its Technological Reproducibility, and Other Writings on Media* (E. Jephcott, trans.), Cambridge, MA: Harvard University Press.

Best, J. (1999) *Random Violence: How We Talk about New Crimes and New Victims*, Berkeley: University of California Press.

Biderman, A. D. (1957) 'Communist Attempts to Elicit False Confessions from Air Force Prisoners-of-War', *Bulletin of the New York Academy of Medicine*, 33(9): 616–625.

Blass, T. (ed.) (2000) *Obedience to Authority: Current Perspectives on the Milgram Paradigm*, Mahwah, NJ: Lawrence Erlbaum Associates.

BMJ (2010) Patient leaflet: Post-Traumatic Stress Disorder. Retrieved 27 March 2012, from http://bestpractice.bmj.com/best-practice/pdf/patient-summaries/ptsd-standard.pdf

Boorstin, D. J. (1992 [1961]) *The Image: A Guide to Pseudo-Events in America*, New York: Vintage.

Bosteels, B. (2006) 'Alain Badiou's Theory of the Subject: The Recommencement of Dialectical Materialism?' in Žižek, S. (ed.), *Lacan: The Silent Partners* (pp. 115–168), London, New York: Verso.

Brannigan, A. (2004) *The Rise and Fall of Social Psychology*, New Jersey: Aldine Transaction.

Brannigan, A. (2009) 'Review: The Defense of Situationalism in the Age of Abu Ghraib', *Theory & Psychology*, 19(5): 698–700.

Brecher, R. (2007) *Torture and the Ticking Bomb*, Malden, MA: Blackwell Publishing.

Bruner, J. (2005) 'Foreword', in Milgram, S. (ed.), *Obedience to Authority* (pp. xi–xv) London: Pinter & Martin.

Buchanan, I. (2001) 'Enjoying "Reality TV"', *Australian Humanities Review*, June–August(22).

Burman, E. (1994) 'Innocents Abroad: Western Fantasies of Childhood and the Iconography of Emergencies', *Disasters*, 18(3): 238–253.

Burman, E. (2006) 'Emotions and Reflexivity in Feminised Education Action Research', *Educational Action Research*, 14(3): 315–332.

Burman, E. (2008) *Deconstructing Developmental Psychology*, Second Edition, Hove/New York: Routledge.

Burman, E. (2009) 'Beyond "Emotional Literacy" in Feminist and Educational Research', *British Educational Research Journal*, 35(1): 137–155.

Cameron, D. E. (1956) 'Psychic Driving', *The American Journal of Psychiatry*, 112(7): 502–509.

Chin-Yi, C. (2007) 'Hyperreality, the Question of Agency, and the Phenomenon of Reality Television', *Nebula*, 4(1) 31–44.

CIA (1963) 'Kubark Counterintelligence Interrogation Manual'. Retrieved 27 March 2012, from http://www.gwu.edu/~nsarchiv/NSAEBB/NSAEBB27/01-01.htm

Claes, J. (1982) *Psychologie, een Dubbele Geboorte. 1590 en 1850: bakens voor modern bewustzijn*, Antwerpen/Amsterdam: De Nederlandsche Boekhandel.

Contu, A., Grey, C., and Örtenblad, A. (2003) 'Against Learning', *Human Relations*, 56(8): 931–952.

Cooper, A. (2004) 'New Photos of Iraqi Prisoner Abuse Released; Bush Backs Rumsfeld' [Television Broadcast], 360 DEGREES: CNN.

Costanzo, M., Gerrity, E., and Lykes, M. B. (2007) 'Psychologists and the Use of Torture in Interrogations', *Analyses of Social Issues and Public Policy*, 7(1): 7–20.

Daunton, M. J., and Hilton, M. (eds) (2001) *The Politics of Consumption: Material Culture and Citizenship in Europe and America*, Oxford: Berg.

De Kesel, M. (2007) 'Bin Laden Cartesiaan: Fundamentalisme als Modern Symptoom', in De Kesel, M. and Devisch, I. (eds), *Fundamentalisme Face to Face* (pp. 7–26) Kampen: Klement.

De Kesel, M. (2008) 'Emocratie als Symptoom: Een Cartesiaanse Causerie', in Hertmans, S. (ed.), *Ratio in een Emotionele Samenleving* (pp. 110–119) Gent: Hogeschool Gent.

De Kesel, M. (2010) 'Goden Breken', *Essays over Monotheïsme*, Amsterdam: Boom.

De Sade, M. D. A. F. (1990) *Justine, Philosophy in the Bedroom, and Other Writings*, New York: Grove Press.

De Vos, J. (2005) 'On Psychology and Other Symptoms', *Journal for Lacanian Studies*, 3(2): 258–270.

De Vos, J. (2006) 'Psychologisation: Psychoanalysis' (Double) Political Appointment with History: The Accoyer Amendment Revisited', *Psychoanalysis, Culture and Society*, 11(3): 304–322.

De Vos, J. (2008) 'From Panopticon to Pan-psychologisation', *International Journal of Žižek Studies*, 2(1).

De Vos, J. (2009a) '"Now That You Know, How Do You Feel?" The Milgram Experiment and Psychologization', *Annual Review of Critical Psychology*, 7: 223–246.

De Vos, J. (2009b) 'On Cerebral Celebrity and Reality TV: Subjectivity in Times of Brain-Scans and Psychotainment'. *Configurations*, 17(3): 259–293.

De Vos, J. (2010a) 'Christopher Lasch's The Culture of Narcissism: The Failure of a Critique of Psychological Politics', *Theory & Psychology*, 20(4): 528–548. doi: 10.1177/0959354309351764.

De Vos, J. (2010b) 'From Milgram to Zimbardo: The Double Birth of Post-War Psychology/Psychologization', *History of the Human Sciences*, 23(5): 156–175. doi: 10.1177/0952695110384774.

De Vos, J. (2011a) 'Depsychologizing Torture', *Critical Inquiry*, 37(2): 286–314. doi: 10.1086/657294

De Vos, J. (2011b) 'From La Mettrie's Voluptuous Man Machine to the Perverse Core of Psychology', *Theory & Psychology*, 21(1): 67–85.

De Vos, J. (2011c) 'The Psychologization of Humanitarian Aid: Skimming the Battlefield and the Disaster Zone', *History of the Human Sciences*. doi: 10.1177/0952695111398572

De Vos, J. (2011d) 'Psychologization or the Discontents of Psychoanalysis', *Psychoanalysis, Culture & Society*, 16(4), 354–372.

De Vries, F. (1998) 'To Make a Drama Out of Trauma is Fully Justified', *The Lancet*, 351(9115): 1579–1580.

Dean, J. (2002) *Publicity's Secret*, Ithaca, NY & London: Cornell University Press.

Debord, G. (1994) *The Society of the Spectacle* (D. Nicholson-Smith, trans.), New York: Zone Books.

Dennett, D. C. (1991) *Consciousness Explained*, Boston, MA: Little Brown.

Dennett, D. C. (1993) 'The Message Is: There Is No Medium', *Philosophy & Phenomenological Research*, 53(4): 919–931.

Dennett, D. C. (2001) 'Are We Explaining Consciousness Yet?', *Cognition*, 79(1–2): 221–237.

Dershowitz, A. M. (2003) *Why Terrorism Works*, New Haven, CT: Yale University Press.

Descartes, R. (1996 [1637]) *Discourse on the Method and Meditations on First Philosophy* (D. Weissman and W. Bluhm, trans.), New Haven, CT: Yale University Press.

Diski, J. (2004) 'XXX · The Man Who Shocked the World: The Life and Legacy of Stanley Milgram by Thomas Blass', *London Review of Books*, 26(22). Retrieved 27 March 2012, from http:www.irb.co.uk/v261n22/jenny-diski/xxx.

Donzelot, J. (1977) *La Police des Familles*, Paris: Editions de Minuit.

Duffield, M. (1997) 'NGO Relief in War Zones: Towards an Analysis of the New Aid Paradigm', *Third World Quarterly*, 18(3): 527–542.

Duffield, M. (2001) *Global Governance and the New Wars*, London: Zed Books.

Duffield, M. (2004) 'Carry on Killing: Global Governance, Humanitarianism and Terror' (vol. DIIS Working Paper 2004/23), Copenhagen: Danish Institute for International Studies.

Eban, K. (2007) 'The War on Terror, Rorschach and Awe', *Vanity Fair*, July 2007.

Egginton, W. (2003) *How the World Became a Stage*, Albany, NY: State University of New York Press.

Egginton, W. (2007) 'The Best or the Worst of Our Nature: Reality TV and the Desire for Limitless Change', *Configurations*, 15(2): 177–191.

Ehrenreich, B. (2004, 4 June 2004) 'Feminism's Assumptions Upended', *Los Angeles Times*.

Family Lives (2011) 'Families Matter. The Realities of Family Life in Britain Today'. A Report from Families, for Families: *Family Lives*.

Fassin, D. (2008) 'The Humanitarian Politics of Testimony. Subjectification Through Trauma in the Israeli-Palestinian Conflict', *Cultural Anthropology*, 23(3): 531–558.

Fiske, S. T., Harris, L. T. and Cuddy, A. J. C. (2004) 'Social Psychology: Why Ordinary People Torture Enemy Prisoners', *Science*, 306(5701): 1482–1483.

Foucault, M. (1978) *The History of Sexuality*, vol. 1 (R. Hurley, trans.), New York: Vintage Books.

Foucault, M. (1979) *Discipline and Punish* (A. Sheridan, trans.), New York: Vintage Books.

Foucault, M. (1988) 'Technologies of the Self', in Martin, L. H., Gutman, H. and Hutton, P. H. (eds.), *Technologies of the Self: A Seminar with Michel Foucault* (pp. 16–49), Amherst: University of Massachusetts Press.

Foucault, M. (2002) *The Order of Things: An Archaeology of the Human Sciences*, London: Routledge.

Foucault, M. (2003) *Society Must be Defended: Lectures at the Collège de France, 1975–1976* (D. Macey, trans.), New York: Picador.

Freud, S. (1957 [1914]) 'On Narcissism: An Introduction', in Strachey, J. (ed.), *The Standard Edition of the Complete Psychological Works of Sigmund Freud*: vol. XIV (pp. 73–102), London: Hogarth Press.

Freud, S. (1955 [1927]) 'The Future of an Illusion', in Strachey, J. (ed.), *The Standard Edition of the Complete Psychological Works of Sigmund Freud*: vol. XXI, London: Hogarth Press.

Freud, S. (1955 [1930a]) 'Civilization and its Discontents', in Strachey, J. (ed.), *The Standard Edition of the Complete Psychological Works of Sigmund Freud*: vol. XXI, London: Hogarth Press.

Girard, R. (2002) 'Psychoanalysis and Sacrifice. A Conversation of Sergio Benvenuto with René Girard', *European Journal of Psychoanalysis,* 14. Retrieved 27 March 2012, from http://www.psychomedia.it/jep/number14/girard.htm.

Haney, C., Banks, C., and Zimbardo, P. (1973) 'Interpersonal Dynamics in a Simulated Prison', *International Journal of Criminology and Penology,* 1: 69–97.

Haney, C., Banks, C., and Zimbardo, P. (1981) 'A Study of Prisoners and Guards in a Simulated Prison', in E. Aronson (ed.), *Readings About the Social Animal* (pp. 52–67), San Franciso: Freeman.

Hardt, M. (2005) 'Autopsy Interview with Michael Hardt', *Autopsy,* (January) Retrieved 27 March 2012, from http://www.generation-online.org/p/fpnegri15.htm

Hardt, M., and Negri, A. (2000) *Empire,* Cambridge, MA: Harvard University Press.

Hardt, M., and Negri, A. (2004) *Multitude,* New York: The Penguin Press.

Hardt, M., and Negri, A. (2009) *Commonwealth,* Cambridge, MA: Harvard University Press/ Belknap Press.

Haslam, S. A., and Reicher, S. D. (2008) 'Questioning the Banality of Evil', *The Psychologist,* 21(1): 16–19.

Hersh, S. M. (2004) *Chain of Command: The Road From 9/11 to Abu Ghraib,* New York: Harper Collins.

Husserl, E. (1970) *The Crisis of European Sciences and Transcendental Phenomenology: An Introduction to Phenomenological Philosophy* (D. Carr, trans.), Evanston: Northwestern University Press.

IFRC (2001) *Psychological Support: Best Practices from Red Cross and Red Crescent Programmes,* Geneva: International Federation of Red Cross and Red Crescent Societies.

Illouz, E. (2008) *Saving the Modern Soul: Therapy, Emotions, and the Culture of Self-Help,* Berkeley: University of California Press.

Ingleby, D. (1984) 'The Ambivalence of Psychoanalysis', *Radical Science,* 15: 39–71.

Jonckheere, L. (2004) Problemen bij de 'implementatie' van het decreet betreffende de Integrale Kwaliteitszorg in de Verzorgings- en Welzijnsvoorzieningen. Presentation at the 'Kring voor Psychoanalyse' of the New Lacanian School.

Jones, E. (1955) *Sigmund Freud: Life and Work,* vol. 2, London: Hogarth Press.

Jones, N., Greenberg, N., and Wessely, S. (2007) 'No Plans Survive First Contact with the Enemy: Flexibility and Improvisation in Disaster Mental Health', *Psychiatry,* 70(4): 361–365.

Keller, A. S. (2006) 'Torture in Abu Ghraib', *Perspectives in Biology and Medicine,* 49(4): 553–569.

Klein, N. (2007) *The Shock Doctrine: The Rise of Disaster Capitalism,* London: Penguin Books.

Kog, M., Moons, J., and Depondt, L. (1997) *A Box Full of Feelings. A Playset for Children from 3 to 8,* Leuven: CEGO.

La Mettrie, J. O. (1987) *Oeuvres Philosophiques* (F. Markovits, trans.), Paris: Fayard.

La Mettrie, J. O. (1996 [1747]) *Machine Man and Other Writings* (A. Thomson, trans.), Cambridge: Cambridge University Press.

Lacan, J. (1978) *The Four Fundamental Concepts of Psychoanalysis* (A. Sheridan, trans.), New York: Norton.

Lacan, J. (2006) *The Seminar of Jacques Lacan: Book XVII: The Other Side of Psychoanalysis* (R. Grigg, trans.), New York: Norton.

Lasch, C. (1978) *The Culture of Narcissism*, New York: Norton.

Le Bon, G. (2002 [1895]) *The Crowd: A Study of the Popular Mind*, Mineola, NY: Dover.

Lessing, D. (1986) *Prisons We Choose to Live Inside*, Montréal: CBC Enterprises.

Levant, R. F. (2007) 'Making Psychology a Household Word', *The Psychologist*, 20(6): 366–367.

Lewis, N. A. (2004, November 30) 'Red Cross Finds Detainee Abuse in Guantánamo', *The New York Times*. Retrieved 27 March 2012, from http://www.nytimes.com/2004/11/30/politics/30gitmo.html?_r=2

Lury, K. (2009) '"For Crying Out Loud": The Repression of the Child's Subjectivity in *The House of Tiny Tearaways*', *Semiotica*, (173): 491–507.

Makino, C. (2009) 'Happiness as a Development Model', Catherine Makino Interviews Bhutan Prime Minister Jigme Y. Thinley. Retrieved 1 September 2010, from http://ipsnet/news.asp=48361.

Mandarini, M. (2009) 'Not Fear but Hope in the Apocalypse', *Ephemera*, 8(2): 176–181.

Marshall, P. D. (1997) *Celebrity and Power: Fame in Contemporary Culture*, Minneapolis, MN: University of Minnesota Press.

Mason, B. (2001) 'Psychologist Puts the "Real" into Reality', *Stanford Report*.

Mathijs, E., and Hessels, W. (2004) 'What Viewer? Notions of "the Audience" in the Reception of Big Brother Belgium', in Mathijs, E., Jones, J., and Corner, J. (eds.), *Big Brother International: Formats, Critics and Publics* (pp. 62–76), London: Wallflower.

McCoy, A. W. (2006) *A Question of Torture: CIA Interrogation, from the Cold War to the War on Terror*, New York: Metropolitan Books.

McGowan, K. (2008, Mar/Apr) 'Second Nature', *Psychology Today Magazine*. Retrieved 27 March 2012, from http://www.psychologytoday.com/articles/2008 02/second-nature.

McLuhan, M. (2006) *Understanding Media*, Abingdon: Routledge.

Médecins sans Frontières. (2006) 'Dossier Freud in the Field', *Messages*, 142: 1–18.

Mikos, L. (2004) 'Big Brother as Television Text: Frames of Interpretation and Reception in Germany', in Mathijs, E., Jones, J., and Corner, J. (eds.), *Big Brother International: Formats, Critics and Publics* (pp. 93–104), London: Wallflower.

Milgram, S. (Writer) (1965a) *Obedience* [Film]: University Park, PA: Penn State Audio Visual Services.

Milgram, S. (1965b) 'Some Conditions of Obedience and Disobedience to Authority', *Human Relations*, 18(1): 57–76.

Milgram, S. (1974) *Obedience to Authority*, London: Tavistock.

Moeran, B. (2003) 'Celebrities and the Name Economy', in Dannhaeuser, N., and Werner, C. (eds.), *Anthropological Perspectives on Economic Development and Integration*, vol. 22 (pp. 299–321), Bingley: Emerald Group Publishing.

Moorehead-Slaughter, O. (2006) 'Ethics and National Security', *Monitor on Psychology*, 37(4): 20.

Nordanger, D. O. (2007) 'Coping with Loss and Bereavement in Post-war Tigray, Ethiopia', *Transcultural Psychiatry*, 44(4): 545–565.

Norwegian Refugee Council (2008) 'Bhutan: Land of Happiness for the Selected', in R. Skretteberg (ed.), NRC Reports (vol. 1), Oslo: Norwegian Refugee Council.

Nussbaum, M. (2007, October 17) 'Texts for Torturers. From Stanford to Abu Ghraib: What Turns Ordinary People into Oppressors?', *The Times Literary Supplement*.

Olson, B., Soldz, S., and Davis, M. (2008) 'The Ethics of Interrogation and the American Psychological Association: A Critique of Policy and Process', *Philosophy, Ethics, and Humanities in Medicine*, 3: 2–8.

Omaar, R., and de Waal, A. (1993) 'Disaster Pornography from Somalia', *Media and Values* (61): 13–14.

Palmary, I., and Nunez, L. (2009) 'The Orthodoxy of Gender Mainstreaming: Reflecting on Gender Mainstreaming as a Strategy for Accomplishing the Millennium Development Goals', *Journal of Health Management*, 11(1): 65–78.

Parker, I. (1995) *Deconstructing Psychopathology*, London: Sage.

Parker, I. (1999) 'Deconstructing Diagnosis: Psychopathological Practice', in Feltham, C. (ed.), *Controversies in Psychotherapy and Counselling* (pp. 104–112), London: Sage.

Parker, I. (2000) 'Obedience', *Granta*, 71(4): 99–125.

Parker, I. (2004) *Slavoj Žižek: A Critical Introduction*, London: Pluto.

Parker, I. (2007) *Revolution in Psychology: Alienation to Emancipation*, London: Pluto Press.

Patel, N. (2007) 'Torture, Psychology, and the "War on Terror": A Human Rights Framework', in Roberts, R. (ed.), *Just War: Psychology and Terrorism* (pp. 74–108), Ross-on-Wye: PCCS Books.

Piven, J. S. (2007) 'Terror, Sexual Arousal, and Torture: The Question of Obedience or Ecstasy Among Perpetrators', *Discourse of Sociological Practice*, 8(1): 1–21.

Polman, L. (2010) *The Crisis Caravan: What's Wrong with Humanitarian Aid?* New York: Henry Holt and Co.

Pupavac, V. (2002) 'Therapeutising Refugees, Pathologising Populations: International Psycho-Social Programmes in Kosovo' (Working paper No. 59), UNHCR.

Pupavac, V. (2004a) 'Psychosocial Interventions and the Demoralization of Humanitarianism', *Journal of Biosocial Science*, 36(04): 491–504.

Pupavac, V. (2004b) 'War on the Couch: The Emotionology of the New International Security Paradigm', *European Journal of Social Theory*, 7(2): 149–170.

Reicher, S. (2006) 'Rethinking the Psychology of Tyranny: The BBC Prison Study', *The British Journal of Social Psychology*, 45(1): 1–41.

Rejali, D. M. (2007) *Torture and Democracy*, Princeton, NJ: Princeton University Press.

Ritchie, J. (2000) *Big Brother: The Official Unseen Story*, London: Channel Four Books.

Roelands, J., and Druine, N. (2000) 'Belgium', in Brock, C., and Tulasiewicz, W. (eds.), *Education in a Single Europe*, Second Edition, London: Routledge.

Rose, N. (1985) *The Psychological Complex: Psychology, Politics and Society in England, 1869–1939*, London: Routledge & Kegan Paul.

Rose, N. (1990) *Governing the Soul: The Shaping of the Private Self*, New York – London: Routledge.

Rose, N. (2008) 'Psychology as a Social Science', *Subjectivity*, 25(1): 446–462.

Roudinesco, E. (2001) *Why Psychoanalysis?* (R. Bowlby, trans.), New York: Columbia University Press.

Rubenstein, L. S. (2007) 'First, Do No Harm: Health Professionals and Guantánamo', *Seton Hall Law Review*, 37(3): 733–748.

Sanders, M. R. (1999) 'Triple P-Positive Parenting Program: Towards an Empirically Validated Multilevel Parenting and Family Support Strategy for the Prevention of Behavior and Emotional Problems in Children', *Clinical Child and Family Psychology Review*, 2(2): 71–90.

Saramago, J. (2008) *Death with Interruptions*, London: Harvill Secker.

Shane, S. (2008, 2 July) 'China Inspired Interrogations at Guantánamo', *The New York Times*. Retrieved 27 March 2012, from http://www.nytimes.com/2008/07/02/us/02detain.html?pagewanted=all

Slevin, P., and Stephens, J. (2004, 10 June) 'Detainees' Medical Files Shared: Guantánamo Interrogators' Access Criticized' , *The Washington Post*. Retrieved 27 March 2012, from http://www.washingtonpost.com/wp-dyn/articles/A29649-2004Jun9.html

Soldz, S. (2008a) 'APA Members Change Association's Interrogations Policy!', 17 September, 2008. Retrieved 27 March 2012, from http://psychoanalystsoppose war.org/blog/2008/09/17/apa-members-change-associations-interrogations-policy/

Soldz, S. (2008b) 'Healers or Interrogators: Psychology and the United States Torture Regime', *Psychoanalytic Dialogues*, 18(5): 592–613.

Stam, H. J., Lubek, I., and Radtke, L. (1998) 'Repopulating Social Psychology Texts: Disembodied "Subjects" and Embodied Subjectivity', in Bayer, B., and Shotter, J. (eds) *Reconstructing the Psychological Subject: Bodies, Practices and Technologies* (pp. 153–186), London: Sage.

Stavrakakis, Y. (2007) *The Lacanian Left: Psychoanalysis, Theory, Politics*, Edinburgh: Edinburgh University Press.

Suedfeld, P. (1990) 'Psychologists as Victims, Administrators, and Designers of Torture', in Suedfeld, P. (ed.), *Psychology and Torture*, New York: Hemisphere.

Suedfeld, P. (2007) 'Torture, Interrogation, Security, and Psychology: Absolutistic Versus Complex Thinking', *Analyses of Social Issues and Public Policy*, 7(1): 55–63.

Summerfield, D. (1997) 'Legacy of War: Beyond "Trauma" to the Social Fabric', *The Lancet*, 349(9065): 1568.

Summerfield, D. (1998) '"Trauma" and the Experience of War: A Reply', *The Lancet*, 351(9115): 1580–1581.

Summerfield, D. (2002) 'Effects of War: Moral Knowledge, Revenge, Reconciliation, and Medicalised Concepts of "Recovery"', *British Medical Journal* (Clinical Research edn), 325(7372): 1105–1107.

Summers, F. (2007) 'Psychoanalysis, the American Psychological Association, and the Involvement of Psychologists at Guantánamo Bay', *Psychoanalysis, Culture and Society*, 12(1): 83–92.

Sundance Channel (2006) *The Human Behavior Experiments* [TV documentary].

Tarde, G. (1989 [1901]) *L'Opinion et la Foule*, Paris: P.U.F.

Taylor, P. A., and Harris, J. (2008) *Critical Theories of Mass Media: Then and Now*, Maidenhead: Open University Press.

Teo, T. (2004) 'The End of Psychology?' *Contemporary Psychology: APA Review of Books*, 49(4): 491–494.

The Sphere Project (2004) *Humanitarian Charter and Minimum Standards in Disaster Response*, Oxford: Oxfam Publishing.

Timimi, S., and Radcliffe, N. (2005) 'The Rise and Rise of ADHD', in Newnes, C., and Radcliffe, N. (eds), *Making and Breaking Children's Lives,* Ross-on-Wye: PCCS Books.

Uzelac, M. (1997) *Za Damire I Nemrie, Opening the Door to Nonviolence – Peace Education Manual for Primary School Children*, NGO MALI KORAK – Centre for Culture of Peace and Nonviolence Zagreb. Retrieved 27 March 2012, from http://www.hrea.org/erc/Library/primary/Opening_the_Door/workshop12.html

Vande Veire, F. (2008) 'De Smoel van de Emotie', in Hertmans, S. (ed.), *Ratio in een Emotionele Samenleving*, Gent: Hogeschool Gent.

Vernon, J. (1966) *Inside the Black Room: Studies of Sensory Deprivation*, London: Penguin Books.

Vidal, F. (2009) 'Brainhood, Anthropological Figure of Modernity', *History of the Human Sciences*, 22(1): 5–36. doi: 10.1177/0952695108099133

Vlaamse Gemeenschap (2010) Development aims for Nursery Education – Dutch. Retrieved from http://www.ond.vlaanderen.be/curriculum/english/corecurriculum/nursery/nurserydutch.htm

Walzer, M. (1994) *Thick and Thin: Moral Argument at Home and Abroad*, London: University of Notre Dame Press.

Weizman, E. (2006) 'The Art of War', *Frieze*, 99. Retrieved 27 March 2012, from http://www.frieze.com/issue/article/the_art_of_war/

Welch, M. (2007) 'The Re-Emergence of Torture in Political Culture: Tracking It's Discourse and Genealogy', *Capítulo Criminológico*, 35(4): 471–505.

Wertz, F. J. (1994) 'Of Rats and Psychologists: A Study of the History and Meaning of Science', *Theory & Psychology*, 4(2): 165–197.

Wessells, M. (1999) 'Culture, Power, and Community: Intercultural Approaches to Psychosocial Assistance and Healing', in Nader, K., Dubrow, N., and Stamm, B. (eds), *Honoring Differences: Cultural Issues in the Treatment of Trauma and Loss* (pp. 276–282), Philadelphia, PA: Brunner/Mazel.

Wolff, H. G., and Hinkle, L. E. (1957) 'The Methods of Interrogation and Indoctrination Used by the Communist State Police', *Bulletin of the New York Academy of Medicine*, 33(9): 600–615.

Woodside, D., Barbara, J. S., and Benner, D. G. (1999) 'Psychological Trauma and Social Healing in Croatia', *Medicine, Conflict, and Survival*, 15(4): 355–367.

Zarembo, A. (2004, 15 July) 'A Theater of Inquiry and Evil', *Los Angeles Times*. Retrieved 27 March 2012, from http://articles.latimes.com/2004/jul/15/science/sci-prison15

Zimbardo, P. (1989) *Quiet Rage: The Stanford Prison Study Video* [Film]: Stanford, CA: Stanford University Press.

Zimbardo, P. (1999) *Stanford Prison Experiment Slideshow: A Visit.* Retrieved 25 June 2009, from http://www.prisonexp.org/slide-27.htm

Zimbardo, P. (2006a) 'The Power of Norms and Groups on Individuals: Parallels Between the Stanford Prison Experiment and Milgram's Obedience Research'. Retrieved 25 June 2009, from http://www.lucifereffect.com/about_content_norms.htm

Zimbardo, P. (2006b) 'Who Was Lucifer and How Did He Become the Devil'. Retrieved 25 June 2009, from http://www.lucifereffect.com/lucifer.htm

Zimbardo, P. (2007a) *The Lucifer Effect*, New York: Random House.

Zimbardo, P. (2007b) 'Thoughts on Psychologists, Ethics, and the Use of Torture in Interrogations: Don't Ignore Varying Roles and Complexities', *Analyses of Social Issues and Public Policy*, 7(1): 65–73.

Zimbardo, P. (2008) 'How Ordinary People Become Monsters . . . or Heroes'. Paper presented at the TED Conference 2008: *The Big Questions*, February 27–March 1, 2008 Monterey, California. Video available on: http://www.lucifereffect.com/aboutphil_media.htm

Žižek, S. (1989) T*he Sublime Object of Ideology*, London: Verso.

Žižek, S. (1991) *Looking Awry: An Introduction to Jacques Lacan Through Popular Culture*, Cambridge, MA: MIT Press.

Žižek, S. (1994) 'The Spectre of Ideology', in Žižek, S. (ed.), *Mapping Ideology* (pp. 1–33), London & New York: Verso.

Žižek, S. (2001) *The Fragile Absolute: Or, Why is the Christian Legacy Worth Fighting For?*, London: Verso.

Žižek, S. (2002a) 'Big Brother, or, the Triumph of the Gaze Over the Eye', in Levin, T. Y. (ed.), *Ctrl [space]: Rhetorics of Surveillance from Bentham to Big Brother*, (pp. 224–227), Massachusetts: MIT Press.

Žižek, S. (2002b) 'A Plea for Leninist Intolerance', *Critical Inquiry*, 28(2): 542–566.

Žižek, S. (2003a) 'Homo Sacer as the Object of the Discourse of the University', Retrieved 27 March 2012, from http://www.lacan.com/hsacer.htm

Žižek, S. (2003b) *The Puppet and the Dwarf*, Cambridge, MA: MIT Press.

Žižek, S. (2004a) 'From Politics to Biopolitics . . . and Back', *The South Atlantic Quarterly*, 103(2–3): 501–521.

Žižek, S. (2004b, 21 June) 'What Rumsfeld Doesn't Know That He Knows About Abu Ghraib', *In These Times*.

Žižek, S. (2005) 'Ignorance of the Chicken, or, Why Many Lacanians Are Reactionary Liberals'. Paper presented at the Centre for Research in Modern European Philosophy, Middlesex University, London.

Žižek, S. (2006a) 'Against the Populist Temptation', *Critical Inquiry*, 32(3): 551–574.

Žižek, S. (2006b) *The Parallax View*, Cambridge, MA: MIT Press.

Žižek, S. (2006c) 'The Pervert's Guide to Cinema', in Fiennes, S. (Producer): Lone Star–Mischief–Films Amoeba Film.

Žižek, S. (2008a) 'Descartes and the Post-Traumatic Subject', *Filozofski vestnik*, 29(2): 9–29.

Žižek , S. (2008b) 'The Ticklish Subject', *The Absent Centre of Political Ontology*, London/New York: Verso.

Žižek , S. (2010a) *Living in the End Times*, London/New York: Verso.

Žižek , S. (2010b) 'Some Concluding Notes on Violence, Ideology and Communist Culture', *Subjectivity*, 3(1): 101–116.

Žižek, S. (2011) 'Lacan and Sexual Difference'. Paper presented at the Masterclass 25 March 2011, The Birkbeck Institute for the Humanities, London.

Žižek, S., and Daly, G. (2004) *Conversations with Žižek*, Cambridge: Polity Press.

Index